EYES
OF THE
FATHER

SEEING MEANING IN THE MIRROR

TODD LEYDEN

authorHOUSE

AuthorHouse™
1663 Liberty Drive
Bloomington, IN 47403
www.authorhouse.com
Phone: 1 (800) 839-8640

© 2019 Todd Leyden. All rights reserved.

No part of this book may be reproduced, stored in a retrieval system, or transmitted by any means without the written permission of the author.

Published by AuthorHouse 02/20/2019

ISBN: 978-1-5462-7471-1 (sc)
ISBN: 978-1-5462-7470-4 (hc)
ISBN: 978-1-5462-7498-8 (e)

Library of Congress Control Number: 2019901486

Print information available on the last page.

Any people depicted in stock imagery provided by Getty Images are models, and such images are being used for illustrative purposes only.
Certain stock imagery © Getty Images.

This book is printed on acid-free paper.

Because of the dynamic nature of the Internet, any web addresses or links contained in this book may have changed since publication and may no longer be valid. The views expressed in this work are solely those of the author and do not necessarily reflect the views of the publisher, and the publisher hereby disclaims any responsibility for them.

Scripture quotations marked NKJV are taken from the New King James Version. Copyright © 1982 by Thomas Nelson, Inc. Used by permission. All rights reserved.

CONTENTS

Inspiration ix
Author's Note xi

Part 1: Pleading before the Throne
Chapter 1:   God, Declare Yourself 1

Part 2: Getting Our Attention
Chapter 2:   The Gift of Payton 13
Chapter 3:   Trees or a Fireplace 24
Chapter 4:   A Spiritual Tug-of-War 29

Part 3: Preparing the Way
Chapter 5:   An Invitation to Fort Wilderness 49
Chapter 6:   The Businessman and Payton Hike the Grand Canyon .. 64
Chapter 7:   A Marathon or a Providential Witness for Suffering? 70
Chapter 8:   Our Last Family Camp 75
Chapter 9:   The Pieces to the Puzzle are Coming Together 81

Part 4: He lived So Long to Reach So Many
Chapter 10: The Last Supper 91
Chapter 11: Man, Medicine, and Machines or God? 97
Chapter 12: Blessed 119
Chapter 13: Fish or Cut Bait 129
Chapter 14: The Breath of Life 146
Chapter 15: Three Crashes and Three Rebounds 154

Part 5: The Glorious Unfolding
Chapter 16: The Lord Speaks, and His Plan Unfolds 169
Chapter 17: A Restless Night and a Surreal Phone Call 178
Chapter 18: A Bittersweet Award and a Community Impacted 188
Chapter 19: Family of Four: We Never Have to Worry Where He Is 194
Chapter 20: A Celebration of Life: Worship Unlike Anything This
　　　　　　Side of Heaven 202
Chapter 21: Life Is for the Living 214
Chapter 22: Payton LLC: A Providential Conviction 222
Chapter 23: A Return to Fort Wilderness: Dedication of Payton's
　　　　　　Place 234
Chapter 24: Dear Heavenly Father 239

Part 6: Rest Assured
Chapter 25: Payton's Dream 249

Epilogue 257
Evidence of God's Plan 265
A Final Word 271
Acknowledgments 273
Scripture Index 277
Notes 279
About the Author 281

To my wife, Robyn, God's greatest gift to me
this side of eternity, and our three sons,
Payton, Blake, and Chase, who are a great
blessing and a source of tremendous joy

INSPIRATION

A special thanks to my fourteen-year-old nephew Jack Leyden, who has published three books, the Tom Bunker series, and encouraged me with the following note as I started this book: "Are you published yet?"

AUTHOR'S NOTE

I've made every effort to accurately depict the situations described within this book, including confirming critical story elements with those cited. A treasure trove of personal journal entries, summary reflections, and website and email communications were available to provide me with detailed and factual accounts. My training as an auditor equipped me with the skillset to construct the story years later with limited deviation from the historical events. I've incorporated certain stories within the general time frame described to offer insight into our season of life. What you are about to read is true.

PART 1

PLEADING BEFORE THE THRONE

CHAPTER 1

GOD, DECLARE YOURSELF

As Payton, our thirteen-year-old son, lay in a hospital bed at the edge of death for thirty-three days, our life stood still. From the time he was admitted, our prayer was the same: glory for God, wisdom for the doctors and nurses, and healing for Payton, in that order—and we did not want to receive a phone call in the middle of the night.

But then the call came. On February 2, 2001, I was startled awake by the piercing ring of the phone. The clock read 3:37 a.m. Having been asleep but a few hours, I lurched across the room. The voice on the other end of the phone calmly but urgently said, "This is Riley Hospital. Payton is crashing. You need to get here quickly."

My wife, Robyn, was now awake, and I shared the news, even though she probably already knew the reason for the call. We scrambled to get ready, but first, I needed to call our closest friends to let them know Payton was dying and ask them to come to the hospital. Robyn was anxious and said with a quivering but firm conviction, "Todd, we need to go now!"

Our sons Blake, who was ten, and Chase, who was seven, were staying with friends during that time. Robyn and I quickly grabbed whatever clothes were available, brushed our teeth, and got in the car to make the now-familiar trip to the hospital. The good news, if there could be such a thing at a time like that, was that there was virtually no traffic at four o'clock in the morning. When we arrived at the hospital parking garage, the brisk air of a five-degree morning in Indianapolis greeted us.

We moved quickly through the double sliding-glass doors of the hospital entrance, which, ironically, was where Robyn had started her career as a pediatric oncology nurse thirteen years earlier. Riley Children's Hospital is the state's largest and most highly acclaimed children's hospital. We were fortunate and blessed to have such great care available so close to home, because as Payton's cardiologist, Dr. Caldwell, had shared with us early during Payton's hospitalization, Payton was "the sickest kid at Riley."

We were anxious to find out who was on call and get the report of Payton's condition. The elevator ride to ICU 4 North seemed to take forever. By then, most, if not all, of the hospital staff knew us. The combination of Payton's condition, the significant number of friends and family who were with us at the hospital during that time, and our faith was not what the staff usually saw in a situation like that, and Payton was not the typical Riley kid. At thirteen years old, six foot one and 175 pounds and wearing a size 13 shoe, he was bigger than many of the doctors and nurses. He was perfectly healthy, or so we'd thought until an emergency trip to the hospital.

We found the resident on call, and he told us Payton's oxygen saturation levels were dangerously low—hovering in the low eighties. That meant his vital organs were not getting the oxygen they needed to work. Normal levels are 95 to 100 percent. We were told Payton was stable for now.

Our friends Keith Ogorek, Nick Taylor, Leisa Ress, and Jeff Terp arrived soon. It was now a little before six o'clock in the morning. I shared the doctor's report. It appeared the end was near—crushing words to convey to anyone, including those who love you most. We went to the hospital chapel to pray. Prayer was a constant during that time, not only by those at the hospital but also by thousands who knew of Payton's plight.

Throughout the previous thirty-two days, we'd shared updates on Payton's condition and prayer requests by email and through a website created for people who wanted to follow his situation. His battle was shared far and wide. It seemed most of Indianapolis was aware of his condition. A little more than twenty-four hours earlier, I had posted a message at 1:44 a.m., sharing the following scripture from Psalm 118:8: "It is better to trust in the Lord than to put your confidence in man."

Providentially, three close friends had posted that exact passage during the preceding twenty-four hours. I now shared the medical team's assessment, which was essentially "There is nothing more we can do. The odds of Payton surviving are not good at all."

In that spirit, we gathered to pray or plead with the Lord for Payton's life. We shared fervent prayers. We shed tears. My body heaved, as I lay prostrate on the chapel floor, and took in the reality that Payton might soon be gone. We were defeated by man's standards, but we were hopeful because we could put our faith and trust in the Lord. Almost ten years earlier, convicted by reading the biblical book of Ecclesiastes, I had accepted Jesus as my Lord and Savior. I'd decided that either all of scripture was true or none of it was true. While I did not know what I was getting into, in the years that followed, I would continue to be anchored in that decision. Could I trust in the Lord and His Word and His plan for my life? If I could trust Him when things were good—which had been my life experience up to that point—then I had to also trust Him when it appeared we might lose Payton.

During our time in the chapel, our prayers had an intensity I had never experienced before. I believe that is what followers of Christ mean when they say, "Deliver your prayers with an expectation for the Lord to respond." We were expecting an answer. Man had said there was nothing that could be done. We needed a miracle for Payton to live, or God had other plans I could not let myself even begin to fathom.

About an hour later, we concluded our time of prayer. I vividly remember one specific prayer request that is forever anchored to my soul: Robyn prayed that Payton's life would have meaning. She was sobbing and gasping for breath. Normally, she was unemotional, but the situation had taxed her in ways she couldn't possibly have imagined. Did she know he would not make it, and was she imploring the Lord to make sure there was a reason we were enduring that horrific situation?

It was now late morning after we had received the dreaded phone call, and Payton remained in critical condition. That had been his medical status since his arrival, but he was now stable. What was going on? It was the third time that week he'd crashed and later bounced back and stabilized. Perhaps the answer lay in something that would happen later that afternoon.

During the preceding thirty-two days, we'd received hundreds of visitors and an overwhelming amount of support. Our every need had been met. Meals, laundry, care for our kids, prayers, work, and transportation were all taken care of. No request was too big or menial for someone to lovingly do on our behalf. We were amazed at how the Lord had provided for us during that time. Experiencing the amount of love and support we received was like standing under Niagara Falls with millions of gallons of water cascading down on us. I never had experienced anything like it before, and I haven't since. Typically, we would visit with friends in the waiting room. Sometimes they would want to see Payton, hold his hand, pray for him, and shed a silent tear.

We asked our friend Jeff to get the word out to the multitude of people praying for Payton about his grave condition and our inability to see visitors. However, word did not make it to Payton's best friend, Scott Macke. Scott's mom brought him to the hospital—he wanted to see his friend. Robyn greeted Scott and shared the news with him: it looked like Payton was not going to make it. She sat with Scott for a while, hugging and consoling him. She told him he could not see Payton. He was crushed. Robyn wished she had not had to deliver the news to him. However, that day in the hospital was the start of a new relationship between Scott and us, one that would continue for the years to come.

About two thirty in the afternoon, Payton's girlfriend, Meredith, arrived at the hospital with our other sons, Blake and Chase. Meredith and Blake had visited the hospital a couple times before. A few days earlier, Meredith had shared her heart with me, saying there was no reason to live if Payton did not make it. I'd taken hold of her shoulders, looked into her forlorn eyes, and told her, "I know my son, and he would be mad if he heard you say that." Payton hated stupid comments and would have viewed it as such. Meredith rebounded a day or two later with conviction after reading the following from Isaiah 57:1: "The righteous perishes, And no man takes *it* to heart; Merciful men *are* taken away, While no one considers That the righteous is taken away from evil." This scripture caused Meredith to do a complete turnaround and realize her life must go on if Payton's prematurely ended. Meredith told me to be strong. I knew she would be all right.

Payton and Blake were close. Even though Payton was about a foot taller and seventy-five pounds heavier, they loved to compete against each other. Basketball, soccer, Ping-Pong—it didn't matter what the game was;

if they could keep score, they played against one another. Blake, with his analytical mind, was the eternal optimist, coming up with ideas and questions to try to solve Payton's condition. However, it was Chase's first visit. We had not allowed Chase to visit his brother. He had not asked. We were concerned how our seven-year-old son would react to seeing his brother in an intensive care unit. Payton was in a medically induced coma; jaundiced; and hooked up to a breathing apparatus (ventilator), a dialysis machine, and a variety of other machines measuring his vital signs. By then, we were used to the panoply of numbers, beeps, and mechanical analyses of his vital functions—or, better said, what was not working. For thirty-three days, it had been as if he were walking a tightrope hundreds of feet above the ground, and with one little slip, he would fall and die immediately. Inexplicably, he continued to live day to day but barely.

We greeted Meredith and our sons at the waiting room, which was now our home away from home, and led them down the long corridor to Payton's room. Meredith walked in first and started to tear up. She spoke softly. We never knew what Payton heard or did not hear, except for on our most difficult day, when he had an emergency surgery and was in a state of semi-consciousness. Blake followed. He shared with Payton the get-well video his fifth-grade class had made. The video was just the right mixture of optimism and fun and a great support to Blake. Chase stood transfixed. I am not sure what he was thinking. He was only seven. His brother was very sick—dying. How could a seven-year-old process something like that? But we had to take him to see Payton. A couple days earlier, we'd decided if Payton were to die without Chase visiting, Chase would never have an opportunity to see his brother or perhaps say goodbye. If Payton lived, even in a vegetative state, we could try to address the scars associated with seeing him in that condition in the future. They spent about thirty to forty-five minutes with Payton. There was no poking at one another; saying, "You're a butthead"; or making similar remarks. It was time simply for two brothers and Payton's girlfriend to see Payton, give him a gentle caress, speak words of encouragement, and say goodbye. They left and headed off to the carnival at Chase's elementary school, Fishback Creek, that evening, which would prove the perfect antidote to a hospital visit like that one.

We headed back toward the waiting room. It was now a few minutes before four o'clock. A business acquaintance, Tom Miller, and his wife, Cheri, met us in the hallway and asked about Payton's condition. Before we could say much more than a hello, the resident on duty interrupted us. She told us Payton's doctor and lead intensivist, Edward Seferian, wanted to see us before his shift ended for the weekend. An intensivist is the quarterback or coach of the medical team responsible for acute-care cases. During one of my quieter moments in the waiting room, I'd compiled a list of all the specialists who worked on Payton: infectious disease specialists, cardiologists, pulmonologists, nephrologists, gastroenterologists, hematologists, occupational therapists, dieticians, surgeons and anesthesiologists, residents, and nurses. More than two hundred committed caregivers attended to our son. I'd expected world-class medical staff and was not disappointed. I was amazed how much they truly cared. We were blessed with an outstanding team doing everything they could to keep Payton alive. Dr. Seferian was in charge.

Typically, those types of meetings take place in the waiting room or an alcove, but for the first time in thirty-three days, the room next to Payton was open. Robyn and I made the walk down the hall to meet Dr. Seferian in the hospital room adjacent to Payton's. Dr. Ndidi Musa, the first of three intensivists responsible for leading Payton's care team, joined us. On our second full day in the hospital, Ndidi asked Robyn and I the most profound and critically important question as our journey was about to begin: "You can trust in what man, medicine, and machines can do, or you can trust in what God can do." We chose God. We'd met Ndidi just a few months prior at a friend's wedding. Keith Ogorek had been there as well. Keith, who served as a youth pastor at our church, Zionsville Fellowship, after walking away from a lucrative leadership opportunity with a national advertising firm, was our neighbor. He'd moved into a home fifty yards across the street from us when Payton was less than one year old. We had become close friends due to Payton's friendship with his daughter Rachel.

We gathered a few chairs from the hallway and created an impromptu semicircle. Robyn sat facing me with her back to the window overlooking the courtyard. Next to her on her right was Ndidi. Dr. Seferian was in the middle, with a direct view into Payton's room through the open door between the rooms. Keith was to his right and next to me. It was time to find out what was on Dr. Seferian's mind.

Eyes of the Father

Dr. Seferian was a relatively young doctor and residency and fellowship colleague of Ndidi. He was quiet and brilliant, with a simple and gracious manner. Short in stature with dark black wispy hair his cherubic face befitted the angel of mercy role he played as the person now leading Payton's medical team. He was not prone to developing relationships but given the nature of Payton's case and our desire to love and support the staff, we had come to enjoy the personal side of getting to know him. We'd had many conversations about medical options and strategies with doctors Seferian, Musa, and Jeff Macke during the long days at Riley. Dr. Seferian started that conversation like none we'd had with him before, struggling to share the following words: "I know of your faith, but absent a miracle, you will need to decide about Payton's life support. I do not believe Payton is going to make it. You do not need to decide right now, but I want to prepare you, as this is something you will need to do in the next day or two." He went on to say, "We have done everything. There is nothing more we can do." His chilling words took the air out of the room.

I immediately responded certain it was inspired by the Spirit of God, "It is not fair for any man or father to decide when his son's life is over. God brought him into this world; He can decide when Payton's time is done."

Keith said, "The sheep will hear my voice," referring to a passage in the book of John that says the followers of Christ will hear Jesus's voice and will follow Him because they know His voice.

Ndidi added, "God will declare Himself."

With an air of boldness, I said, "I don't care if it is two days, two months, two hours, two weeks, or two minutes. God can decide when Payton's life on earth is done."

My declaration was barely out of my mouth, when we heard a series of rapid and haunting beeps in the next room. Robyn said, "Maybe God is speaking right now."

Dr. Seferian glanced to the other room and immediately walked over to the machine that was monitoring Payton's oxygenation levels. Payton's levels, which had been hovering in the low eighties, with 100 percent oxygen support, crashed to the forties. Dr. Seferian returned, his face pale, and, looking at us in disbelief, said, "Payton is gone." His stunned reaction conveyed that Payton's final hour was upon us.

I turned to Ndidi and said, "God is good." She agreed. All it took was to ask Almighty God to respond to the question posed by Dr. Seferian. Right on cue, God responded. The Lord of the universe cares that much for us. Payton was in the hospital for almost three million seconds, yet the Lord chose that second to end Payton's time here on earth, graciously allowing Meredith, Blake, and Chase to come see him a final time and allowing Chase to say goodbye.

Robyn, Keith, Ndidi, and I walked through the door into Payton's room, not knowing what we would see. It was an opportunity to say goodbye as the machine helped him to draw his final breaths this side of eternity. There are simply no words to describe the feeling you experience as your firstborn son, barely a teenager, passes from this life to the next. We told Payton we loved him as our faces were wet with tears. Keith pulled out his Bible and read the following passage from 2 Timothy 4:7–8: "I have fought the good fight, I have finished the race, I have kept the faith. Finally, there is laid up for me the crown of righteousness, which the Lord, the righteous Judge, will give to me on that Day, and not to me only but also to all who have loved His appearing." Amen!

We looked upon Payton a final time as he was near his last moments on earth. We were numb. As we headed out of the room, one of the nurses, Kim Stull, started to unplug the myriad of tubes and lines attached to Payton's body. What an awful thing for a nurse or any caregiver to do. They'd fought so hard for so long, and now she had to stand by his lifeless body and detach the very things that had kept him alive. Kim would later tell me that when we'd made our request of God, the machine providing oxygen to Payton's lungs had suddenly stopped. It was something she had never witnessed before. It was as if the Lord, who controls all things, said, "It is done." It was one of countless amazing ways the Lord showed Himself to us during that time.

Kim handed us a small bag with his belongings. We would not take Payton home but would take a few of his things—a cruel way to exit.

As we walked down the hallway and past the nurses' station, we saw our next-door neighbor Cindy Kaufman and her friend Diane Harty. Cindy lived next door to us at our first home after Robyn and I were married. We moved there when Payton was six months old. Cindy had watched Payton grow up for the first twelve years of his life. It was somewhat fitting that Cindy, an employee of the Indiana University Health System, would see us first after leaving Payton for the final time. We told her the news and exchanged tears and hugs—the first of hundreds, if not thousands, of tears and hugs that would flow in the days, months, and years to come. She asked if she and Diane could go in to say goodbye to Payton. I said, "Yes, of course; however, he is no longer there. A few minutes ago, he breathed his last breath, at five thirty. He is now in his eternal home."

Biblical Principle

The apostle John wrote in John 14:1–4, "Let not your heart be troubled; you believe in God, believe also in Me. In My Father's house are many mansions, if it were not so, I would have told you. I go to prepare a place for you. And if I go and prepare a place for you, I will come again and receive you to Myself; that where I am, there you may be also. And where I go you know, and the way you know."[1]

Jesus is telling his disciples to trust in Him. The same Jesus who was born of a virgin, lived, died on the cross for the sins of mankind, resurrected on the third day, was seen by many witnesses in the following forty days, and then ascended into heaven. It was the most painful day of my life, yet I was comforted in that truth.

Surely, God loved Payton as much as Robyn and I did. Upon reflection, it became clear to me in the days and years that followed that Payton's situation was part of a plan—not my plan but God's plan for Payton's life, which extended beyond Payton's time on earth.

Robyn prayed and sobbed in the chapel at Riley Children's Hospital in the early hours of February 2, 2001, on Payton's final day, "Lord, I pray that Payton's life would have meaning." To see how God answered her prayer in ways unimaginable, we must go back to the beginning of this improbable story.

PART 2
GETTING OUR ATTENTION

CHAPTER 2

THE GIFT OF PAYTON

After a month of mandatory bed rest due to preeclampsia (elevated blood pressure), Robyn was more than ready to go to the hospital for the scheduled delivery of our first baby. As with many first-time births, she was late based on the initially established due date. Fifty pounds heavier and missing her last clinical rotation necessary to complete her Bachelor of Science degree in nursing at Indiana University-Purdue University in Indianapolis, Robyn headed to the hospital with me by her side. We were excited to become first-time parents and for Robyn to return to normal physically. We would deliver at the clinic at St. Vincent's Hospital as a result of our decision to use a low-cost medical coverage option through my employer.

Upon arriving for her scheduled appointment, Robyn was given an epidural for pain and Pitocin to start her labor. We'd made about two or three of the Lamaze classes prior to Robyn's bed rest. I did my best to try to keep her calm during the labor but was not much help. After an hour or two, I asked the doctor if it was all right to leave and get a bite to eat. I was hesitant to go too far, so I headed to the nearest vending machine and bought a Hostess cherry pie, something Robyn would never let me eat today. I was gone only a few minutes, and when I returned to the delivery room, I was startled to see Robyn with an oxygen mask. I quickly learned our baby had turned in a manner that had caused the umbilical cord to wrap around its head.

Robyn's labor continued for several more hours, and a few minutes before seven o'clock on the evening of May 15, 1987, we welcomed Payton

Alexander Leyden into the world. Payton was a beautiful, somewhat jaundiced baby with a heart murmur. Prior to discharge, we were advised to have Payton checked at Riley Children's Hospital in the coming weeks.

When it came time for the appointment, Robyn was in the middle of completing her final clinical rotation and asked fellow nursing student and friend Ann Hale to accompany her mom on the trip to Riley. An electrocardiogram (EKG) and echocardiogram were ordered, and the tests confirmed our baby had a small ventricular septal defect (VSD). Dr. Hurwitz advised monitoring with an annual checkup and said Payton would need to take antibiotics prior to dental procedures due to the risk of his developing bacterial endocarditis. He further explained that dental work could stimulate bleeding of the gums, allowing bacteria to travel through the bloodstream to his heart and potentially attach to an area of irregular-shaped tissue, such as a VSD. Otherwise, Dr. Hurwitz said, the nature of his heart murmur should cause no problems and might close on its own. He did not think it would limit Payton in any significant way. When we heard the news, we were relieved-. Today Robyn finds it strange she did not attend the initial appointment and thinks the Riley staff must have thought she was not a good mom. Later, she acknowledged she was young and naive and did not believe anything was wrong with her perfect baby.

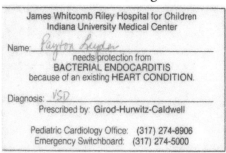

We called Payton Alex for the early years of his life—partly, I suspect, due to my close friendship with the Booth family growing up. The parents, L. Thomas and Norma Sue, both used their middle names, as did my first childhood crush, Carolyn Suzanne, who went by Suzanne. Suzanne's younger brother, Tommy, was a frequent golf partner at junior tournaments, and Tom and Sue served as our chauffeurs to various golf tournaments, given my mother's work schedule. Payton continued as Alex until he started school. I told Alex, "When the teacher does roll call, he or she will say, 'Payton Alexander,' and you will need to let them know your name is Alex."

Alex, as he was prone to do, responded immediately, "That's okay. They can call me Payton." Eventually, we made the change and called him Payton as well.

Robyn attempted to breastfeed but struggled to meet our growing baby's demands. He was a horrible sleeper, largely due to his insatiable appetite. Robyn's mom suggested putting a little cereal in his milk. Robyn knew that was a no-no, but it worked. Alex continued to grow at an alarming rate and was almost thirty pounds by his first birthday.

Robyn and I came from vastly different backgrounds. My high school graduating class at Northrop in Fort Wayne, Indiana, was a tad shy of six hundred students. It was much bigger than Robyn's entire high school in Bremen, Indiana, a rural agricultural community with little diversity in Amish country near South Bend, Indiana. Robyn was excited to attend college, longing for a more sophisticated life than what Bremen offered. I, on the other hand, viewed college as the next rung on the ladder toward moving to adulthood and getting a good job. I was in college to get an education. I self-funded college through loans, work, and grants, and I did not want to waste any time or money.

My early years were shaped by a lot of worldly success but limited spiritual formation. The 1970s were an economic mess, with the highest inflation rates in my lifetime, weak economic growth, and a depressed stock market. My parents divorced in 1975, when I was twelve. Theirs had been a largely loveless marriage often fraught with bickering and angst. My mother and dad were both college-educated but ill-prepared for their roles as parents, given their upbringing. The marriages of their parents and siblings all ended in divorce.

My mother, Patricia, assumed the responsibility of raising three young boys while working full-time in sales to make ends meet. She was a dreamer with noble aspirations, trying to make decisions on her own. My dad, Thomas, was highly intelligent but lacked motivation to do much beyond engage in and brag about his son's athletic pursuits, watch sports, and enjoy a libation with his buddies at a favorite watering hole. Anger and hypocrisy were the norm. I rejected parental authority, as I considered myself more mature and grounded than my parents. I held leadership positions in school government and achieved academic and athletic success. I excelled at golf, consistently performing in the top five in my peer group in city and area tournaments; played Little League baseball; was the quarterback for the junior high football team; and won two YMCA city championship basketball tournaments against future NCAA

Division I athletes. Academically, I finished in the top 10 percent of my high school class and was the student council president in both junior high and high school. Add a spelling bee championship and a finish as runner-up in the high school speech competition, and you get some idea of my achievement-oriented youth. My grandfather Dale was influential in my early years, given his strong work ethic and workplace success. More importantly, he demonstrated a desire to care for and support others, a trait I inherited and would carry forward to future years. My extended family often called me Dale Jr.

I was baptized as an infant and recognized the Christian faith but had limited understanding as to what it meant. My mother had a desire for our family to attend church, but church was a turnoff considering the ongoing conflict at home. I recall my middle brother, Scott, making an altar call at a Billy Graham event as a teenager. I refused my mother's request to participate in confirmation class in 1977, given my disdain for the hypocritical environment I was living in. Selfish desires were the norm, and weekend beer parties were on tap my junior and senior years in high school. I had few, if any, Christian friends, and a couple were self-appointed members of the Federation of Atheist Athletes (FAA).

Robyn, on the other hand, lived her entire life in the same small town where her high-school-sweetheart parents, Mike and Ann, had grown up. Mike had been on the high school's first football team. Ann had been a homecoming queen. Mike's dad, Bud, had wanted him to drop out of school after the ninth grade to help the family, but Mike had been determined to get an education. Mike was a simple man. He said what he meant and believed people could do anything they put their minds to. He lived that credo and could do anything. Robyn was just like her dad: strong-willed, down-to-earth, and related well to the average person. Many were drawn to them through their gifts of hospitality and willingness to serve and help one another. Robyn was a classic overachiever, not girlie and always wanted to be the best and have the best. Unlike her younger sister, Cari, she never wanted to cross her dad. Robyn was athletic and spent a lot of her free time, when not studying or making clothes, playing tennis. She was quite accomplished, losing few matches during her high school career. Like me, she grew up in the United Church of Christ (UCC) and had knowledge of the Christian faith; however, it was not a guiding force in her early years.

One September afternoon in 1981, shortly after beginning college at Indiana University, I ventured down the long V-shaped corridor on the third floor at Briscoe-Gucker Quad. Once classes were done, there was a general gathering in someone's room to chat, play cards, or do just about anything other than study. Hopefully, studying happened later in the evening. Doors were typically open, which meant all were invited to join in. I heard some conversation emanating from the far end of the hall, in the room next to the resident assistant's room. Jerry Hammel was in 330 along with Scott "Howie" Morrison. I knew Jerry, as we had been on the junior high football team at Jefferson and continued our relationship in high school as Jerry pursued an interest in accounting, as I had. I entered the room to familiar voices and noticed a cute girl sitting in the chair next to the door, wearing her letter jacket and with her dark brown hair in French braids. She was studying calculus with Jerry, as they were in the same class. I quickly noticed the twinkle in her pretty gray eyes and her round face and cheeks. She was naturally pretty and did not need makeup to look good. I would learn she was athletic, smart, and not ditzy, which were attractive qualities to me. I hadn't dated much in high school and was not on the prowl to date in college either. It was not for a lack of interest; rather, I was busy working in the cafeteria, going to school, and enjoying time with my fellow dorm mates.

A few months later, in November, I received an invitation to attend her floor party, Come Mix with Six. She was on the sixth floor, in room 622, and I was on the third floor, in room 307, which provided ample opportunity for us to bump into each other from time to time. She would later tell me, "I invited you to the floor party because you paid no attention to me, and I had already dated everyone else on your floor." Robyn is a little prone to exaggeration. She had not really dated everyone on my floor, but she wanted to have fun, and her grades showed it: she ended the first semester on academic probation with a 1.7, or C-, average. She was far smarter and started to kick it into gear in the following semester. I would take some credit for settling her down, as we had our first date on December 5 and spent a significant amount of time together in the semesters to follow.

Our relationship was interrupted for a short time the following semester, as I told Robyn I did not want to get serious. My grandfather had told me I was there to go to school, and I found myself spending a lot of time with her. Immediately after making that proclamation, I was calling her multiple times a day. This was in the day prior to cell phones, which meant I had to try to time my call to when she was in her dorm room. After three or four days, I realized I was hopelessly in love and begged some sort of forgiveness to reinstate our relationship. Robyn agreed, and I was thankful. We were not yet going steady, but we did see a lot of each other.

We had one additional relational hiccup the following month when another girl in our dorm offered to take me to an Indiana University basketball game. She had prime seats on the floor, right behind the basket. Indiana's basketball team was coming off a national championship the prior spring, and the head coach, Bob Knight, was already legendary. Her offer was far too good to refuse. It took me but a few seconds to agree, my feelings for Robyn easily dismissed by the thought of floor seats at the basketball game. I do not remember anything about the game, but I vividly remember walking into the dorm with a conscience seared with guilt, which caused me to feel a little sheepish about the stunt I had pulled. I thought it was a good idea to head up to Robyn's room to check in with her.

Within seconds of stepping onto her floor, I ran into Monique. I was friendly with Monique and engaged in conversation with her from time to time, but on that occasion, she was in no mood to talk. Before I could even get out a hello, Monique, with a piercing gaze that penetrated the depths of my soul, said, "Where were you?"

I tried to avoid looking at her, as she was an intimidating woman, and said in a hushed tone, "The basketball game." She informed me Robyn had been taken to the hospital, and they had been frantically looking for me, as they'd needed a car. I would later learn Robyn had a bout of colitis, likely brought on by stress or anxiety—perhaps a result of the need to improve her grades, her perfectionist tendencies, or a hectic social schedule, which ensnared many a freshman. I never made that mistake again and vowed to date only one person at a time. I was fully committed to Robyn.

In early May, after completing freshman finals, I headed to Michigan to work at Heatherwood Farms in Lansing. I stopped en route for a few days in Fort Wayne for a short visit to see my mom and two younger brothers,

Scott and Tom. My grandfather, as the recently retired former president of the dairy, had arranged the job for me. Grandad, as he was prone to do, gave me the following instructions with an expectation I would follow them: "Keep your head down and your mouth shut." Basically, he was telling me to do my job. Period. Frankly, that advice served me well in the years to come, as most often, workplace problems are a result of straying from mastering the task at hand.

It was difficult to leave Robyn, as we had dated for almost six months, far longer than any relationship I'd had in high school. We agreed to stay in touch, and once I got situated, I would go to Bremen to see her. That summer, I lived with my maternal grandma, Violet, in her duplex in East Lansing, not far from the Michigan State University campus. My grandparents had divorced nine years earlier, on June 8, 1973, the fifth birthday of my youngest brother, Tom. My grandfather had remarried four years later to Verlene Vaughn Blackie, who worked with him at Heatherwood. That was a significant sore point with my mother and grandmother, to say the least.

I loved my grandma and was looking forward to spending time with her. I was her favorite, as we both loved golf, and I enjoyed her cherry pies, among other things. I quickly realized Robyn reminded me of Grandma Vi, with her similar interests, love of clothes, and willingness to state her mind.

If I'd had any thought I was going to have a cushy job, it was quickly removed. The job at the dairy was not easy. Typically, I worked the 3:00 p.m. to 11:30 p.m. shift and returned home each night grimy and sweaty from loading boxes of juice products onto a pallet for eight hours. The plant foreman, John Batista, or Big John, quickly took me under his wing and said, "Make sure you get your education because you do not want to do this type of work the rest of your life." I did not need that encouragement, but it certainly reinforced my belief about the importance of an education and my commitment to school. My grandfather and parents were constant advocates for a college education. My grandfather told me not to pursue professional golf, not that it was my plan. He said I would go broke and starve my family. My mother had broken down in tears my senior year in high school when she thought my best friend, Dave Brown, was going to room with me in college. Dave was the class clown, and Mom had been certain he would lead me down a path of destruction.

It was mid-June before I made the three-hour trip to Bremen to see Robyn. It was my first opportunity to meet her mom. I'd met her younger sister, Cari, during an unchaperoned trip with Jodi Pfefferle the prior fall. Our first encounter had been at her sister's floor dance party, where I'd tried to impress them with my athletic prowess as I bounced from the floor, trying to knock beer caps off the ceiling with my head. My first encounter with her dad, Mike, had been in the main lobby of our quad on Friday, March 5, 1982, when he came to pick up Robyn for spring break. That day is forever etched in my memory, as John Belushi, a cult hero from *Saturday Night Live* and *Animal House*, had passed away earlier that day. Mike was a big guy, a man's man, outdoorsman, and hunter, who made it a habit to clean his guns or sharpen his knives when prospective suitors came over to date his daughters. That was the case when I arrived ten to fifteen minutes later than expected as a result of turning at the first stoplight I hit once I reached town and ending up lost and out in the country. Robyn's mom, Ann, had forgotten to mention to me that a second stoplight had been added a few years prior as a result of the construction of a bypass around the town of five thousand residents. That gaffe, like others in the years to come, would provide me with ample material to pick on my future mother-in-law, whom I dearly love.

We continued dating during our sophomore and junior years as I pursued an accounting degree from the Kelley School of Business, and Robyn pursued a nursing degree after multiple changes to her educational plans. Switching majors put Robyn a year behind me in her timeline to graduate. We spent significant time together, except for Robyn's occasional underage trips with her girlfriends to the bars for drink specials—they didn't even need fake IDs. I used my relationship with Robyn as an excuse to avoid much of the drunkenness and debauchery that came with college living. By our junior year, we each had a single room and, for all practical intents, were living together. One room served as the living room and study room, and the other was for sleeping.

My financial instincts began to take over, and I thought, *if we are going to live together, we should get married, as it is far easier to go to school as a poor married couple than in our present situation.* I was funding my education, and Robyn's parents were funding hers. If we got married, we would only have to pay for one dorm room, and we would receive more financial aid and support than under our parents' incomes. Don't get me wrong: we loved each other—whatever that meant for two twenty-year-olds—so we had a few conversations about getting married. With that in mind, we were at the College Park Mall in Bloomington on Friday afternoon, October 7, 1983, and we casually walked past Goodman Jewelers. Robyn was already an expert in the field of shopping, so her eyes glanced at the window display. I said, "You can go in if you want to." She started to look around as a sales associate seized on the opportunity to assist and quickly showed us the engagement rings. I asked, "What size do you typically get?"

Robyn responded, "Oh, a third or maybe a half carat." She continued to look and found one she really liked. It was .39 carats, which fell within the typical range, and more importantly, she loved it.

I said, "You can get that if you want to."

Robyn was a little stunned and, with the same twinkle in her eye I first had seen two years prior, said, "Really?"

I replied, "My bank is right across the parking lot. I will go over and get the money." I was a fastidious saver as a result of working various jobs since I was fourteen: a paper route, jobs at McDonald's and a cinema, jobs as a golf caddy and quad store accountant, and my summer job at Heatherwood Farms. My best friend, Dave, often chided me about my frugal tendencies.

Fifteen minutes later, I returned and paid $519.75 cash for the engagement ring. There was no formal proposal and certainly no romantic sweeping her off her feet. We were now engaged. Robyn could not wait to show her friends her early birthday present, call her mom, and begin planning for the big day.

I was excited to start the next chapter in my life but had no earthly idea what it meant to be married, as every family member dating back two generations had been at one time divorced. We were married the following summer, on August 18, 1984, in Robyn's hometown, Bremen. My youngest brother, Tom, who was sixteen years old, offered me sage advice: "Never let the romance go out of your life." He was obviously astute, given the lack of romance associated with the engagement decision and my dating life. Two weeks later, Robyn and I moved to Portage, Indiana, to start married life together in a trailer park. Earlier that year, I'd secured an internship with Arthur Andersen's audit practice and regulatory services division in Chicago. Andersen was regarded as the number-one professional services firm, and Chicago was their headquarters. I was twenty-one years old, was married, and had great prospects for a career with a preeminent firm—it seemed everything was off to a good start.

The internship experience provided assignments of a veritable blue-ribbon list of some of the Chicago office's biggest and most important clients. I was offered a full-time position upon my future graduation, and it did not take me long to accept. However, I decided to join the Indianapolis office, which was closer to Indiana University and our hometowns. The decision was perplexing to Dick DeCleene, one of the partners in Chicago, who wondered why anyone would want to live in Indiana. "All they have is corn," he said. Little did he know Indianapolis was on the verge of a meteoric rise, and my position with Arthur Andersen's Indianapolis office would contribute in some small part to the city's success.

Robyn started nursing school at Indiana University's Indianapolis campus, which was the hub for their medical programs. Robyn had made dramatic strides in her academics the prior two years to raise her GPA above a 3.0. She had two years of schooling left to graduate with a BS in nursing after changing majors and taking the majority of the last year off from school to follow me on my internship and work to help us make ends meet as I studied for the CPA exam prior to graduating from college.

We were seemingly prepared for starting out our adult and professional lives in Indianapolis, but we would gradually learn that like many young married couples, we lacked a foundation or compass to address many of life's challenges that would come our way.

Biblical Principle

King David, the author of most of the psalms, wrote the following in Psalm 139:13–16:

> For You formed my inward parts;
> You covered me in my mother's womb.
> I will praise You, for I am fearfully and wonderfully made;
> Marvelous are Your works,
> And that my soul knows very well.
> My frame was not hidden from You,
> When I was made in secret,
> And skillfully wrought in the lowest parts of the earth.
> Your eyes saw my substance, being yet unformed.
> And in Your book they all were written,
> The days fashioned for me,
> When as yet there were none of them.

God knew Payton before he was in Robyn's womb. He was fearfully and wonderfully made despite the hole in his heart. Payton was formed in God's image, as it is written in Genesis 1:27.

Upon reflection, God had a plan for Payton and our lives. Though we would have loved more time with him, we are eternally thankful for the time we had.

CHAPTER 3

TREES OR A FIREPLACE

We moved to Indianapolis a few weeks after I graduated from college in mid-May 1985, excited to begin our adult lives together in the big city. We found a small two-bedroom apartment at Chesapeake Landing on the west side of Indianapolis, about a fifteen-minute commute to downtown. My office was about one mile from where Robyn would attend nursing school. Life was busy as I started my full-time career in public accounting at Arthur Andersen and spent the bulk of my time performing audit services for General Telephone (GTE) at their Bloomington, Illinois, service center. That assignment, combined with a summertime trip to Jasper, Indiana, for the year-end audit for Kimball International, meant I was on the road for almost half of my first year with the firm. My traveling provided ample opportunity for Robyn to focus on her studies and made our weekend reunions all the better. My starting salary was $20,000. We were not flush with cash but compared to the $8,000 we'd earned the previous year, we thought we were living high off the hog!

Life was busy. We enjoyed married life together and learned the ropes of becoming a couple. We were immersed in the world of big-city living, with spare time to take in our favorite sports and pastimes: NBA basketball, particularly Magic Johnson and the Los Angeles Lakers, and professional golf and tennis. The Chicago Bears and Cubs were not far behind. The Bears won their last Super Bowl title in 1985, the year we arrived in Indy, and undoubtedly, their star player, Walter Payton, had some impact on our first son's birth name. In the fall of 1986, we learned Robyn was pregnant.

We were surprised, as she was on birth control pills. She likely had missed her required dosage due to her busy schedule. Couple that with my travel schedule, and we had no reason to expect a pregnancy.

Four days after Payton's birth on May 15, 1987, I was promoted to an audit senior. There had been eleven individuals in my starting class two years prior, and three of us were fast-tracked to that role. The communication from Jack O'Donnell, the office managing partner (OMP), went on to say, "Since client service is our main mission, we naturally expect all of our personnel to contribute to this goal. In our office, the partners and managers have grown accustomed to working with exceptionally competent and dedicated personnel. The demands, at times, seem to be substantial. The pressure for answers and leadership seems never ending in the firm. Somehow, most of our people accept the challenge and the opportunities and make the personal sacrifices that help to distinguish our organization from all the competitors." He then went on to offer congratulations on behalf of the office's partners and managers. Jack arrived in the Indianapolis office from Oakland in 1983, ostensibly to either shut down a poorly performing office or make it profitable. Years later, the Indianapolis office would become one of the most profitable and highly regarded offices in the firm, and my role leading the GTE engagement would play a significant role in our growth and profitability. Jack's fingerprints were all over the office. He set the tone and led by example. Jack was driven, almost fanatical in his disciplined approach to serving clients, developing his people, and supporting them. He never shied from a difficult discussion or conversation. His approach was the outgrowth of his competitive upbringing as a basketball player at Marquette.

At his core, Jack was a teacher. He invested in people and their careers and cared about their lives outside of work. He placed a high value on family. His leadership and example served as a testament to me and many others for the years to come.

However, it was not my promotion or early success at Andersen that would ultimately alter the trajectory of our life. People make many decisions that seem inconsequential at the time but have a huge impact on their lives—for example, when Robyn and I made the decision to move into Briscoe Quad at Indiana University. If I'd not made that decision, I would not have met Robyn. My decision was based principally on the proximity of the dorm to the athletic facilities on campus. Indiana University was a foregone conclusion for me, given the outstanding reputation of their business school and the success of their basketball program.

In the same way, a seemingly inconsequential article in the Sunday newspaper ultimately impacted our future in a big way.

Ever since my early teen years, I'd woken each morning and stumbled half asleep out to the curb to pick up the newspaper after rolling out of bed. Often, I did so with no shoes and barely any clothing, quickly sprinting to the end of the drive and back inside in ten seconds or less. It didn't matter if it was the middle of summer or the coldest day of the year. Growing up in an era without ESPN, social media, and cable TV meant I learned how my favorite team had fared when I read the morning newspaper. I would go to the sports section first to learn how my teams had done. I spent little time and attention on world, national, and local events. I studied the box scores and read with interest stories about my favorite teams and heroes. An early version of ESPN's *SportsCenter*, in print media, was the *Sporting News*, which I received weekly and scoured to review the interesting stories of the day.

On a warm Sunday morning in July 1987, I picked up the *Indianapolis Star* newspaper and, after digesting the sports and other stories of interest, stumbled upon an article that seemed too good to be true. On that Sunday, it was not a sports story that grabbed my attention but a piece about an incentive program geared toward first-time home buyers. The program offered upward of a $2,000 annual mortgage credit applied against your federal tax liability for the life of your mortgage. There were a couple key caveats: the buyer had to make less than $37,000 in annual income, and the purchase price had to be less than $95,000 for new homes. My recent promotion and salary increase to $24,800 put me comfortably under the threshold, as Robyn was not working. Her plans were to get a nursing job by the end of the year, as she was only two months removed from delivering Payton, so we met the financial requirements for the time being.

My financial instincts immediately went into overdrive, and a quick calculation demonstrated the potential staggering benefit of seizing the opportunity. Given my income, the potential credit and the traditional mortgage interest deduction would result in almost half the potential mortgage payment coming back to me through a reduction to our federal income taxes. The article went on to say the state of Indiana had a pool of $2 million in available credits. That meant possibly a thousand people could hit the lottery with a $2,000 maximum annual credit. I was motivated to act.

We had no immediate plans to buy a house for our family of three; however, Robyn previously had expressed interest in buying a house at some point down the road. I shared the news of the program, and she was excited about the possibility. Robyn trusted—and still trusts—my financial instincts and shared later in life that she had no knowledge or understanding of money growing up and, absent my involvement, would have been broke. I, on the other hand, spent too much time stewarding our resources. In that respect, we were good for each other: Robyn had a desire to enjoy what we had, and I was a saver.

I was concerned about a state-wide rush to tap into the lucrative opportunity, and we began to look at homes later that week. Within ten days, we executed a purchase agreement with Ryland Homes to build a house in Liberty Creek North subdivision on the northwest side of Indianapolis, in Pike Township, a few miles from our apartment. We ultimately settled on lot number twenty-five, on a cul-de-sac, as it was about $1,000 less than the wooded lot catty-corner on Petersburg Parkway, which was our other choice. Ultimately, we opted for the lower priced lot, as it would allow us to have a fireplace.

We moved into our new house the first week of November, excited to have our first home. Of the approximate eighty lots in the subdivision, about seven to ten were built, which would allow us ample time to meet our neighbors as the subdivision was built out over the coming years. The following spring, Keith and Becky Ogorek and their daughter Rachel moved into lot number thirty, the lot with trees in the backyard that we'd passed over. Years later, we would learn of Becky's passion for nature and wooded surroundings. She would not have moved into our subdivision absent our decision, as there were only a couple lots with any measure of trees other than the perfunctory sapling planted in front of each of the starter homes. The seemingly inconsequential decision of having trees or a fireplace ultimately forged a lifetime friendship and one the Lord would use for His glory.

The next couple years would result in feelings of guilt for Robyn as she worked full-time at Riley Hospital on the 3:00 p.m. to 11:00 p.m. shift. Work was a necessity, as we'd purchased the most house we could afford, and the evening shift allowed us to split childcare responsibilities, except for a few hours every afternoon until I picked Payton up in the late afternoon or early evening. My recent promotion also included a big assignment as the lead audit senior: supervising a large team of talented individuals for GTE at their Midwest regional headquarters in Westfield, Indiana. The overall GTE corporate audit was one of Andersen's top five US audit clients. My role as the audit senior in charge would result in almost three-quarters of my billable hours. Thus, my schedule was predictable, albeit demanding, and allowed Robyn and me to reasonably manage our dual careers for the near future.

Some twelve years later, we outgrew our starter home and moved a few miles away, staying within Pike Township and the city of Indianapolis. It pained me to move and lose the benefit of the tax credit, but I knew it was the right decision for our family. Financial stewardship was a significant focal point of our married life, to a fault. But the Lord was about to grab our attention and put some major life-altering decisions in front of us that would cause us to evaluate our priorities.

≈ Biblical Principle ≈

The Old Testament prophet Ezekiel addressed the politically and spiritually corrupt nation of Israel and spoke the following in Ezekiel 36:26–28: "I will give you a new heart and put a new spirit within you; I will take the heart of stone out of your flesh and give you a heart of flesh. I will put My Spirit within you and cause you to walk in My statutes, and you will keep My judgments and do them. Then you shall dwell in the land that I gave to your fathers; you shall be My people, and I will be your God."

I did not know it at the time, but Robyn and I had hearts of stone. There was nothing in our lives that directed us to acknowledging, living for, or serving the Lord. Yet God pursued us and put His Spirit in us.

Upon reflection, we were on the verge of a big change in the direction of our lives, one that would cause us to examine His Word and whom we were living for. Only then would we come to understand and see His plans for us.

CHAPTER 4

A SPIRITUAL TUG-OF-WAR

Payton was growing quickly and off the charts. I am six feet three inches tall and come from a family of tall men. There is an old wives' tale that says if you double your child's height at age two, you can predict his or her ultimate height. If that were true, then Payton would exceed my height and then some when he reached adulthood. Robyn's mom, Ann, was available to come help at our beck and call. Payton was her first grandson, and we learned that grandparents could and would spoil their grandchildren, but we were thankful for her help. She loved Payton, and it showed. Payton ruled the house, and much of Robyn's life revolved around him. It did not take long for Payton to learn the art of manipulation, and he would scream if we put him in his crib, seemingly wailing forever. He would lift himself out of the crib, drop to the floor, and crawl to the door in his futile attempt to come sleep with us. He would cry himself to sleep, and we would find him the next morning with his little hand sticking out from underneath the door into the hallway. It made us feel terrible. We were amazed at the persistence of our two-year-old but frustrated at our inability to have him sleep in his bed. Eventually, we gave in, as Robyn felt a lot of guilt over her work schedule and was more than willing to have Payton sleep between us, a habit that would take years to break.

In 1989, we decided to have baby number two. It did not take long for Robyn to become pregnant. About six weeks later, Robyn began bleeding and had a miscarriage. She was devastated. To ease her pain, she drove two and a half hours to Bremen with Payton to spend a few days with her mom and dad, especially Ann, whom she needed most. They spoiled Payton, as he was a representation of what we had lost.

It wasn't long until Robyn became pregnant again. This time, the pregnancy was successful. Robyn was exhausted; the combination of working full-time at Riley and her pregnancy was almost more than she could bear. We were not in a position, or so we thought, for Robyn to quit work, but having learned her lesson from her miscarriage, she vowed to take better care of herself. Blake Michael Leyden was born on June 20, 1990, the last day prior to summer. Robyn's employer provided six weeks of maternity leave, which went by quickly. By comparison, Blake was a breeze. It was not long until he was sleeping through the night and on a regular schedule.

At about that time, we started attending a small church with an aging congregation: Garfield Park United Church of Christ, or Garfield Park, a few miles southeast of downtown Indianapolis. Garfield Park was about a twenty-minute car trip. We set out to find a church after prompting from my mother, who shared the concern of my youngest brother, Tom, that we needed to attend church with young children at home. I asked Robyn to call my home church, Plymouth Congregational, in Fort Wayne to ask if they could recommend a church in Indianapolis. The church secretary said their members George and Lucille Blossom had a son, Tom, who was a pastor at a UCC church in Indianapolis. As was often the case in denominational churches, he was expected to do everything.

Tom would soon serve as a spiritual mentor for me, along with two work colleagues, Laura Mayhall and Tim Doyle. Laura was an attractive young lady with a gleam in her eye and an unstated humility who quietly witnessed for the Lord. Laura was a runner, and we often ran together in 8K and 10K races. Robyn and Payton often joined me, cheering from the sidelines.

Tim had been a gifted athlete in his youth and contemplated suicide when he was fifteen because he knew something was physically wrong and was concerned about his ability to continue playing baseball. While sitting alone in a field, he'd heard a voice say, "Go to the hospital," and he'd obeyed the command. His thoughts of suicide had vanished. Tim had been diagnosed with muscular dystrophy on his sixteenth birthday—one of five siblings with the disease—and by thirty, he'd been wheelchair bound.

I did not know what it was at the time, but I saw something different in Tom, Laura, and Tim that was attractive to me. They did not seem overly preoccupied with the world and demonstrated a sincere love and affection for others.

Neither Robyn nor I really understood much about the Christian faith beyond the surface level and the general tenets of salvation, hell, and Jesus's sinless life. I enjoyed the Hollywood adaptations of certain biblical stories, regardless of their accuracy, such as the Exodus journey as portrayed by Charlton Heston in *The Ten Commandments*. I watched the movie every Easter for decades. Tom, Laura, and Tim demonstrated a certain aroma for Christ. They were selfless, humble, and directed in their desire to see the Lord work through them. I took notice, but it would take time and much personal churning to figure out the Christian faith and what it might mean to orient my life under His Lordship. Fortunately, the Holy Spirit was working on me amid my confusion.

The following May, in 1991, I was promoted to audit manager, the only one in my starting class to achieve that promotion. Arthur Andersen, at that time, was an up-or-out firm, and I was definitely on track, moving up the corporate ladder of success. If Tom Blossom was my spiritual mentor, Jack O'Donnell, the managing partner at Andersen, was my business mentor. Jack's retirement from the firm in the spring of 1992 resulted in Gil Viets taking the reins as the OMP. Gil was someone I knew well, as I'd worked with him on GTE the prior five years following his transfer from the Kansas City office.

During that time, I gave my life to Christ and accepted Jesus as my personal Savior. I do not remember the day, but I vividly recall the circumstances that led to my decision. I was growing in my faith through Tom's teaching at Garfield Park, and I stumbled upon—or, better said, the Lord directed me to—the book of Ecclesiastes. Ecclesiastes, written by King Solomon, son of David, unlocked answers to questions I was inherently searching for. Solomon, reputedly one of the wisest men who ever lived, had great wealth (and many wives) but found emptiness in the continued striving for and accumulation of worldly wealth and knowledge.

For many, the book of Ecclesiastes is depressing, as it puts man in an insignificant light and goes on to talk about the many seasons of life, including death. That reality struck a chord with me, as my logical orientation searched for the overarching governing principle(s) for life, and I found it, big-time, in the book of Ecclesiastes. Everything now made sense—at least from a starting point. Either the Bible was true and the singular source of truth for our lives, or it was not.

However, my newfound infant faith did not have my full attention. I also immersed myself in the teachings of Tony Robbins, the noted self-help guru with a new-age spiritual mysticism. Tony's thirty-day program entitled "Unleash the Power Within" addressed the central premise of man's existence to avoid pain or gain pleasure while delving into more complex subjects, such as neurolinguistic programming. His programs were entertaining and provocative, and he interviewed famous and highly acclaimed individuals on a range of topics. As a result, I started to outline a blueprint for my life and family, with intermittent journaling to ensure I was on track. My diet changed. I established goals. I created rituals. I was taking a much more active role in the direction of my life. I always had been driven; now I was focused. Frustration would set in when I did not follow through on my new game plan for my life. Professional opportunities were abundant at Arthur Andersen. Robyn and I were maturing in our relationship with one another. Externally, it appeared everything was great. Internally, it was a season of struggle for my heart as I started down a path to grow in my faith: Would the world get my affections, or would God?

The following year, on August 31, 1993, we rounded out our family with the birth of our third son, Chase Hamilton. Robyn had a salaried position with the Indiana University Medical Center, assisting one of the top breast cancer doctors in the country, George Sledge. The position provided much-needed flexibility with both her pregnancy and her maternity leave. Payton and Blake adored their baby brother, and Payton sent Robyn into a dizzying search for clothes for baby Chase, wanting him to have a white T-shirt and jean jacket.

Two weeks prior, prompted by Tony Robbins's disciplines, I'd embarked on an almost two-year period of journaling to ensure progress against desired objectives. The practice often resulted in journal entries every few days. Entries in late August and early September did not make mention of Chase's birth but only spoke to business and personal goals. That was shameful. I was embarking upon a significant time of searching and spiritual awakening that would usher in a new era for our family.

There was a lot of stirring, as Robyn and I were trying to make sense of the American dream while trying to figure out our faith. As I've said, our early years growing up in the church had provided only a faint understanding of what it meant to be a Christian.

On August 18, we celebrated our ninth wedding anniversary, and I gave Robyn an anniversary card that said, "I am committed to making this next year [the tenth] the most enjoyable and rewarding year for our family. With your continued support, we can accomplish anything we want to. I am very lucky to have someone like you." A few days later, Payton started first grade.

In October, I noted the following in my journal: "I'm not done with the operational consulting plan because other day-to-day activities have taken up my time." Recent business-improvement work in support of GTE and interest in understanding our clients' business, a result of Jack's leadership, was the impetus to initiate discussions with office leadership to start a new practice area. That was no small undertaking, as the firm already had a bellwether consulting organization in Andersen Consulting. Most of Andersen's large offices had nascent operational consulting practices to mitigate potential inroads by Andersen competitors, given Andersen Consulting's focus on top market opportunities and not protecting traditional audit and tax-client relationships. I was excited about the possibility but never measured the risk of success or the resources required and had tacit or lukewarm support from office leadership to pursue this as a potential career path within Andersen.

Two months later, I got the opportunity to lead the Arthur Andersen business unit Indianapolis office's first consulting project, and it was a doozy. The Indiana Department of Environmental Management (IDEM) was a government agency under attack for poor service with their regulatory permitting process and increased fee levels. They needed both business help and political cover. Andersen Consulting, with significant relationships and service to the State of Indiana, wisely understood the risk associated with taking on that project and passed it along to me, given my newfound role. It was a political hot potato, with the lieutenant governor of Indiana as the chair of a blue-ribbon task force and industry stalwarts, such as Jim Rogers, CEO of Cinergy, and Pat Kiely, head of the Indiana Manufacturers Association, playing key roles. We were under the gun to deliver a report prior to Christmas to help them figure out the mess. I was still working on finalizing the report at ten o'clock five nights before Christmas. It was a great first project for our fledgling practice, with one practitioner—me—and a couple individuals with interest in joining the team if we could acquire enough work. Most would have recommended building early wins with some safe projects to demonstrate success. I, on the other hand, stumbled upon a behemoth to start our foray into the world of consulting.

On Sunday, January 2, 1994, I journaled the following prescient and profound message from Pastor Tom Blossom's sermon: "The Lord is the center of our life. And I need to trust in the Lord's direction. I recognize there must be disciplining to accomplish the Lord's objectives." Little did I know, two weeks later, a major life-changing opportunity would come my way—the first of several that would grab my attention in 1994. It would serve as an early test to see how I might respond considering my newfound faith.

On January 19, Dave Foster, the overall engagement partner for GTE Telephone Operations, asked me about transferring to the Dallas office to serve as the overall engagement manager for GTE. My initial conclusion was no. I struggled with Dave's highly technical approach to an audit as compared to the business-driven approach in the Indianapolis office. He was a nice man, but I was also concerned with my perception of his work–life balance in light of his propensity to work long hours. Furthermore, I was increasingly committed to the community of Indianapolis, given family, church, and other considerations. In the coming months, Robyn and I visited Dallas as part of a recruitment effort and ultimately did say no to the opportunity. It was not an inconsequential decision, as GTE was one of the largest clients in our firm, with annual billings in the tens of millions of dollars, and if I'd continued to progress consistent with past results, I would certainly have made partner and received a lucrative financial package.

In May, six months after going back to work following Chase's birth, Robyn longed to stay home with our three boys. Payton was in the first grade and starting to have behavioral issues at school, exerting his unusual size and an independent streak, learned from his parents, to his advantage. Blake and Chase were in day care. Robyn felt a great deal of guilt for sending them to school and day care with the typical community colds and sore throats, fearing she'd miss too much work. Our finances were tight, primarily due to her overspending and her desire to dress her and the boys in the latest designer clothes. She had been sucked into the world of materialism, which became her identity. Robyn loved fashion and wanted to keep up with the Joneses, as our friends in the professional workplace valued a certain image. She thought if we all looked good, then everything was good. Her satisfaction and fulfillment came from shopping, and after all, she felt we deserved it because we worked so hard.

Our marriage was good but not great, as I was overzealous in my disciplined approach to pursuing my goals for me and our family. During one heated discussion, Robyn welled up with tears and said, "Life should not be this hard." She did not appreciate my misguided role as the consultant trying to figure out solutions to her and our problems. In one forceful exchange, she exclaimed, "I am not your client!" She resented my desire to control situations from afar, as she was the primary caregiver, dealing with the day-to-day grind, while I popped into the parenting role when work permitted me to do so. I was on the verge of learning a critically important lesson, one that served me well in the years to come: my wife was not an extension of me, and I could not change her; I had to change myself. Robyn's "I am not your client" remark hit home with me. I needed to listen, empathize with her situation, and determine the best way to lead our family but not solve all her problems. Slowly but surely, I was starting to come to grips with my strengths and limitations.

On May 8, Robyn and I developed a high-level financial goal. She wanted to stay at home beginning in August 1995. We agreed to make it happen. That was perhaps the most important goal we would establish in the first ten years of our marriage. The benefits far outweighed my overt preoccupation with our finances.

Two months later, I made the following entry in my journal: "Payton is not showing respect for Blake [our four-year-old] and treating him poorly. Robyn and I discussed appropriate ways to discipline, which does not include sarcasm and constant yelling."

However, it was an entry on July 21, 1994, that heralded a significant shift in my thinking and outlook on my career and our family life: "Today I set a goal that I will leave Arthur Andersen by March 31,

1995—hopefully by January 1, 1995. I am tired of feeling like a piece of raw meat." My post went on to express my concerns about the perceived callousness of the investment we made in our careers and the time taken away from our family. Nine years of constant deadlines, critical client demands, significant travel, financial sacrifice, and working in a fast-paced environment did not offset the benefits of working for arguably the world's best professional services firm, one where I had learned so much with great mentors, interesting client assignments, and an incredibly talented team of professionals. I was ready to give it all away. Ten days earlier, I'd noted, "I am more despondent at Gil's cavalier attitude toward operational consulting. I can't let this bitterness control me." I was despondent about Gil's buy-in with my significant investment and early results with the new practice area. Whether that was reality or Gil's desire for me to continue to serve lucrative clients, such as GTE, I do not know. I was not sure what Gil, or the firm, wanted from me. The firm's motto of "Think Straight, Talk Straight" rang hollow. I began to question my ongoing commitment to a firm I loved and where I had spent the past nine years. My annual review was two months later, which would hopefully bring this matter to a head.

On August 3, I called Mark Holden somewhat out of desperation and a desire to control my own destiny. I could share my frustrations with Mark, given our long work relationship. I'd worked almost exclusively for him for the first five years of my career. I wanted to let him know my plans to leave the firm the following year. We agreed to talk more after my return from vacation. Mark had been the audit manager on GTE until his departure the prior year to take the CFO role at Wabash National Corporation, a public company in Lafayette, Indiana, about an hour northwest of Indianapolis.

On September 11, Robyn and I were trying to get the school year off to a good start, as the following entry showed: "Great day. Robyn, the boys, and I each drafted our responsibilities and a daily chore schedule. Payton [now seven] surprised me when we discussed him signing the agreement, and he indicated he wasn't making a covenant. What a bright kid." During that same season, a work colleague, Tom Woodason, helped me install a parquet floor around our breakfast bar and kitchen. I told Payton, "If I were you, I would pick up those toys," meaning "We need your help, as we are trying to put in this floor."

Without hesitation, Payton responded, "You're me." I thought Tom was going to die of laughter. I'd set up Payton by the way I'd asked the question. We had our hands full with Payton.

On September 23, I had my annual review with Gil. Accompanying me were three pages of notes, which outlined several concerns. What was my incentive—the five-year carrot of partnership and significant future financial rewards? The prior November 15 to April 15 my work–life balance and the process related to my potential transfer was awful. I shared the following picture

to illustrate my frustration and need for an appropriate balance among faith, family, and the firm. This was a little bold, but I needed to get Gil's attention. I was at a point where something needed to change. My evaluations were stellar, exceeding expectations in most categories. Mark Fagan, a New Yorker who'd transferred to our office two years prior, served as the lead partner on GTE. Mark was extremely intelligent and hardworking, and I enjoyed working with him. He was a strong advocate for me.

Gil summarized my performance for the prior year as follows: "As a result of a corporate move by GTE Telephone Operations' plan for the coming year, one of Todd's major engagements will disappear. Todd has recognized this as a challenge to his career and has accepted the challenge to build an operational consulting practice in the Indianapolis office. This will be a major effort on Todd's part. He has shown that he is willing to make sacrifices for that effort, including significant amounts of training and patience to build desired confidence in the practice. Marketing these services to our clients is a risk he has accepted in his career, but one for which the partners in the office are delighted to give him the opportunity." Looking back with the benefit of hindsight, I realize Gil's comments were fair. I knew I had demonstrated and delivered a significant contribution to the office during my first nine years. Did I leave the review believing we were all in? No. But I was willing to move forward for the time being.

I'd been given an opportunity, and now I needed to make the most of it—unless, of course, the Lord had other plans.

The roller coaster of 1994 continued October 28, when I received news of a discussion involving Mark Holden. Mark called Tom Ertel, the audit division head, and inquired about my coming to work at Wabash National. The following entry shared my thoughts at the time:

> I am trusting in the Lord to direct us in the right direction. Gil spoke briefly to me and cautioned me to look long term. It is interesting this is the fourth major opportunity to present itself this year: first the relocation to Dallas for GTE; second an opportunity to transfer to Chicago and work with Carl Geppert on Ameritech [one of the Bell regional operating companies]; third with Vance and Dinsmore OC project; and now this. There are tradeoffs with any decision. I will have to work harder at Wabash, yet I will have a quality of life, a mentor, the ability to broaden my business skills, Fortune 500 credentials, and apparently good growth opportunities. On the other hand, Andersen provides prestige, unlimited opportunity, demands, flexibility yet lack of it, limited mentors, appreciation at times when the firm needs me, etc. This is a big and important step, and it impacts many things: church, home, work.

The tug-of-war continued as I reflected on December 5 on the pull of the workplace, my need to control my situation and outcome, and the Lord's leading through His Spirit. The possibility of a career change seemed to accelerate an already intense internal wrestling match for my soul, as the following entry highlights:

> What a beautiful day the Lord hath provided for me. I know it is time to change. Time to come to peace with the Lord. I am so thankful for His continued forgiveness, especially despite my failings. How thankful we are for His forgiveness and never-ending love if we trust in Him

and seek salvation through Christ Jesus. Tom Blossom spoke of contentment yesterday and referenced the lottery. What if we were content in what the Lord provided to us? What if we really made the best use of the resources, He has given us? I am very thankful today for another chance, another day, and another opportunity!

Years later, I could address with a mature perspective life-altering questions that were impossible for me to consider at that time in my life. My flesh was torn between the desires of upward mobility and the associated lifestyle and the Lord's truth, which was gradually revealed to me as I started to look at life through a new lens.

The Holy Spirit and Tom's teaching continued to work on me as I recorded the following on January 16, 1995:

> Tom's sermon was superb and brilliant and clearly articulated his personal mission and vision. He has given so much recently. I pray for his strength and continued commitment. I love him and what he stands for. I pray for this Wabash situation to come to a timely resolution. I really want this opportunity to come to pass if it is the Lord's will. This would be an additional dimension to my credentials and provide more security for our family and stability long term in my career. I am growing tremendously in the consulting arena; however, this does not provide for the financial and business perspective as it relates to stakeholders, customers, and vendors. Robyn has been fantastic lately—very committed to our financial plan. Two weeks until her retirement. This will be great for our family.

We achieved Robyn's goal of leaving the workforce seven months earlier than our original plan. She was ecstatic.

A week later, I was in the Chicago area and journaled the following:

> What a powerful day. In St. Charles, Illinois, to attend Andersen market share program. I heard a whisper to call Scott [my brother] and encourage him in concluding his studies and with his employment search. Peg [his wife] led us in reading scripture with many powerful passages ... Scott prayed for me, the Wabash situation, and the kids and family. Peg prayed for Scott and his studies and for Robyn to open up to the Word ... I prayed yesterday for the Lord to guide my steps in service.

A month later, almost four months had elapsed since Mark Holden contacted Andersen leadership about my joining Wabash National. My entry on February 21 said the following:

> The Lord woke me up at 10:30 p.m. in Columbus Holiday Inn and told me to reverse the typical hold pattern of pizza, a movie, and early to bed with laziness and lack of discipline and conviction. I turned to the book of Job, chapter 31, and readings in Proverbs and Matthew. Job 13:15 says, "Though he slays me, yet I will hope in Him." After all, if faith depended on visible evidence, it would not be faith. I am reminded of patience and to trust in the Lord. Robyn and I talked about this today as I met with Mark Holden regarding Wabash. Robyn is frustrated about the time to decide and move forward. I felt our meeting went very well. Mark was honest about other candidates but implicitly indicated I was the front-runner or his choice, but it is important top management is comfortable with the decision made. I will have patience; there is a reason behind all of this. This will allow more time to move forward with strategic planning initiatives with the church, advance the Columbus schools initiative, and demonstrate my capabilities with the Indiana Gas project.

Despite the inconceivable delay with the Wabash decision, life moved on, and the following entries recorded during the Lenten season demonstrated the Lord was winning the spiritual tug-of-war for Robyn's and my souls.

- March 1: "A great day. Lenten service was nice. Tom had a nice meditation describing the relevance of the forty days [e.g., Noah's ark, Jesus's temptation in the wilderness, and the exodus of Jews from Egypt] and ashes and sack cloth and our humanity. Robyn is very committed to serving Christ. I am so proud of her. Her support for Moms Together, desire to attend all Lenten services, purchase of my Bible for Valentine's Day, and discussion with Eda [Jeff Terp's wife] about Bible study class. Tony Robbins tape this month is on love. I need to write a love letter. I will."
- March 5: "Relationship with Robyn grows closer every day. I sense we are really beginning to look inward before condemning the other. She is very supportive of me, especially as it relates to the career uncertainty. She is doing very well meeting our financial objectives and is truly enjoying retirement. This was the best decision we made."
- March 6: "A passage in the book of Luke really caught my attention … Luke 12:15: 'And He said, to them, Take heed and beware of covetousness, for one's life does not consist in the abundance of things he possesses.' Am I funding my needs or greed?"
- March 8: "Am losing interest in Wabash daily. I am disappointed not that the process has taken so long but rather in the poor communication from Mark."
- March 25: "Tonight is a watershed event. I am going to share my principles with Robyn. I was very disappointed at her reaction to my request to attend the Tony Robbins seminar in Chicago. I spent two hours with Blake, walking through the woods at Eagle Creek Park. I had quite a chat with Gil Thursday regarding my career. It is nice to feel appreciated—although it may be self-serving. Even though Mark has not called, I better understand the reasons for delays in his making a move. Gil said Tom Ertel told him Mark was going to make an offer to me. Who knows? … I had Robyn rate me on various aspects of my life [on a ten-point scale]

compared with three to five years ago to support my attendance at the Robbins event.

	Today	3–5 years ago
Spiritual	9	3
Family and marriage	8	5
Physical	9	7
Career	7	3
Financial	7	3

An entry on April 16 summed up the culmination of several years of struggle as I attempted to balance the prospects of a career with Andersen, my growing family, and my recent faith:

> I learned from a Zig Ziglar tape the importance of trusting in the Lord regarding the decisions that affect you, the need to glorify God in all you do, the importance of witnessing to your faith, and salvation through acceptance of Jesus Christ and not through works. The Lord knows what is around the corner for each of us, and that is why we must trust in the Lord. This past week, I told Robyn I would contact Mark by May 1 if I have not heard from him, as we need to move forward with our life. I have an inner peace, as I know that our steps are ordered by the Lord, and He delighteth in the way.
>
> Zig's message was underscored by a sermon we heard from the pastor at First United UCC in Bremen [Robyn's home church]. It was outstanding—he was warm and engaging. His sermon addressed the need to recognize Jesus, and when we lose our focus, looking to the past and our selfish desires, it will make it difficult to see Jesus in our lives and how the Lord can shape decisions for us. We focus on the wrong needs—secular.

> I now realize prayer is even more important than I can comprehend. Daily prayer and scripture are the backbone of life. This will bring me spiritual fulfillment and contentment.

This journal entry brought into focus discernment regarding the Lord's will through prayer and the reading of His Word. It was a harbinger for the Wabash decision, which would occur in the following month. I was on the teeter-totter of life, with one leg on the things of the world and the other tiptoeing into the realm of reliance of Jehovah Jireh, my provider as the source of divine direction.

On April 21, I noted the following:

> I called Mark Holden this afternoon, as I know the time has come to move forward. The next move is his. My interest has waned substantially. I put this decision in the Lord's hands. Gil was extremely complimentary (to me) given the potential consulting work on our plate. I must temper this excitement with my long-term realization of my goals. I was touched by Robyn wanting to make this a special evening for me: ice cream, Jacuzzi with Blake, a nice dinner. She is happy to be off work. I am tired after a long week! I will continue my quest for success and personal fulfillment. Robyn is now resolved to stay at Andersen and change some things around in the house to make our living conditions more bearable.

On May 15, we celebrated Payton's birthday, which I noted as follows: "Payton's eighth birthday—I worked late. Hectic day for Robyn with soccer, Payton's school, shopping, etc. I must continue to support her with love. I am so thankful for children and the joy they bring to our lives. Mother is very approachable as I have worked at developing and strengthening our relationship."

On May 17, I finally received an answer. It was the answer I was prepared for but not the one I originally had sought.

> Yesterday Mark Holden called and indicated he was hiring Rick Davis [a fellow coworker and younger staff person]. He didn't want to hurt our relationship. I was relieved he didn't make an offer, as I did not want to turn the offer down. The Lord made it very clear to me that our future was not in Lafayette. The Zig Ziglar tape I listened to on April 20 indicated Zig prayed very hard for two things the Lord turned down. The Lord knows what is around the corner, and we do not. I continue to put my faith and trust in God. I am looking forward with excitement to developing the business consulting practice. There are significant opportunities. I want to do it in the best way possible and be a model to others in the firm.

God responded, just as Zig had said He would, with a no—a response I received but a few times in my professional career. Mark's call was the right call, and I knew it. Why did the call happen nine months after my initial cry for help and almost seven months after Mark called office leadership to express an interest in hiring me?

Matt Erickson, senior pastor at Eastbrook Church in Milwaukee, summed it up well in his remarks at a Fort Wilderness family camp in June 2018 when he reflected on our lives: "Apart from God, we often live by one of three story lines: the story of achievement, the story of reputation, or the story of consumption." I was living the story of achievement, with the central goal of life to achieve. Matt described it as "I am what I do." I associated my intrinsic value with what I did or did not accomplish.

I was stuck—living in two worlds. I could not see it at the time, but God's plans were much broader and bigger than mine. Only He can see around the corner. God wanted all of me. My decision-making framework was beginning to change. The decisions made would serve as a critical anchor and prepare us for some big things the Lord had in store for our family, starting with an invitation from our neighbor Keith to attend a Christian camp, Fort Wilderness.

⇥ Biblical Principle ⇤

King Solomon, the son of David, king in Jerusalem, wrote in the first chapter of the book of Ecclesiastes,

> "Vanity of vanities," says the Preacher;
> "Vanity of vanities, all is vanity."
> What profit has a man from all his labor
> In which he toils under the sun?
> One generation passes away, and another generation comes;
> But the earth abides forever.
> The sun also rises, and the sun goes down,
> And hastens to the place where it arose.
> The wind goes toward the south,
> And turns around to the north;
> The wind whirls about continually,
> And comes again on its circuit.
> All the rivers run into the sea,
> Yet the sea is not full;
> To the place from which the rivers come,
> There they return again.
> All things are full of labor;
> Man cannot express it.
> The eye is not satisfied with seeing,
> Nor the ear filled with hearing.
> That which has been is what will be,
> That which is done is what will be done,
> And there is nothing new under the sun.
> Is there anything of which it may be said,
> "See, this is new"?
> It has already been in ancient times before us.
> There is no remembrance of former things,
> Nor will there be any remembrance of things that are to come
> By those who will come after …

> What is crooked cannot be made straight,
> And what is lacking cannot be numbered …
> For in much wisdom is much grief,
> And he who increases knowledge increases sorrow.

The above passage played a major role in my understanding and acceptance of the Christian faith. Upon reflection, I realized my value and importance were not in the striving and ceasing but must have a higher and nobler pursuit in the understanding of God and my relationship with Him who created all things. We are restless until we rest in Him and His plans and purposes, not ours, as we will eventually wither and fade away. Whatever we do, whatever we achieve, and whomever we know, we will leave it all behind. I cannot understand all that God has put in place for me and my life.

PART 3

PREPARING THE WAY

CHAPTER 5

AN INVITATION TO FORT WILDERNESS

Looking back with the benefit of age, maturity, and wisdom, I can see that the decision from Wabash ushered in a two-year transformative period in our lives, especially for Robyn. Robyn, with an increased amount of freedom, loved her new life as a stay-at-home mom and was starting to explore and engage in the study of God's Word. At the urging of a friend, she started to attend Bible Study Fellowship (BSF), an internationally renowned weekly Bible study that covered the whole of the Bible over a seven-year period. Robyn recalls an initial conversation with her group leader about joining BSF, in which she said she loved to study literature. Later, she realized how stupid that remark was. After the first year, she was surprised she was not put up for leadership, as she had all the right answers and looked great in her designer clothes. Her desire for a leadership role continued to fuel her competitiveness as a classic overachiever; she wanted to know more so she could meet the mark. She kept at it and acquired a lot of head knowledge as she strove to complete the weekly lessons and questions. But God did not want her head; He wanted her heart. She did not understand that one could have a personal relationship with Jesus, having grown up with a traditional belief of separation between the sacred and secular worlds. Her ongoing study, including the writings of Francis Schaeffer and the L'Abri model of living in community for Christ, caused her to reexamine her belief system and how she was living her life. She observed godly women living their lives with real problems but acknowledging Christ, not themselves, as the source for their faith and help. Little by little, she became convicted of the truth of scripture and gave her life over to Christ.

I was now challenged with running the rapidly growing business consulting practice for Arthur Andersen's Indianapolis office while also responsible for delivering outstanding service and solutions for key clients. While growing my faith and family—a challenging task—I began to look to the Lord rather than self-help gurus for direction. During that time period, I was blessed to lead critical projects that would not only deliver significant benefits to our clients but also impact the city of Indianapolis and central Indiana. The pinnacle was serving as the lead consultant for the Mayor's High Technology Task Force, under Mayor Goldsmith, which created an economic development strategy around technology and the new economy. It was preceded by another project with the mayor's office and the first base privatization in US history, which saved more than two thousand jobs for the city of Indianapolis and averted a shutdown of the Naval Air Warfare Center. In between, I led a project to integrate the back-office functions for Simon Property Group (owners of the Indiana Pacers) and DeBartolo Realty after their merger in May 1996. Mixed in was a project to assist Jim Irsay, owner of the Indianapolis Colts, with a financial forecast to support a stadium lease renegotiation with the City of Indianapolis.

All the above happened because two years earlier, an opportunity had presented itself, and I'd taken a calculated risk to lead a critically important project for the Indiana Department of Environmental Management and a task force convened by the lieutenant governor. I never looked at any project or assignment and said it was too big or too tough. In my view, there are always harder or more difficult assignments. Candidly, I love to solve complex problems and bring people together to find a solution.

During that time, I was also replaced as the practice leader by Bill McConnell, the former partner in charge of Andersen Consulting's Indianapolis office practice. Bill, hands down, is the best consultant I have worked with. I am not certain as to the circumstances that resulted in Bill's return to the firm on January 20, 1997, but I do know this: The Lord was directing my path, and Bill's rejoining the firm provided me the opportunity to lead several critical initiatives that had a huge impact on the city of Indianapolis and my career. In many respects, I was pleased to pass along the administrative and political aspects of leading the practice to Bill.

On the home front, there was also a big change: we decided to enroll Payton in Traders Point Christian Academy in the fall of 1996 due to frustration with his academic progress and the school administration's desire to medicate him with Ritalin during the craze to stymie creative, bored kids with mood-altering drugs. We tried Ritalin for a couple weeks and took him off the medication a couple weeks later, as his entire personality changed. I suspect some need Ritalin, but Payton did not. Putting Payton on Ritalin was one of the worst decisions we ever made. Admittedly, Payton struggled with authority and was impulsive. Teachers either adored him or could barely tolerate him—there was no in between.

For the first dozen years of our married life, we climbed the proverbial ladder of success. But the Lord had other plans in mind for us and would use our neighbors the Ogoreks and their daughters, Rachel and Emily, to get our attention. Little did we know that a seemingly innocuous relationship between our son Payton—and his friend Paul—and Rachel would alter the trajectory of our lives.

Payton, like many his age, was a mischievous boy, and he and his friend Paul Ketterer enjoyed playfully picking on the neighbor girl Rachel. As I came to learn in later years, she had large buttons to push. It was easy to get her amped up about almost anything. Today I can tell you she is the most passionate individual I have met on the planet. Nonetheless, those nine-year-old boys would concoct series of tricks or ways to get Rachel's goat, including putting a bucket full of water balloons above her door, ringing the doorbell, and asking her to come outside to play. She eventually became wise to their ways, but that did not deter Payton or Paul. It was simply too much fun! After one of those encounters in the summer of 1996, upon returning from Fort Wilderness, or Fort, a Christian camp in the Northwoods of Wisconsin, her dad, Keith, asked Payton if our family liked to camp. Payton responded, "We don't do camping. My dad is a businessman!" Upon hearing that and taking seriously the biblical command to know your neighbor and a desire to further Christ's mission, Keith extended an invitation for our family to come over for a campfire in their backyard one late summer evening—the backyard with the trees, the lot we'd passed up almost ten years prior. We knew of the Ogoreks because one of my coworkers at Andersen, Jim Pajakowski, had been his college roommate at Indiana State. Truth be told, I do not remember much about the conversation or the evening. I recall some discussion about Fort Wilderness as we roasted marshmallows and made s'mores, but what created a lasting impression was the willingness of Keith and Becky to invite us to come over and enjoy some time together.

This was the beginning of a long friendship with the Ogorek family. We would come to love and appreciate Keith's big personality and an even bigger heart. His commanding presence and physical stature diminished by the ease at which he desires to intentionally engage with those whose path he crosses. His gregarious nature and ability to use story often a draw to create comfortable and memorable conversations. You always knew when Keith was in the room with his wisdom and counsel on full display.

A couple months later, Robyn signed us up to attend family camp at Fort for the summer of 1997. The Ogoreks later found out and knew they had to return. We did not know it at the time, but our lives would never be the same again. This businessman, his wife, and their three children would start to forge a family identity through camp, and the Lord would use Fort and that season of life to prepare us for His plans—plans that would include one of the most difficult circumstances parents could ever face: the mortality of their child.

Fort Wilderness is in McNaughton, Wisconsin, in the Northwoods, about 350 miles north of Chicago and a little less than one hundred miles south of Lake Superior. The main camp is eighty acres and located on beautiful Spider Lake, adjacent to thousands of acres of state forest with an array of magnificent trees, including huge red and white pines, white birches, hemlocks, tamaracks, and aspens, to name a few. Lakes dot the landscape, with one seemingly every mile or two. The camp was founded in 1956 by Truman "Tru" Robertson for $8,000, with a sacrificial gift of $4,000 from a couple in Indiana to purchase the pristine property. Imagine land costing only a hundred dollars an acre. Tru, a pastor with a heart for evangelism and ministering to youth; his wife, Jan; and their five children led much of the activities during the early days of camp. Later, the camp added an additional 230 acres on nearby lands to include dedicated facilities to serve youth ages eight to eighteen at what is now known as Adventure Outpost and Leadership Lab and a gun range, with the main camp primarily hosting family camps and adult and youth retreat weekends.

We caravanned with the Ogoreks on the 520-mile car ride the following summer to camp. The pastor at the Ogoreks' church, Tom Streeter, had a long-standing relationship with the camp dating back to his days at Moody Bible Institute and previous pastoral roles in the Chicagoland area. Tom, with prodding from the early congregants at Zionsville Fellowship Church (ZF), located a few miles northwest of Indianapolis, made an annual trek to Fort with thirty to forty families from the church. So, we were party crashers, as we did not attend ZF, but we were quickly grafted into ZF's temporary community at Fort.

We had no idea what to expect. My camping experience was limited to a couple years of Cub Scouts and Boy Scouts as a young boy, which had included a few opportunities to camp in a tent. Robyn, the daughter of an outdoorsman, quickly had outgrown her upbringing and life in a rural farming town with light industry amid Amish country and enjoyed the benefits and amenities of living in the big city, particularly shopping. Our boys were game. The outdoors, activities, a lake—it all sounded good to them, and Payton and Blake were excited to hook up with a couple of their classmates from Traders Point Christian Academy, where they'd just completed their initial years at the school: fourth grade and kindergarten, respectively.

After five hundred miles, our excitement grew as we exited the two-lane Highway 51, which travels north and south through the middle of Wisconsin and headed east toward Rhinelander on Highway 8. Rhinelander is the closest town to McNaughton, about twenty minutes from camp, and provides some semblance of civilization with a population of 7,500 residents. Soon enough, we made the left turn to head north on Highway 47 for the final fifteen miles of the trip.

You know you've reached Wisconsin's Northwoods when the landscape begins to change. Birch and pine forests increasingly replace cities and farms, and the highways turn to two-lane roads. Signs with white arrows along the sides of the roads mark businesses, schools, churches, camps, friends' cottages or cabins, resorts, and restaurants.

The arrow signs are a fixture in the Northwoods' landscape and a visual reminder of yesteryear.

As we exited Highway 47, we saw the white-arrow sign, and there amid several other names was *Fort Wilderness*. We turned onto Spider Lake Road, which would take us to camp. The road wound through the massive pines of the Northwoods. The final turn onto Wilderness Trail would take us the final half mile up the hill, where the now-familiar Fort Wilderness sign greeted us, declaring the camp as the "Stronghold of Christian Adventure." We did not know what that meant, but we were excited, if for no other reason than to get out of the car after a nine-hour trip with three young boys who'd spent the last two hours asking if we were there yet.

We arrived, and the camp staff greeted us warmly. They genuinely seemed excited to have us at camp. We were provided a stapled six-page set of instructions that shared necessary information about camp activities, meals, medical emergencies, and billing procedures. The introduction on the first page brought to light what was in store for us as we ventured into that new realm of outdoor adventure with our family:

> Dear family campers:
>
> Welcome to Fort Wilderness! Our theme is Fort Family Adventures. We hope you vacation with your family unit in mind. Most of our programs provide family togetherness. We hope your family will grow and be strengthened while you are here. Relax, and let the charm of God's creation and our Fort staff minister to your needs this week. Tom Robertson [Tru's son], our general director, and our permanent staff enjoy these weeks of fellowship with your families. So stop us, and let us get to know you as we share this great camping spot for the week.
>
> Your servants in Christ,
> The Fort Staff

As we were a new family to Fort, the camp director, Tom, led us on a short walk past the dining hall and the community bathroom and shower facility, the Moonbeam, to a group of three smallish cabins: the Klondikes. He opened the door to our unit, the Silver Dollar, and the boys exclaimed, "Bunk beds!" and quickly threw their stuff onto the floor and laid claim to beds. Robyn and I were excited to arrive after the long trip and did not immediately notice the musty smell and limited sunlight in the old, dated cabins with vinyl mattresses. It was certainly a far cry from our Hilton Head Island vacation a couple years prior or our ten-day trip to Orlando and Disney and Universal Studios when Payton and Blake were young, or so we thought. We would soon learn to double up the mattresses to provide additional cushion to prevent the inevitable backaches after sleeping on the single foam mattress. Tom would remark years later that he was certain we would see the cabin, turn around, and head home. He did not see us fitting in, especially Robyn, with her wedge shoes and designer clothes. Little did he know, that experience was the start of something new and dramatically different for the Leyden family.

After unpacking the car, we explored camp to see what was in store for the week, until we heard the cascading rings of the dinner bell reverberate through camp at 5:30, heralding the arrival of Fort's famous chicken dinner. We gathered at the dining hall for brief announcements followed by prayer and then headed outside to get our meal. The chicken was moist, cooked in the kitchen prior to transfer to the large outdoor grill in the center of camp for a perfect smoky char. Baked beans, coleslaw, and watermelon made for a delightful meal as we gathered for the first time with the other campers.

Each morning, there was a different specialty breakfast served at a wooded lakeside site under the open skies. Fort's signature wranglers' breakfast—to which we traveled by horse drawn wagon—included a hearty meal of eggs, crispy hash browns with bacon and onions (if we so desired), and wranglers' toast, which was buttered toast on the griddle with cinnamon and sugar to follow. If that were not enough, we could also partake in the men's breakfast, which included ribeye steak in addition to the above. Another option was the lumberjack breakfast: made-to-order pancakes with various fruit, nut, and sweet toppings served with bacon. Somehow, I caught wind of the breakfast bonanza and made it my goal to take one of the boys to each of the meals. Robyn, on the other hand, was not keen to wake up early for food, when she could go to the dining hall for a leisurely breakfast at eight thirty.

As good as the breakfasts were, the topper was the adult banquet on Thursday night. Camp staff provided special programming for the kids, and the adults were treated to a special meal in the dining hall. It was every bit as good as a meal at a fine restaurant. We ate on linen tablecloths with a fancy place-setting and water goblets, and the meal featured an appetizer, salad, main course, and dessert—and entertainment to boot. I'd had an expectation for camp food, and that was certainly not it!

After we finished the opening night chicken dinner, there was a welcome and kickoff session in the Big Top. The Big Top served as the gathering place for worship, teaching, and general camper get-togethers. It looked just like its namesake from the circus: a large yellow canvas structure fifty-one feet in diameter with wooden benches for about two hundred people to gather with protection from wind, rain, and sunlight—but with more than ample opportunity for the large flies of the Northwoods to annoy us as they circled during our gatherings. The welcome session provided an opportunity to meet the staff, including a significant number of summer staff made up of high school and college students serving in various programming and camp roles. Ron Robertson, Tom's older brother, served as the emcee for the gathering. Ron, short in stature and bereft of an ear, was celebrating thirty years of service at camp, and after that many years, he had the routine down. I was not sure if he was a comedian, an evangelist, or both. At the end of the week, when I asked each of our family members what he or she'd enjoyed most about camp, Robyn said, "Ron's announcements."

I thought, *We traveled five hundred twenty miles for a vacation so you could listen to announcements!*

The session was a surprisingly high-energy introduction to camp and gave us an overview of what to expect for the week, including available activities. Most importantly, we were to head to the dining hall, where there were sign-up sheets for all the week's programming. A mad rush ensued once we left the Big Top. We signed up for everything, or so it seemed. We would later figure out that was a rookie mistake, as we were dragging by the end of the week. Meanwhile, the kids headed straight for the fry bread, which the staff were serving across from the dining hall. Fry bread is something like a doughnut in the shape of a breadstick, covered in either cinnamon and sugar or powdered sugar—just what we needed to top off the evening. Did I mention the canteen was also open for ice cream, drinks, and treats?

Mealtime was much more than an opportunity for nourishment or a tasty meal. It provided the perfect opportunity to meet other campers and the missionary staff who raised their financial support to come on staff and share conversation and stories and enjoy time together. The men's breakfast on Monday morning was particularly memorable. It was led by Todd Dunham. In the years to follow, I would learn Todd shared many similarities with my father-in-law, Mike Scott. Todd was a man's man. He told you what he thought. His goal was not to make you feel good. He was a hunter and outdoorsman who seemingly could do anything. He was married to Jackie, who worked in the camp's office.

A group of about thirty men gathered at the beachfront on Monday morning at seven thirty for the ten-minute leisurely walk to breakfast. Dew was on the trees, and a mist was coming off the lake. We could hear loons at a distance. The smell of the pine trees was in the air, and a gentle, cool breeze greeted us as the sun rose across the lake. As we started our walk out to Cranberry Point, Todd spoke in a direct and convincing tone. He said we needed to slow down and be quiet. We needed to hear what Dad had to say to us. I could tell by looking at the men around me that he had everyone's attention. It was the first time anyone had told me I needed to slow down to listen and hear what our heavenly Father had to say. Todd's admonition would resonate with me for the remainder of the week and the years to follow.

If there was a perfect man to deliver that message, Todd was it. In his younger days, he'd been a raging alcoholic with a foul mouth and anger to boot. His wife, Jackie, one of the sweetest women I have ever met, had forced a separation and divorce in April 1981, telling Todd, "I hate you and want you to leave me and the kids alone." She'd had enough of his manipulation and put no trust in his empty promises. A stint in a treatment center had led to acknowledgment of his hopelessness, and Todd had prayed to the Lord, asking God to kill him, which had led to the Lord killing Todd's old self. Todd's newfound relationship with God had healed and restored him. He and Jackie had remarried in October 1982. Ten years later, he'd joined the Fort's missionary staff, and he'd evangelized to the life-changing power of the gospel ever since. Todd's life story and role in leading Fort's Stockade 80 shooting program impacted countless lives, just as his simple words spoken to me and the other men on that Monday morning years ago did (Author's note: the story about the Dunhams was reviewed and approved by them to share the power of the gospel to change and impact lives for eternity.)

The boys were perfect ages for camp: ten, seven, and almost four years old. Camp provided a good environment for the boys to roam and have fun. It was odd to not know where our kids were, but there were caring adults everywhere, who seemingly had their eyes open to monitor the children's whereabouts and, more importantly, their behavior. Mind you, they were not perfect families but ones who had a family-centric focus. That was refreshing, particularly given a comment made by one of my supervisors at work, who chose not to go on a family vacation with his wife and youngest child due to the demands of work and mockingly referred to his wife as the last great "moralist."

Blake was excited to spend time with his classmate Sean McCloskey and soon was going through camp with the McCloskey clan to catch the perfect frog for the frog-hoppers contest on Friday. Their family was legendary for an uncanny ability to find the perfect frog; some argued they brought their own for the competition. Payton spent time with Jason Chapel and his dad, Mike, and enjoyed fooling around on the guitar. Jason's mom, Dot, was a free spirit much like Payton. Dot served as a surrogate mom for Payton. He loved hanging out with the Chapels. Chase stayed close to Robyn but enjoyed time at the beach with his assortment of plastic pails and shovels as he built sand castles while an admiring group of teenage girls and young mothers talked about how cute he was.

Opportunities abounded to have fun at the lake; ride horses; or avail ourselves of the craft shop, archery, the shooting range, or off-camp programs if we wanted to venture out. Most of the time, the older two boys were off on their own. We quickly instituted a rule for Payton and Blake to check in at mealtime. That way, we knew they were alive.

Perhaps the highlight of the week for the Leydens was the canoe trip on Tuesday afternoon. We gathered at the parking lot shortly after lunch and loaded into a bus for a short canoe trip to the Wisconsin River and an overnight camping experience, including dinner over an open fire. Bright blue skies greeted us with a few stray clouds as we unloaded from the van after a bumpy ride down dirt roads to get to our launch site. We gathered our canoe and life vests and applied some last-minute sunscreen prior to heading down the ramp to place our canoe in the water. Fort staff, as expected, were leading the trip down the river, with one of the most seasoned staff bringing up the rear. Robyn sometimes questioned my desire for adventure but seemed game for the trip with our boys.

We started down the river, and the current was not much more than a tranquil flow, which made navigation manageable despite our inexperience and young family. Robyn was in the front, and I manned the rear, with Blake and Chase in the middle seat. Payton had ditched us for a newfound friend, a teenage boy named Alex from Quebec.

It was noticeably peaceful, even with many canoes afloat, as birds flew overhead, returning to the tall trees along the shoreline. We were excited as we rounded the bend and saw an eagle off to our right. About forty-five minutes into the trip, we entered the Rainbow Flowage, a three-thousand-acre lake with the river channel meandering through the reservoir. Fishing was popular in the Northwoods, and Rainbow Flowage had an abundant amount of panfish and a good amount of northern pike, walleye, muskie, and bass. Clouds were beginning to roll across the reservoir, with a slight headwind slowing our pace. Nonetheless, we were game for the journey. The breeze stiffened as we reached the middle of the lake, and then out of nowhere, it suddenly started to pour—the drenching sort of rain. It seemed buckets of water were dumped from the sky. For a good ten to fifteen minutes, it seemed we were doing everything in our power not to go backward, and then, just as quickly as it had started, the rain stopped. We were soaked. Worse yet, we had fallen behind our group and needed to catch up.

As we continued toward our destination, word made its way back to us that our trip leader, Tom, was looking for a site where we could stop to set up for dinner. We would bypass the overnight portion of the trip for obvious reasons. We paddled on seemingly forever, as each suitable location was occupied. Finally, we reached an available site and headed to shore to join the two dozen or so wet and brave souls who'd endured the past two to three hours on the Wisconsin River and Rainbow Flowage. Tom prepared perhaps the best meal I have ever eaten in my life: chicken fajitas over the open fire. The combination of a warm fire and a hot meal was the perfect end to that unforgettable experience. To this day, Robyn swears the mosquitoes were the size of small birds. She was more than excited to take the van trip back to camp that evening with our wet clothes, which ensured a musty aroma in our cabin for the remainder of the week. Years later, we would question our decision to try a family overnight canoe trip for the first time with a three-year-old, seven-year-old, and ten-year-old. As Keith would remark at the end of our week of family camp, "Making memories." Making memories indeed.

Food, activities, and campfires were staples of camp life; however, the life-giving conversations, often centered on the teaching or a shared experience, were some of the most impactful aspects of our time at camp. Each day, campers would gather at the Big Top at nine fifteen for announcements, a time of worship, and teaching. Ron was in rare form, with his slapstick humor and impeccable timing. As funny as he was, it was clear he really cared for people; it showed. I often saw him, and many of the other Fort staff, in conversation with campers about the important things in life. Worship was upbeat, with songs intended to both bring you alive in your relationship with Christ and draw you into an intimate time of praise to the Lord. We had two teachers for the week: Mark Duffey, who was a few years younger than us and had played an active role with the Fellowship of Christian Athletes beginning in college, and Frank Dragash, a man from Croatia, who provided a much different perspective to the gospel and life than I had ever heard. Prior to camp, much of the biblical teaching Robyn and I had received had been from seminary-trained middle-aged white males within the United Church of Christ. Family camp teaching was led by two non-seminary-trained men, one in his early thirties and the other from overseas, with a distinctly European perspective. Mark, with a youthful countenance and energy to boot, was in the cabin next to us with his wife, Gina, and his preschool-age children, Nolan and Kristen. He taught from John 17:3: "And this is eternal life, that they may know You, the only true God, and Jesus Christ who You have sent." The early church fathers used the word *knowledge* (*gnosis*) to mean spiritual or specific knowledge of the divine. We are to know God just as we might know our neighbor or a fact. That idea was new to Robyn and me and gave us pause as we considered the teaching from Mark, an enthusiastic layperson who seemed knowledgeable about the Word of God.

Our kids were well taken care of in the children's ministry. Chase, a preschooler, was with the Buckaroos and met in the Homestead. Blake and Payton headed to the Inn, where Blake met with the Mavericks in the Bears' Den and Payton met upstairs with the Trailblazers in the Elk Room. They seemed genuinely excited to be at camp, and if they had an issue with attending Sunday school every morning for forty-five minutes, we did not hear it.

While the Ogoreks had invited us to camp, we did not spend significant time with them. We shared a few meals together and saw them occasionally. We quickly met lots of new friends and had a full schedule of activities, which left limited time to connect. Robyn liked to refer to Keith as Beach Jesus. Keith was the perfect blend of relationship and intentionality, trying to draw all circumstances to Christ. Occasionally, he was down at the beach, where his wife, Becky, spent a fair amount of time, conversing with anyone on the topic of the day and drawing Christ and His teachings into the discussion. Keith had a disarming and engaging way of sharing the gospel. It was never heavy-handed; rather, he used the scriptures as a historical truth rendered under God's authority to speak into our lives—and there were lots of things in our lives that required speaking into.

On our last day, Keith asked me what I thought of our week at camp. I said we'd had a great time, the food was great, and we'd met a lot of great people, both staff and campers. Then I said, "But I don't know who your pastor is." Likely, I'd met Tom Streeter and his wife, Judy, but I did not know them. For all thirty-four years of my life, the pastor had been front and center with the teaching of God's Word and setting the direction for spiritual life. Church was on Sundays, and only in recent years had I started to consider what it meant to integrate all my life under the lordship of Christ. What I did on Tuesday afternoon was equally as important as the time at church on Sunday morning.

By the time it came to pay our bill, we knew we were coming back. Seeds had been sown that would begin to forge a new family identity—one not about activity and pursuit of the American dream but, rather, about seeing the Lord at work. We saw the church in a whole new light. My historical view of the church was largely what I experienced on Sunday morning, bound by a strong liturgical service. I was now seeing the church lived out by real people replete with problems, not guarded in their relationships, enjoying time together in creation, and studying God's Word, and with plenty of opportunity for fun and adventure. Fort was a place of refuge where one was accepted and loved despite his or her baggage. Refreshed by listening ears, sincere encouragement, and freshening spirits, we were challenged to live for Christ in a deeper way. Church was fun and real, and furthermore, church was not confined to a building or a specific hour of the week. As we departed camp, a place that seemed too good to be true, the staff's prayer and desire was that we'd be resupplied in body and soul, ready to reengage with the world.

We returned home exhausted but exhilarated from a wonderful trip and some great family memories. Robyn quickly instituted a rule that would serve us well for future return trips from Fort: the wet, sandy, musty clothes, which were in garbage bags, could not enter the house. They would remain in the garage, and Robyn would begin the process of separating and laundering them over the next several days. I would return to work, and the boys had a few weeks until school started.

But there was something different about our family life after our week together at camp. We could not wait to return the following year.

~ Biblical Principle ~

Matthew, a tax collector and disciple of Christ, wrote the following in Matthew 22:37–39:

> Jesus said to him, "'You shall love the LORD your God with all your heart, with all your soul, and with all your mind.' This is the first and great commandment. And the second is like it: 'You shall love your neighbor as yourself.'"

A neighbor, Keith Ogorek, based on the prompting of my son, extended an invitation to a backyard campfire to get to know us. That led to a second invitation to join them at camp.

Upon reflection, I see that Keith was living out the biblical command to love us as he loved himself. A twenty-plus-year friendship ensued. Our lives would never be the same.

CHAPTER 6

THE BUSINESSMAN AND PAYTON HIKE THE GRAND CANYON

Evidently, sleeping in a cabin for a week in the Northwoods of Wisconsin with prepared meals and activities was not enough camping for me. The following year, in 1998, I learned Fort Wilderness was offering an opportunity to hike the Grand Canyon, and I was intrigued. Fort and Camp Forest Springs, a camp an hour and a half southwest of Fort, offered a joint trip with five days of backpacking in the canyon. It sounded like a lot of fun and an opportunity to spend some great time with Payton. Payton was homeschooled, so getting time off for the fall trip was not a problem, as I was married to his teacher! Robyn was supportive, as she is with most things, and thought it would provide an opportunity for Payton and me to further develop our relationship. Robyn and I were unified in our approach to parenting, but Robyn had a much more engaging style. I was more of a disciplinarian, wanting to make sure our children knew the rules and followed them. My approach was likely a result of my father's limited involvement in my life growing up, outside of sports.

I did not often take the opportunity to spend extended one-on-one time with my boys, given the demands of my job and other interests. Payton was growing up quickly, and I thought the ten-day trip, which would include a forty-hour bus ride from Wisconsin to the Grand Canyon, was the perfect opportunity to see the majesty of the Grand Canyon and spend some quality time with my son.

Eyes of the Father

Payton was a smart, creative, and artistic boy and was beginning to express his personality in his dress; he wore weird clothes and necklaces and loved to experiment with his hair. He was gifted in the arts and started art lessons as well. He excelled in music and joined the nationally renowned Indianapolis Children's Choir the following year. It was quite a feat to make that choir and perhaps a more demanding feat to stick with it, given the time commitment, strict attendance policies, and his desire to continue playing basketball and soccer. Payton dutifully participated until the end of the year, when his group performed a Barney song, "Kookaburra," which was more than Payton could bear. He told us that was his last performance.

Christian contemporary music got his attention most, as Robyn was able to get tickets for her and Payton to see Audio Adrenaline play in Anderson, which was about thirty miles from Indianapolis. They attended the concert with his friend Jason and Jason's mom, Dot, and were thrilled to meet the band and get autographed T-shirts. Robyn and Payton became Christian concert junkies. Payton loved rock and roll, and the fact that it was also Christian was all Robyn needed. She took him to see Jars of Clay a few months later, and a T-shirt was launched into his lap. Wrapped inside was a devotional book. Robyn told him it was a clear message that God was trying to get Payton's attention.

His love of music continued, and he spent all his spare time listening to and writing music and playing the guitar. He was largely self-taught and could play the piano by ear and the harmonica. We were certain he would grow up to have a career in music. He had a God-given talent for sure.

A trip to the Grand Canyon seemed a perfect way for me to spend intentional time with Payton and get to know him better as he moved into that age of self-expression. We could spend time in creation as he began the process of considering what it meant to enter the teen years and ultimately become a man. For weeks, I implored him to get in shape for the five-day, twenty-five-mile hike. He ignored me and would ultimately regret that decision.

Tom Robertson, Fort's general director, asked me to journal our trip and share our story with the Fort family. The following is our trip as shared first through the eyes of an eleven-year-old and then through the eyes of his noncamping father.

Todd Leyden

Payton's Entry

We started off in our car. We drove from Indy to a huge church in Wisconsin [Elmbrook]. We were late too, so we had to hurry. We had to drive right through Chicago during rush hour. We finally made it and put our stuff in the bus. After the longest car or bus trip I've ever been on, we were there! The Grand Canyon was huge. After we got all our instructions the next day, we went to bed, and were we ever ready for it.

The next day, we tried to put on our packs, and they weighed thirty to fifty pounds. I thought, *Oh crud!* I'm eleven years old, and that's a lot for anyone to carry, especially while hiking the canyon! We drove to the canyon, and we were off. It was hard going downhill. As we were hiking, we saw beautiful rock formations. When we were at the most treacherous part of the trip, it started hailing. We waited in one of the very few restrooms [a shelter] in the canyon. When it started hailing, you could have fallen a thousand feet very easily with one wrong step. It was pretty cool. We started going this time, and it wasn't as hard. The conditions were better, but it still wasn't easy either. We ate our lunch, got back on the trail, and were on our way to our destination. This was a long way down to the Colorado River. I had to stop a lot at the end [eight and a half miles and eight hours later]. We walked over the bridge, I took off my pack, and I fell over. My dad carried both our packs for the last half mile. We got to the campsite, ate a great dinner, and we went to bed. We got our first sleeping place. It wasn't bad sleeping on the ground, except when Dad rolled over on me during the night. We woke up and had breakfast and then went back on the trail.

We ate a great dinner and went to bed. We woke up, ate, and went back on the trail. This time, we were going back to the top. We stayed a day before we went back up.

If you decide to go on this trip, make sure you're in shape. This was an experience!

Dad's Entry

What a wonderful blessing to have ten days to spend with your son on a trip to one of the greatest gifts that God gave us—the Grand Canyon. Okay, so a two-day bus trip doesn't sound like fun. Especially sleeping one of the nights on the bus. It is the fellowship and bonding.

I strongly urged my son to get into shape for this trip. My wisdom was ignored, as Payton assured me he was in shape, given his participation on the local soccer team. Wrong. Hiking over twenty miles in one week doesn't seem bad until you consider the elements: the terrain and five-thousand-foot vertical drop or incline on your way back up.

I want to share some of the highlights of our trip. The people, the majesty, the memories, and God's gift to Payton and me.

It is probably not surprising to hear you develop close relationships with your fellow hikers. There were forty-four brave souls who went on the trip. Our group set out on the South Kaibab and Bright Angel trails [corridor trails]. This is where ninety-five percent of the Grand Canyon foot traffic takes place. Now, the canyon is not small: about 275 miles long and, on average, eighteen to twenty miles across. We had a great group: Russ and Carol, Bill and Barb, Dave, Ken, and Jim. And our two trip leaders—the two Marks. We laughed together, were in fellowship together, hiked together, and even slept together (more later). Carol was a good "mother" for Payton. Russ and Ken enjoyed Payton's company. Payton was always looking for Bill and Barb on the trail, who were slower than the rest of the group. Sometimes this would make Dad nervous, as he would turn around, oblivious to the steep descent, and look for them. It was nice to see Payton's concern.

I will always remember our last day hiking back up out of the canyon. When you are looking up to the top, you are convinced there is no humanly possible way to climb the steep face. It was tiring. We were supposed to camp up at the rim the last night. Well, it was kind of cold, we were tired, and there was a dry bus where we could sleep. Well, our two married couples decided to get a room at the hotel. And guess what. After much prodding, they convinced all of us to join them. What a relief. Hot showers! I am convinced we would have stayed on the bus, except Payton, upon hearing their gracious offer, agreed. There is only so much hiking and camping an eleven-year-old can take. He did, however, leave his cherished Adidas fisherman's hat in the room, or so we thought, until Payton received a Christmas present from Ken.

The canyon is unbelievable. It is difficult to imagine the majesty, size, difficulty, and sense of awe in seeing God's handiwork. There is a quiet peace that comes upon you; maybe that is due to the physical exhaustion after a day of hiking. It was a place where I became closer to my son and began to understand him more as a young man. It was great for him to hear witness from other Christians and develop relationships with people much older than he. We had the chance for some quiet time together. What a blessing.

I am thankful for the Fort Wilderness and Camp Forest Springs team who put this trip together. They were a great group of leaders. Thanks!

My desire for significant adventures would continue the following year with a stirring to run a marathon for a good cause and take a special trip with Blake, but the Lord had other plans and would use that race to introduce me to a young boy and his mother, who would serve as a powerful witness for Christ and prepare us for a critical moment in our family's life.

Biblical Principle

This poem, a song of ascent or a song for the road, is from Psalm 121:

> I will lift up my eyes to the hills—
> From whence comes my help?
> My help comes from the LORD,
> Who made heaven and earth.
> He will not allow your foot to be moved;
> He who keeps you will not slumber.
> Behold, He who keeps Israel
> Shall neither slumber nor sleep.
> The LORD is your keeper;
> The LORD is your shade at your right hand.
> The sun shall not strike you by day,
> Nor the moon by night.
> The LORD shall preserve you from all evil;
> He shall preserve your soul.
> The LORD shall preserve your going out and your coming in
> From this time forth, and even forevermore.

We are all on a journey in this life—a physical journey as we move to and fro and a spiritual journey as we look either to ourselves or to our Creator as the source and sustainer of life and all things.

Upon reflection, Payton's and my hike in the Grand Canyon was a wonderful opportunity for me to enjoy time in God's creation, spend precious time with my son, and continue to grow in my faith. As we journey through life both physically and spiritually, God is the source of our strength and protects us along the way.

CHAPTER 7

A MARATHON OR A PROVIDENTIAL WITNESS FOR SUFFERING?

A young family and demanding job left precious little time for hobbies and free time. Truth be told, I am wired to do the job at hand—perhaps a function of the influence of my grandfather, who was an example of the German work ethic. Running was something I'd picked up in college as I moved on from the traditional American competitive team sports of football, basketball, and baseball, which had occupied much of my youth. I love to golf, but it does not provide the sort of physical benefits necessary to maintain one's body, which I was committed to do. I enjoyed the freedom provided through running, as it allowed me to have quiet time away from the busyness of the day, although my mind would often wander to things requiring my attention. I ran my first half marathon in 1986, the year after I graduated from college, and I was hooked. Over the ensuing years, I would participate in a lot of 8K (5-mile) and 10K (6.2-mile) runs throughout the Indianapolis area.

After returning from the Grand Canyon, buoyed by my excellent physical shape, I began to entertain thoughts about running a marathon. Half marathons were plenty challenging, involving weeks of training and subsequent muscle strains and injuries, not to mention the time commitment. I suspected a marathon was at a whole different level. If it took me roughly two hours to run 13.1 miles, how in the world was I going to run for four hours or more? In that amount of time, I could have watched eight consecutive episodes of my favorite sitcom, *Seinfeld*!

A few years prior, I'd started to develop an interest in giving back to the community through board service and been asked to join the Indiana chapter of Prevent Child Abuse, so when I saw an opportunity to raise money for the Leukemia Society and run the Mayor's Midnight Sun Marathon in Anchorage, Alaska, on the first day of summer, it caught my attention. How cool to run on a day when there was sunlight for almost twenty-four hours and the temperatures were cool enough (in the upper fifties) to possibly allow one to complete the race without fear of heatstroke. Plus, I could raise money for a good cause and visit Alaska. I signed up and made plans to run my first marathon in Alaska on June 21, 1999.

I would take Robyn and Blake, as his birthday was June 20, the day before the marathon. My trip to the Grand Canyon the prior fall had convicted me of the need to schedule a special trip or event with each of my boys. Raising the necessary funds was relatively easy, given my circle of friends and business acquaintances through Arthur Andersen, and soon enough, I met the $7,800 goal for Robyn and me to attend. I would pay for Blake to join us.

I started the Leukemia Society's Team in Training (TNT) program in January, which presumably would provide ample time—five months—to train for the marathon. Training runs in January in Indiana are a little tricky due to the ice and snow and related injuries with running on slippery and challenging conditions, not to mention dealing with single-digit temperatures and below. But I was committed, and I knew a trip to Alaska was a once-in-a-lifetime opportunity. One of the first things the Team in Training program does is assign your team an honoree. Our honoree was Brandon Gore, a fourteen-year-old boy who'd been diagnosed with acute lymphoblastic lymphoma (ALL) on May 8, 1996.

We met every Saturday morning at Eagle Creek Park, a mile from my house, to do our weekly long run. Training was going well, and I learned that running long distances involved both putting in the miles and having a positive mental outlook. I routinely did training runs that exceeded half marathons and thought nothing of it. That was difficult for me to comprehend, as prior half-marathon races had found me mentally and physically exhausted by the ten-mile mark!

We met Brandon and his father, Jim, at an Indianapolis Indians AAA baseball game in April. He seemed like a great young man, with an infectious smile and personality. He'd started a chemotherapy regimen shortly after his diagnosis three years prior and was now cancer free. It is hard to imagine someone at that age fighting for his life. Even more impressive were his positive disposition and outlook, considering that dreadful disease.

A week prior to the marathon, our TNT leader, Andrea Roberts, told us she was unable to attend the race. Andrea, a bright, energetic, and personable young lady, had been a motivating force for all of us to get our miles in and made it enjoyable as we logged our miles on cold winter and spring mornings. Andrea was an attorney at a major firm in Indianapolis, and the judge on one of her cases had told her she could not leave Indianapolis due to an important trial scheduled the week of our marathon. Our team was bummed. Andrea took it in stride, knowing we were prepared, and that type of inconvenience came with the territory as an attorney.

The trip to Alaska was memorable. We saw our first glacier and had dinner at ten o'clock at night in bright daylight. After a while, Robyn and I became more than annoyed with Blake's incessant chattering and his continued desire to cross paths with a bear, but he assured us he could outrun it. What he was really saying was that he could outrun us, and the bear would get us first. Ah, a ten-year-old.

The marathon route itself was beautiful, through the rolling hills in the outskirts of Anchorage, mostly on trails or country roads. The race ended in downtown Anchorage at a school. For the first twenty or so miles, I did reasonably well, with a pace of 8:15 miles. I struggled with the last six miles, particularly with the steep ascent over the last mile to the school. I finished in four hours and twenty-four minutes, extremely sore and tired but glad I'd done the race.

Upon our return to Indianapolis, we were crushed to learn heartbreaking news: Brandon had relapsed on June 23, just a few days after the marathon and prior to his last scheduled treatment. How could that be? He had completed thirty-six months of the thirty-eight-month protocol. Statistically speaking, if Brandon completed the full protocol, he would have an 85 percent chance of survival. Now what? Hearing the news made me sick to my stomach. His mother, Robin, was a tireless woman of faith and prayer during Brandon's battle and shared with us the reason for the hope she had in her relationship with Jesus Christ. She would always say, "I am keeping my eyes on Jesus," and claim the truth of scripture as her own. One of her favorite verses was 1 John 5:14–15: "Now this is the confidence that we have in Him, that if we ask anything according to His will, He hears us. And if we know that He hears us, whatever we ask, we know that we have the petitions that we have asked of Him."

In the days and weeks to follow, we routinely prayed for Brandon and the Gore family. One Sunday afternoon, we gathered as a family for lunch, and I shared Brandon's medical situation and history and expressed my concern. Payton, who was often blunt and to the point, said, "It doesn't matter. He is going to die anyway." While that perhaps was true based on the medical opinion of certain doctors, Payton's apparent indifference to Brandon's suffering and struggle made me mad. I called Payton out for his lack of compassion and committed to praying for Brandon and the Gores.

In September, Brandon had a bone marrow transplant. He would continue his treatments. His odds of survival were low.

During that time, our faith and relationship with the Lord grew in a significant and meaningful way. Keith and Becky Ogorek started a small group study to complement Keith's teaching at Garfield Park. He taught from Henry Blackaby and Claude King's book *Experiencing God*. It was perhaps the most impactful study Robyn and I have ever done. I memorized and often refer to Blackaby's central tenets, which are as follows:

1. God is always at work around you.
2. God pursues a continuing love relationship with you that is real and personal.
3. God invites you to become involved with Him in His work.
4. God speaks by the Holy Spirit through the Bible, prayer, circumstances, and the church to reveal Himself, His purposes, and His ways.
5. God's invitation for you to work with Him always leads you to a crisis of belief that requires faith and action.

6. You must make major adjustments in your life to join God in what He is doing.
7. You come to know God by experience as you obey Him, and He accomplishes His work through you.[2]

That study and our increasing knowledge in the Lord's Word provided the framework for Robyn and me to respond to a potential crisis of belief when Payton's life was not spared. The following summer at family camp, the message delivered during the teaching time was directed at us. God's preparation was intensifying, but we had no idea what was about to hit us.

Biblical Principle

The Old Testament prophet Isaiah wrote the following in Isaiah 40:29–31:

> He gives power to the weak,
> And to those who have no might He increases strength.
> Even the youths shall faint and be weary,
> And the young men shall utterly fall,
> But those who wait on the LORD
> Shall renew their strength;
> They shall mount up with wings like eagles,
> They shall run and not be weary,
> They shall walk and not faint.

I thought I was running a marathon to raise money for a good cause.

Upon reflection, I realize the Lord was using the marathon and my relationship with the Gores as a God-appointed lesson in trusting Him in the face of life's most difficult moments. He is the source of our strength and hope in all circumstances. Human strength and desire cannot compare to or compete with God.

CHAPTER 8

OUR LAST FAMILY CAMP

We were excited to join our friends from Zionsville Fellowship for the fourth year in a row at their week of camp at Fort in July. For a family with little to no roughing-it experience, we sure enjoyed the time at camp. Even though we did not attend ZF, we felt as if we were one of the body and looked forward to renewing relationships with fellow campers from ZF and the wonderful Fort missionary staff.

Prior family camp weeks had been replete with a boatload of wonderful memories: the canoe float; the frog-hoppers contest; and the "ancient" Olympic Games complete with Roman togas, when Payton's saggy pants kept falling to his ankles as he tried to navigate a wheelbarrow with his partner, Jerry Klavon, in the tub. Payton said, "I am not going to do any sort of game with a man who is wearing a dress!"

One of the most popular camp games for kids and teenagers was carpetball. Imagine a combination of shuffleboard and bowling using billiard balls, and you essentially have carpetball. The tables were eighteen feet long by two feet wide, with four-inch-high sideboards and a seven-inch-deep box or well at the end of the table to receive the balls. Each player strategically placed six balls in front of the box on his or her end of the table, and then took turns rolling, bouncing, or spinning the white ball overhand or underhand down the table or off the side rails to try to knock his or her opponent's balls into the tray. Debris, such as leaves and sand, infiltrated the uneven tables with slight rolls in the carpet. Matches were quite competitive and often intense, and occasional injury occurred as a ball bounded from the table and struck the opponent or an innocent bystander. Blake's lowlight of his years at Fort was a loss to a girl in the end-of-week tournament. He did not say much for the rest of the day. Chase, on the other hand, had no competitive bones in his body and played once or twice with Mom or Dad as something to do in between more interesting activities.

During the end-of-the-week tournament, Blake and I received an important life lesson. After one of Blake's matches, one of the campers, Dave Greiwe, pulled me aside. Dave was in a two-year men's discipleship group with me. Six months earlier, in January, Keith Ogorek had formed a discipleship group with seven men to study church history, theology, calling, spiritual gifts, and worldview. It was the second men's discipleship group offered by Zionsville Fellowship and largely patterned after the initial study led by their pastor, Tom Streeter, in which Keith had been a participant. We learned a lot, but more importantly, we lived life together and sought each other's prayer and counsel with decisions ranging from the routine to significant, life-altering situations. Dave was a particularly kind and gracious man, and while watching Blake during the tournament, he noticed Blake was highly competitive, perhaps to the point of not setting a good example. Dave pulled me aside not to embarrass me or Blake but to share his observation out of love for me and our family. Perhaps I had a blind spot and did not see the same thing or was willing to overlook my ten-year-old son's aggressive competitive posture for the result Blake often achieved as a competitive and successful young athlete. Competition is good; however, when it generates an all-out desire to win or an inability to exhibit grace in defeat, competitiveness is not a good quality. I thanked Dave for his insight and shared with Blake at the appropriate time.

Eight years later, in the fall of 2008, Blake was named the city of Indianapolis's male soccer player of the year—quite an honor. However, another recognition that year was perhaps his most significant achievement throughout his years of playing competitive soccer from a young boy through college at Butler University, a strong Division I program. Robyn and I were invited unexpectedly to attend the sports banquet at Washington High School, a largely Hispanic high school just a couple minutes west of downtown Indianapolis. Unbeknownst to us, Blake was to be honored as the athlete or competitor who most exemplified the character and qualities of sportsmanship to the Washington High School soccer team. Truth be told, Blake was a dominant force as his team, Covenant Christian High School, won the city championship that year, beating the city schools, including the mega powerhouse Cathedral, a large Catholic school with a history of piling up city and state championships. During that time, Blake had made an impression on his competitors—the right impression, as he would put his arm around a member of the other team in a friendly gesture during stoppage of play, speaking Spanish, which he'd learned from his award-winning Spanish teacher, Andy Goodwin. It was impossible to know the impact that one gentle but needed remark by Dave Greiwe would have many years later.

Meanwhile, Payton developed a mysterious rash while at camp. Fortunately, one of the family campers was a doctor and prescribed oral steroids to address the problem. The weather was unusually damp and cool, unlike during our prior three years at camp. The camp did not have a medical facility or place for Payton to go, so he would bundle up his six-foot frame in his sleeping bag and lie by the fire.

We were thankful there were several godly men interested in Payton's musical capabilities and supportive of his efforts. Payton often played his guitar with one of the family campers, Scott Puckett, who was convinced the Lord would use Payton's gifts in a big way. One afternoon, I went into town, which meant a twenty-minute trip to Rhinelander, to purchase a tuner for Payton's electric guitar. At dinner, I surprised him with the tuner. He was appreciative and thought it was one of the nicest things I had ever done. I do not recall what I paid, perhaps twenty or thirty dollars. In retrospect, I wish I'd taken the effort to do more simple gestures like that. Payton was invited to play with the praise worship band, which meant getting to play alongside some talented adult musicians. Payton would say later that was one of the top five highlights of his life.

However, it was not camp activities or relationships with other campers that would indelibly impact our family or me during our fourth consecutive summer visit to Fort. By that time, we had attended many camps and teaching sessions. Most were good or excellent; however, they often faded to a distant memory like a sermon on a Sunday morning. However, the message that week was directed at us and would serve as a harbinger of one of the most important things our family would ever face. It was a message the Lord wanted me to hear; understand; take to heart; and, ultimately, respond to. Eric Bobbitt, the associate pastor at Zionsville Fellowship, had a central message during the morning teaching time from 1 Peter 1:6–7: "In this you greatly rejoice, though now for a little while, if need be, you have been grieved by various trials, that the genuineness of your faith being much more precious than gold that perishes, though it is tested by fire, may be found to praise, honor and glory at the revelation of Jesus Christ." It was one of the most perplexing messages I had ever heard. We were to rejoice through our time of trial or suffering if the testing of our faith brought glory to God. Our family had never suffered to any appreciable degree. We had a good life. Nothing bad of any significant consequence had happened to me or my family during Robyn's and my then sixteen years of marriage. I was thirty-seven years old, and no one close to me had died. As Eric spoke, I pondered the message and wondered what it meant. It was a passage of scripture that would sear my conscience in the months and years to follow.

Often, during the worship session, there was an opportunity for corporate prayer to allow participants to share a song of worship, a prayer, or a praise. Greg Cavanagh, who would subsequently endure a lifetime of significant health issues, began to pray during Monday morning's time of worship in a manner I had never experienced. He pleaded with the Lord that he not have to suffer, but if he needed to suffer to be refined, then he prayed for that to occur. If that was what was needed, then God should bring it on. He did not want it, but if he needed to suffer, then he fervently prayed for it to happen. It was as if I were listening to an audio play-by-play of a tremendous rally in a championship tennis match wherein there was one great shot after another only to see a powerful return. Often, it seems that Christian prayer is asking the Lord to protect, provide, or deliver us from some circumstance. Greg was a man wrestling with the Lord's infinite wisdom in the circumstances that would afflict him and how his affliction could bring him to a more perfected relationship with Christ. His prayer was a passionate plea for what the Lord needed to do in his life, but it was also clear that was not what he desired. The prayer and back-and-forth with the Lord seemed to go on forever. I was struck by Greg's prayer and its intensity and his desire for God to work through him.

The message of suffering had immediate relevance when we received a call while making a rare trip out of camp to Eagle River that Brandon, the young man I had run a marathon for the prior summer, had aspergillus in his lungs and a seven-centimeter tumor in his stomach, likely a result of his distressed immune system and the continued high doses of steroids. He was given one week to a month to live. I was devastated. He was such a great young man with a wonderful outlook on life despite his miserable circumstance. His mother was a godly woman of prayer, clinging to the truth of scripture with a fervent hope and knowledge to place her complete trust in Jesus. Now the medical community was saying Brandon's life would soon end. Through a fortuitous discussion with a couple leaders on the NFL Indianapolis Colts staff, the Gores were able to take a trip to the Cayman Islands using the private jet of the owner, Jim Irsay. The flight and trip would require his mother, Robin, to administer the necessary medications and IV fluids, as Brandon had no immune system. A few months later, in October, in a miracle the doctors still cannot explain, tests revealed both the aspergillus and tumor were gone. We were excited to hear the news. The outpouring of prayer was working, or so we thought. But the Lord was not done with our relationship with the Gores. We would reunite in a few months in late January. It was more than an improbable reunion, as both of our sons would face the fights of their lives at opposite ends of Riley Hospital, in the pediatric critical care units—with remarkable and implausible endings to their stories.

Biblical Principle

In Paul's letter to the church of Ephesus, he wrote in Ephesians 1:17–21,

> That the God of our Lord Jesus Christ, the Father of glory, may give to you the spirit of wisdom and revelation in the knowledge of Him, the eyes of your understanding being enlightened; that you may know what is the hope of His calling, what are the riches of the glory of His inheritance in the saints, and what is the exceeding greatness of His power toward us who believe, according to the working of His mighty power which He worked in Christ when He raised Him from the dead and seated Him at His right hand in the heavenly places, far above all principality and power and might and dominion, and every name that is named, not only in this age but also in that which is to come.

The phrase "eyes of your understanding" refers to our spiritual understanding. We are given eyes, or divine illumination, to see what our Father sees or has for us. Our hope is in Jesus Christ, and in Him, we can rest.

Upon reflection, I realize Eric was God's messenger to share with us Peter's message to prepare us for Payton's illness and passing. As I seek Him, my eyes are opened to see His plans and purposes for us and His use of us for His glory.

CHAPTER 9

THE PIECES TO THE PUZZLE ARE COMING TOGETHER

A day or two after we returned from camp, Payton was in the living room, putting his shoes on as he got ready to head outside. He was sitting on a high-backed green corduroy chair as I came down the hallway to head upstairs. Payton called to get my attention. It was not one of those "Hey, Tito" comments that annoyed me. Unlike Blake, Payton was not a big talker, and like his mom, he did not hesitate to say what was on his mind. He caught me off guard as he abruptly blurted out, "Dad, why aren't we going to Zionsville Fellowship?"

Four years of family camp and seeing life lived out in a temporary community with purposeful, fun, and warm Christian fellowship had caused Payton to consider our relationship with our local church. Frankly, I was glad he asked the question. Thirteen-year-old boys have lots of things on their minds, and where they attend church is not typically high on the list. He was asking to attend Zionsville Fellowship. I do not recall my answer, but his question certainly had my attention in the days and weeks ahead, not to mention a remark he made about one of his friends: "That idiot does not even know how to be saved." Perhaps not the best way to witness for the gospel, but that was Payton: direct and to the point.

Payton noticed the difference, if only through the actions and camaraderie created at camp. That community of campers created a picture of church life and worship dramatically different from the one he experienced at Garfield Park. I suspect his view of the church was largely impacted by the setting—the camp environment and activities—but a fair amount was due to the people. Payton's question caused me to reflect on the discussion I'd had with Dave Greiwe, and I recognized that type of conversation did not happen in most churches—or elsewhere, for that matter. Dave was a mature believer following the biblical command to speak into another's life with grace. More importantly, Dave modeled his beliefs well, which made it easy to take instruction from another brother in Christ.

Robyn had asked me from time to time about attending Zionsville Fellowship, including during our most recent trip to camp; however, I was certain we had work to do at Garfield Park. She was concerned about the boys' spiritual development, as Garfield Park had a less robust Sunday school program, and the church did not have the same level of spiritual maturity throughout the body. Robyn was less concerned for herself, as she attended Bible Study Fellowship to supplement her knowledge and, as a voracious reader, expanded her knowledge through various sources.

The biggest drawback to leaving Garfield Park was my perceived self-importance with the key leadership roles I held at the church. I served on the church council and was the financial secretary responsible for the financial reporting. Perhaps most importantly, in late 1997, a few months after our first family camp and exposure to Zionsville Fellowship church, I'd led an ad hoc group of men—Paul Thistle, Charley Grahn, and Jim Jensen—alongside our Pastor Tom to develop a strategic plan for the renewal of the church. Strategic planning was a skill set I'd worked hard to develop and hone through my consulting work at Arthur Andersen, and I was eager to put it to work for the church. Those early discussions led me to remark that we needed to talk to Keith Ogorek because Zionsville Fellowship had "really figured it out." That impression, at the time, was based on attending family camp with ZF. Years later, I realized I had never stepped foot in their church. My observations of Zionsville Fellowship were a result of seeing the church in action in real life through participation in family camps, men's retreats, and a small group study. I had no idea what their Sunday morning church looked like.

The discussions with Keith ultimately led Garfield Park, including our pastor, to formally ask the elders of Zionsville Fellowship to have

Keith and his wife, Becky, come to Garfield Park for a period of about a year, beginning in January 1999, to start and lead a praise worship and teaching time on Sunday mornings between our two liturgical services. To me, it was a miracle to get a traditional, mainline denominational church to agree and for Zionsville Fellowship and the Ogoreks to commit to the experiment for a season. Ultimately, my involvement and drive to advance the renewal of Garfield Park was likely borne out of my skill set and my desire to help the church rather than an obedient call to further the Lord's work. Often, we see the world solely through our own prism and do not grasp the reality of our self-indulgence as we do things of our own accord. Nonetheless, the Lord would use that work, like everything else, to further His plan.

All of that was weighing on my mind as I considered Payton's question in early August 2000, a few weeks removed from our trip to camp. One evening, I was driving home from work on I-65, a route I had taken thousands of times over the past fifteen years. I was approaching the Major Taylor Velodrome as I headed northwest, when the Lord spoke clearly to me—not audibly but through His Spirit: "I will take care of Garfield Park and give them what they need." I was arrogant in my belief I was critically important to the future of Garfield Park. The Lord's message, in addition to the gentle admonition by Dave Greiwe regarding Blake's behavior and requests from both Robyn and Payton to move to Zionsville Fellowship, made it clear. I needed to pay attention, follow His direction, and meet the needs of my family. I was excited to get home and share the news with Robyn.

We would join the body of Zionsville Fellowship in late August. First, I needed to meet with Tom Blossom, the pastor at Garfield Park, to share with him our decision and the reason for it. The conversation was difficult, as I love Tom, but easy, given the nature of our close relationship. I strongly believe we are called to something and should not simply leave a place or situation because we do not like something. Tom was disappointed but understanding. Our relationship continues to this day.

The Terps, Jeff and Eda, joined us the following month. We had a long relationship with the Terps that dated back to our first visit to Garfield Park in 1990 and had continued through our joint participation in the men's discipleship group with Keith. That was one of the few times Jeff followed me. Often, Jeff was telling me what to do or what was in my best interests. Usually, he was right, though not always. When others speak into my life, I am always attentive and try to discern if the Lord is making something clear through someone else.

Jeff with his high-level corporate background in crisis communications and extensive involvement in the political arena would play a critical supporting role in Payton's upcoming hospitalization. His penchant for action, attention to detail and ability to dissect differing points of view made him an ideal person to help us manage an impossible task. Jeff was ideally suited for this role as he thrives on interactions with others, especially when he can help or offer advice and counsel.

A few weeks later, we had a providential introduction to a couple at the wedding of Chris and Kristin Bass. Chris was one of seven men going through the discipleship group process with me. Chris, the youngest man in the group, had an exuberance in life due in part to his career in advertising but more likely a result of who God had made him to be. He brought a lot of joy and energy to everything he did. Robyn and I were looking forward to their wedding. They'd struggled to find a church available on September 23 and ended up having the ceremony at Garfield Park, per Keith's recommendation. Thus, Robyn and I would return to Garfield Park less than one month after the Lord had called us to Zionsville Fellowship.

The ceremony was Christ honoring. Keith officiated the service and did his usual impeccable job. Always engaging and entertaining, Keith brought the art of story to life whenever he spoke. After the service, we headed to a downtown hotel for the reception, where a chance meeting would herald the start of a critically important relationship for Robyn and me. We were seated next to David and Ndidi Musa, who also attended Zionsville Fellowship. David and Ndidi were in their native African garb, which, for a wedding, was resplendent. African culture is known for exquisite clothing on special occasions. Ndidi wore a *gele*, a traditional Nigerian cloth, which was wrapped around her head. David was in an *agbada*, a beautiful robe worn over his clothes. However, their nature was dramatically different than their elaborate, eye-catching clothing —quiet, thoughtful, joyful, engaging, and humble. Our short time at the wedding reception left me with an indelible image of two godly people committed to serving Him.

There were more than two hundred people at the reception, and the Lord wanted us to know the Musas. Exactly one hundred days later, Ndidi would reappear as Payton's lead doctor at Riley Children's Hospital. That could not have been a coincidence.

The Lord continued to put the puzzle pieces together the following month as He prepared us for Payton's impending hospitalization. Zionsville Fellowship had a practice of assigning prayer partners to middle and senior high school students. Neither the students nor their parents knew their partners' identities. They would correspond in an anonymous manner during their time in middle or senior high school, and the prayer partner would pray for the student. In the summer following their graduation from middle or senior high school, there was a reveal, often at a pancake breakfast, and the prayer partner and student would meet knowingly for the first time.

Payton had just started eighth grade at the time of our move to Zionsville Fellowship, and unbeknownst to us, he was assigned a prayer partner, Scott Cooper. Scott had played with Payton on the praise worship team at camp the prior summer and was a gifted musician. I am certain they enjoyed that aspect of their relationship. However, more importantly, Scott worked for Indiana University Hospital, in the bone marrow transplant area, and his office was on the same floor as and directly across the courtyard, about seventy-five feet, from the hospital room Payton would later occupy.

It is staggering to know that immediately upon our arrival at Zionsville Fellowship, which was the result of Payton's inquiry about joining the church, he was assigned a prayer partner who would have a direct sight line to the hospital room he would lie in during the fight for his life three months later. It is impossible to describe with words our overwhelming joy when we later learned that God had established a prayer partner for Payton who could literally see Payton's hospital room from his office. Years later, Scott told me he thought he was a failure, as it appeared his constant prayers returned void. Little did Scott—or we—know the extent of God's plan through Payton's circumstance and passing at the time.

We had one more meaningful marker in the fall of 2000 upon attending Zionsville Fellowship: Robyn and I joined a parenting class based on *Growing Kids God's Way: Biblical Ethics for Parenting* by Gary and Anne Marie Ezzo.[3] An older couple in our church, Gordon and Jean Godsman, led the class. Jean served as the church secretary. We'd gotten to know Gordon and Jean through family camp and enjoyed spending time with them. There is much you can learn from people who have life experience and have matured in their faith and understanding over the years. The course covered several topics, including character development, obedience, discipline, repentance, and touchpoints of love. There were seventeen chapters in the course, which would result in seventeen meetings for our group. Chapter 4, "The Father's Mandate," included a set of principles I would carry on a card for years to come and often recite from memory:

- Cultivate a sense of family identity.
- Demonstrate an ongoing love for your wife.
- Understand your child's private world.
- Give your child the freedom to fail.
- Encourage your child.
- Guard your tongue and your tone.
- Routinely embrace your child.
- Build trust on God's Word.

I would try to live by those precepts or principles over the coming years. Payton, as a quick-witted thirteen-year-old, shared the following remark with us when he learned we were taking the class: "It's not my fault you guys don't know what to do!" (meaning "It's not my fault you guys don't know how to parent me!"). Typical Payton—funny but with a degree of truth. When he was born, we did not know those principles, nor did we live them. However, we did take seriously our role as parents, and over the course of his, Blake's, and Chase's years, we made the necessary steps to grow in our roles as disciples of Christ, husband and wife, and father and mother.

There were three other couples going through the study with us. One couple, Ron and Mary Wertz, would play a pivotal role in the Lord's story through Payton after his passing. Of course, we did not know that at the time, but looking back, it is humbling to see how the Lord was preparing us for the inevitable circumstance that was about to rock our world.

Seemingly innocuous relationships or chance meetings or assignments played critical roles in the unfolding of the Lord's plans—a critically ill child with a death sentence or a God-appointed lesson in response to suffering, a wedding reception church-member seatmate or a critical-care doctor who would lead the efforts to keep our son alive, a member of the worship team at family camp or a prayer partner with direct physical proximity to Payton's hospital room, a member of our *Growing Kids God's Way* class or a supernatural response to Payton's passing. The Lord's plans were unfolding. There was no way to know it at the time, but now we see clearly how He was providing an intricately detailed plan to sustain and comfort us as Payton faced the fight of his life.

Biblical Principle

David wrote in Psalm 37:23, "The steps of a good man are ordered by the LORD, And He delights in his way."

Psalm 37 is a wisdom psalm with an overarching message to maintain patience during life's troubles. Our eternal reward far exceeds any temporal troubles. God oversaw the playbook, ordering our circumstances in such a way to provide for us in a way only He could have at the time of our greatest need.

Upon reflection, I am comforted God made unmistakably clear the path He'd laid in advance for Payton and our family. Otherwise, our loss would have crushed us.

PART 4

HE LIVED SO LONG TO REACH SO MANY

CHAPTER 10

THE LAST SUPPER

It was Thursday, December 20, just five days until Christmas. Christmas is great anytime but especially good when you have a thirteen-, ten-, and seven-year-old. Robyn's family was coming to visit from northern Indiana. Robyn had to work a few days the week following Christmas, but we would have plenty of time together to enjoy time with family, open presents, reflect on the reason for the season, and enjoy time away from work and school.

I had a few things to get done at work before I could enjoy, with limited distraction, the week between Christmas and New Year's. That afternoon, I had a board meeting with the Indianapolis and Central Indiana Technology Partnership (ICITP) at Intech Park on the northwest side of Indianapolis. ICITP, a nonprofit organization started a year or two prior, was an initiative that had come out of the Mayor's High Technology Task Force. Working with CEOs and high-level individuals at many of the area's major employers and universities was a wonderful opportunity to grow and develop as well as drive a critical effort for our community.

The board was energized to tackle many of the initiatives coming out of the study, and that meeting was no different. It is enjoyable to work with individuals committed to getting things done. It was the holiday season, and naturally, there was an elaborate spread of food, including bakery fresh breads, deli meats and cheeses, and various side dishes and cookies. When the meeting concluded, many hustled to the exits to finish last-minute preparations and enjoy planned time off. As we looked to clean up the conference area, I noticed the attendees had eaten little. It seemed no one was going to claim the food, and I mentioned I was on the way to my oldest son's basketball game and was certain the team would enjoy the meal after their game. There were no disagreements from anyone, so I took a boatload of food and was anxious to get to the game to share the bounty with the team. They were in for a special treat.

Fortunately, the game was nearby, at Payton's middle school, New Augusta North. The eighth-grade team was coached by Norm Leonard, a man I had met a few years prior at Zionsville Fellowship's fall men's retreat. Norm was a good man and cared about the boys. He had an enviable task, as New Augusta typically had a significant pipeline of talented young men on the basketball team and molding their talent into a cohesive team was a big challenge. Norm had the right type of disposition and leadership for the role.

Upon arriving at the gymnasium, I took the food to the locker room and proceeded to join Robyn in the bleachers to watch the game. As I watched Payton, he did not seem into the game. I often challenged him about his work ethic as he often relied on his height, so he did not have to work as hard. If he'd had half the work ethic of his younger brother Blake, no one would have stopped him. Payton was good, mind you, just not dedicated to doing what it took to really excel. His height and body size, at six foot one and 175 pounds, gave him an enviable advantage, and he had a nice shot perfected the past couple years on our basketball hoop in our driveway.

It didn't take long for Coach Leonard to notice Payton's lethargic play, and Payton spent most of the game on the bench. Robyn and I were not sure what was wrong. After the game, I went to talk to Payton, and he said he did not feel well. He asked if I could give him some money to get a can of pop from the vending machine, and I was glad to oblige. We then gathered with the rest of his teammates in the

locker room to celebrate the victory. Coach Leonard asked me to share a few thoughts prior to the meal and pray before we broke bread together. It was a sweet and special time for the team to enjoy the food and time together, as it was their last game before the Christmas break. Payton ate little. He was not hungry. We did not know it at the time, but that was his last supper, a final time to share a meal with his twelve teammates (IMAGE #6 – Basketball team picture).

The next day, Payton stayed home from school sick with what we thought was the flu. The planned Christmas gift exchange with his girlfriend, Meredith, would need to wait. About two months prior, Payton had let us know there was a girl he liked. We were concerned about dating relationships in eighth grade and were curious to know more about her. Payton assured us she was from a good family, and through the course of our conversation, we learned Meredith and her family were next-door neighbors to Derrick and Celeste Burks. Derrick was the office managing partner at Arthur Andersen, and we had worked together for fifteen years. That provided Robyn and me with a great opportunity to inquire of the Burks regarding Meredith and make sure she was a good girl. Not that Payton was an angel, but we wanted to ensure any relationship was God honoring. I would tell Payton and his brothers, "You need to treat a young lady like you want your mother treated." A high bar.

For the next several days, Payton periodically spiked a fever. Robyn, with her nursing background, was well equipped to assess his situation. Christmas Day came, and he was still the same. He was weak, tired, and sluggish. He joined us for the traditional opening of Christmas gifts. The tree was always overloaded with gifts. Robyn's love language is giving gifts, and her mom and dad and Aunt Jo also contributed to the overload. Payton's illness muted our celebration. I tried my best to keep Payton from infecting the rest of us by using Lysol disinfectant to minimize the spread of any germs. Boy, I felt terrible later about my insensitivity to how Payton was really feeling.

The coming days were a continuation of the same. Robyn called his pediatrician, Dr. Harper, and both thought it was likely viral, and Payton would eventually get better. Robyn checked Payton periodically to make sure there was nothing alarming warranting more extreme measures. I was planning on taking vacation days between Christmas and New Year's and would stay home with him and the other boys, as Robyn was scheduled to work at the Indiana University Medical Center.

New Year's Eve arrived, and Payton seemed to perk up a bit. He did not attend church that morning, as we did not want to spread whatever he had to Zionsville Fellowship and his Sunday school class. His teachers, Joey Stein and Pam Basch, taught on invincibility and concluded that no one was invincible. In the weeks ahead, the middle school class would get a firsthand perspective on that teaching.

For the preceding week, I'd asked Payton to call Meredith to let her know what was going on. He always said he did not feel up to it and would sometime. That was unusual, as they talked almost every day. I anticipated a fourteen-year-old girl would have some level of concern if she had not heard from her boyfriend for ten days. Payton, unbeknownst to us, did call Meredith on New Year's Eve. We would find out about their conversation many weeks later.

We planned an early evening New Year's Eve gathering with some close friends. It's hard to call it a celebration; rather, it was an opportunity to get together. Payton was on his computer with young Austin Taylor on his lap. We were close with Austin's dad and mom, Nick and Traci, having met them in 1998 at family camp at Fort Wilderness. Their interaction was encouraging, as Payton had spent most of the past ten days on the La-Z-Boy recliner in the family room.

After our friends left, Robyn said she was concerned about Payton and his breathing. He did not sound good. Payton had mild asthma, mostly exercise induced, which was typically not a problem. He had outgrown the use of an inhaler, which he'd used when he was younger. Robyn was giving serious consideration to taking him to the emergency room. She said, "It just does not make sense—he should be getting better." I asked if we really wanted to go late on New Year's Eve, when the hospital was dealing with all sorts of interesting problems associated with partying and revelry, and the new insurance year started the next day. We agreed if he was not better, we would take him to the hospital in the morning.

Payton's best friend, Scott Macke, had come over for the gathering earlier that evening with his dad, Mike, and stepmom, Peggy. He wanted to spend the night, and his parents quickly obliged. Scott had an infectious smile and was always a joy to see, and we saw him frequently. However, in the prior ten days, Payton had not seen much of anybody, and we were glad to see a little return to normalcy, hoping the supposed flu bug was coming to an end. Looking back, I believe perhaps that was God's way of providing Payton with a final time to enjoy a special time with his best friend and call Meredith earlier in the day. We would soon adjust to a new and stark reality.

Robyn told me she was going to sleep with Payton, which brought back memories of Payton as a child, when he'd slept with us all the time. Robyn wanted to be near him in case he had trouble breathing and to comfort him and herself. Scott slept on the floor in the same spot our dog, Bandit, had occupied until a few weeks prior, when he'd run off and never returned. We feared Bandit had run onto the ice on the reservoir and fallen in. Bandit, a beautiful dog, part husky and part Lab, was Payton's dog, and the rest of us were outsiders. Payton loved Bandit and spent lots of time grooming Bandit, and he kept his hair in a Ziploc bag on his bookshelf. I cannot imagine Bandit without Payton.

Our typical New Year's celebration was muted as we counted down the minutes till midnight. We never could have imagined that was Payton's final night with us in our home.

Biblical Principle

Luke, a physician, wrote the following in Luke 2:8–20:

> Now there were in the same country shepherds living out in the fields, keeping watch over their flock by night. And behold, an angel of the Lord stood before them, and the glory of the Lord shone around them, and they were greatly afraid. Then the angel said to them, "Do not be afraid, for behold, I bring you good tidings of great joy which will be to all people. For there is born to you this day in the city of David a Savior, who is Christ the

Lord. And this will be the sign to you: You will find a Babe wrapped in swaddling cloths, lying in a manger."

And suddenly there was with the angel a multitude of the heavenly host praising God and saying:

"Glory to God in the highest,

And on earth peace, goodwill toward men!"

So it was, when the angels had gone away from them into heaven, that the shepherds said to one another, "Let us now go to Bethlehem and see this thing that has come to pass, which the Lord has made known to us." And they came with haste and found Mary and Joseph, and the Babe lying in a manger. Now when they had seen Him, they made widely known the saying which was told them concerning this Child. And all those who heard it marveled at those things which were told them by the shepherds. But Mary kept all these things and pondered them in her heart. Then the shepherds returned, glorifying and praising God for all the things that they had heard and seen, as it was told them.

    The shepherds were the first to hear of the Christmas story and Jesus's birth. Mankind has heard the story for the past two thousand years. Today the story is often overshadowed by family gatherings, celebrations, gift giving, and the busyness of the season.

    Upon reflection, I recognize that Christmas 2000 was special, as it was our last Christmas as a family. God's gift to us in his Son, Jesus, provides hope for those who believe in Him to share this gift in eternity, and for that, we are thankful.

CHAPTER 11

MAN, MEDICINE, AND MACHINES OR GOD?

January 1, 2001

Robyn woke the next morning and went downstairs to make her ritualistic cup of coffee. The boys were still sleeping upstairs. She is a woman with good intuition, particularly with teenagers, which is a great gift. Robyn was concerned. She did not like how Payton sounded and thought he should have shown some sign of improvement by then. Robyn, despite her nursing background, is not prone to unnecessary medical care or treatment. She had my full attention when she said, "Todd, we need to take Payton to the emergency room. I am scared." We decided to take him to St. Vincent's Hospital, which was about fifteen minutes from our house—the same hospital where Payton was born.

The boys woke up a little after ten o'clock, and Robyn made a New Year's morning brunch. Payton, consistent with the past ten days, did not eat much. He had little appetite. We told Payton we were going to take him to the emergency room to see what was going on. Payton, who had strong views and opinions on most things, said that was okay. We asked Scott to stay with Blake and Chase while we were gone. Scott contacted his family, and they were fine with Scott staying so he could take care of Blake and Chase.

I told Payton to get ready to go and get cleaned up. It was his first trip out of the house in eleven days—highly unusual for a thirteen-year-old boy—and the trip was an unusual start to the New Year. Typically, the New Year was steeped in optimism, resolutions, college football bowl games, and our traditional New Year's trip to Kentucky Fried Chicken to splurge on a family package of chicken, baked beans, coleslaw, mashed potatoes, and biscuits. That was not our typical fare, as Robyn is a tremendous cook, but it had been a long-standing tradition since the kids were little.

A few minutes later, I heard a thud in our bathroom just down the hall from our family room. I thought Payton had knocked something down while getting into or out of the shower. I opened the door and the shower curtain and was shocked to see Payton slumped down in the tub. My heart sank. He did not have the energy to stand up. I yelled to Robyn, "We need to get Payton to the hospital right now!" She found the boys and told them we were leaving, while I did my best to help my 175-pound son get dressed. Fortunately, the bathroom was right across from the door leading to the garage, and I only needed to help Payton move a few feet to get into the front passenger seat of the car. He could not move—it was as if the life had been sucked out of his body. Robyn came in a hurry a few moments later.

Early afternoon on New Year's Day is a great time to drive if you need to get somewhere quickly, as most people are just getting moving, watching parades or football, or staying indoors. The car trip was quiet. Payton was in no mood to talk. Robyn and I did not want to alarm Payton, but our minds were racing. What was going on? We quickly arrived at the emergency entrance at St. Vincent's, and Robyn entered the building to have an orderly get a wheelchair for Payton. I helped Payton get out of the car and clutched him with a deep and longing hug as I moved his body into the wheelchair. I told Robyn I would park the car and meet her inside. A few minutes later, I entered the hospital door, and Payton was already back in one of the rooms with Robyn, getting ready for blood work. The attending nurse took Payton's blood pressure, and it was dangerously low, which meant an immediate trip back to the emergency room. There was no time to wait.

Soon enough, the attending doctor came to see us in the waiting area and said, "Payton is in renal failure." He went on to describe other counts and his condition, but I did not hear any of it. Renal failure was enough. His kidneys were not working. The situation sounded serious. Then the doctor said, "We are going to transfer him to Riley Children's Hospital. An ambulance will take him, and you can meet him there."

What had just happened? He was so sick they needed to transfer him to the acute-care hospital for children in the state of Indiana.

We quickly gathered our things and headed back to the emergency entrance and out to our car. As we reached our car, we saw an emergency vehicle scream south on Naab Road. We were certain Payton was in the vehicle. We were stunned, not knowing what had just happened. What in the world was going on?

Robyn was quiet on the twenty-five-minute trip, which meant she was concerned. Normally, Robyn was full of energy and life. As a health-care professional, she knew something was not right. I asked a few questions, as I was trying to understand Payton's medical situation, but I also wanted to respect Robyn's need to process what was taking place.

Robyn was familiar with the hospital, having started her professional career there about eight months after Payton was born. We pulled into the parking garage and found a spot on the first level, which negated the need to walk through the skyway connecting the garage to the emergency room entrance. We entered through the sliding glass door, and within a few feet, there was a small office with a sliding glass window behind which sat a middle-aged lady who would take the necessary information. She informed us Payton was in intensive care on 4 North.

We walked down the corridor to the elevator. As the doors closed, I put my arms around Robyn. The situation was tough for both of us, but Robyn was a mom and a nurse. She needed to know I was there for her. We exited the elevator and headed to the nurses' station. We were told Payton's room was down the hall on the right. We entered his room, and Payton was in the hospital bed and hooked up to various machines to check his blood pressure and oxygen saturation levels. His six-foot-one, 175-pound frame took up every part of the bed.

Payton particularly enjoyed the pulse oximeter device attached to his middle finger. Think of it as a splint with a small, bright infrared light on the tip of the finger, used to measure the amount of oxygen his body was receiving. Throughout the evening, Payton would ask us for something to drink. He was thirsty, and we had to tell him no. Payton said, "If I don't get some water, I am going to die."

I responded, "If you do drink something, you are going to die." Payton's body was not allowing him to excrete any fluids, as his kidneys were not working. Payton's response was to lift his middle finger with the bright red light ever so gently to let us know he did not like our answer. It was a moment of levity in an otherwise difficult and unfunny circumstance.

There was a significant amount of activity taking place in Payton's room, which gave us further understanding of the serious nature of Payton's condition. I suspect that comes with the territory in ICU; however, it was clear the team assembled on New Year's Day was trying to figure out what was wrong with Payton. Tests continued with an echocardiogram done in his room. Payton asked Robyn to get him some McDonald's, as he was hungry, and he wanted a Coke as well. I do not think he was delusional, but he did not want to accept the reality that he was not going to eat or drink. That was consistent with Payton's character, as he liked to push us.

While we waited for the results of the tests, I turned on the television set to check the New Year's Day bowl game scores. Oregon State was playing Notre Dame in the Fiesta Bowl. Robyn had grown up in northern Indiana, in the shadows of South Bend. It took only a few moments before I noticed that Oregon State was up big, 34–3, in the third quarter. A few minutes later, the resident on duty came in and shared Payton's medical situation, and the television went off for the evening—and the days to come – as my attention diverted from most everything happening in the outside world.

We listened intently as he gave us the initial assessment of Payton's condition. He was straightforward in his approach, bereft of years of experience and trying to discern a significant amount of known and unknown conditions with Payton's situation. The echocardiogram had identified a vegetation on Payton's heart, likely a result of an infection inexplicably making its way into a small hole in Payton's heart—the same VSD diagnosed at Payton's birth, which we'd presumed would not cause any problems.

The initial game plan was to use medication to support Payton's blood pressure and a broad spectrum of high-powered antibiotics to address the infection while allowing time for the results of the culture to identify the specific treatment protocol and for Lasix to stimulate the kidneys. The resident also discussed the possibility of intubating Payton (putting him on a ventilator) in a medically induced coma to help him breathe. We would consult with the lead doctor in the morning regarding that decision and the overall game plan. The message was clear: Payton was very sick.

Payton seemed a little oblivious to his illness and more concerned about eating, drinking, and his comfort level. He was understandably sluggish and tired from almost seven or eight hours of medical attention. It was nearing ten o'clock, and Payton was tired. Upon arriving at Riley, Robyn had called her parents, Mike and Ann, and sister, Cari, to inform them of the situation with Payton. Her parents had arrived earlier that evening to relieve Scott of child-care duties or whatever he and our boys were doing. That was the least of our worries.

We gave Payton a hug and slowly started to leave the room. Payton needed rest, and we did too. It is an odd thing to leave your child in the hospital. There is a feeling of helplessness impossible to describe. But we were thankful he was at Riley. We had profound respect for the quality of care. Surely, they could figure out what was going on and address the problem. We did not know it at the time, but that was the last time we would ever have a conversation with Payton.

We left the hospital and headed home. Robyn was numb and exhausted. Her health-care training and experience were now working against her. She knew too much about the gravity of Payton's situation. In the days ahead, she would avoid the moment-by-moment analysis of the machines like the gyrations of the stock market. It was more than she could bear. Later that week, I found her nursing school anatomy textbook and looked up sepsis and a patient with multiple organ failure. The diagnosis was grim. Most patients lived a few days or maybe a week. I ripped the pages out of the textbook to protect Robyn from ever seeing the information. While I believed that outcome was a possibility, my view was that Payton was alive, and God could provide what we needed.

We arrived home and shared the news with Mike, Ann, and the boys. They were hoping for the best. Surely Riley Children's Hospital could help Payton, they said. We agreed, but we made it clear Payton was very sick. We would need the Lord's help like never before.

Blake, at ten years of age, was the eternal optimist, always ready with an approach to solve a problem, likely a result of his upbringing and the discipline he'd learned as a young athlete gifted at soccer. Chase was just seven. His age and predisposition to fantasy and playing out life made it hard to understand what Chase knew or understood. Ann said, "You do whatever you need to do. We are here and will take care of these boys." Her voice quivered at the gravity of her first grandson's life-threatening illness. The situation was hard for her and Mike. She'd spent hundreds of hours caring for Payton during his first couple years of life. She was trying her best to remain strong. Mike, a big, strong guy, was hurting too. Payton was their first grandchild. Payton was a big and strong kid and built and looked like Mike. Robyn gave Blake and Chase big hugs and said it was time to get ready for bed. We would need our strength and energy to see what tomorrow would bring.

I was up in the wee hours of the morning, which was commonplace in the days to come. I sent the following email to a few close friends and business associates, including Robin Gore; Jeff Terp; Alan Boress; Michael Maley; Dave Greiwe; Chris Bass; Nick Taylor; Keith Ogorek; Tom Blossom; Jim Jensen; Markham Hines; Tim Doyle; Bryon Parnell; Ted Kramer; Charley Grahn; my mother, Patricia; and my brothers, Scott and Tom.

Subject: URGENT PRAYER REQUEST

Tuesday, January 02, 2001, 4:26 a.m.

Yesterday my oldest son, Payton, was admitted to the intensive care unit at Riley Children's Hospital in Indianapolis. He has battled a flu or virus since December 21. He started getting a little better during the middle of this past week but took a turn for the worse over the past forty-eight hours. I am not a health professional but will try to share with you what is going on and the urgency of prayer. Payton is in renal failure, as his kidneys are not working. As a baby, he had a very slight heart murmur, which can create the opportunity for infections to get in the heart. Unfortunately, the infection is in the heart. He has a toxic rash around his joints due to the inability of the kidneys to do their job. The challenge is the doctors need to stabilize his breathing and respirations and are using Lasix to stimulate the kidney function—but not much has happened. The good news is Riley is staffed with world-class physicians and health professionals. They believe they know what is causing this to happen. The challenge is the infection or problem has a big head start. I don't want to mislead anyone: he is very sick. Proverbs 18:14 says, "The spirit of a man will sustain him in sickness, But who can bear a broken spirit?" Payton, like most healthy thirteen-year-olds, is quite apprehensive and anxious about all of this. The more anxious he is and persistent he needs water—even though he can't have any—causes his breathing to be more labored and his strength to diminish.

Please pray for Robyn and our family that we can support Payton and one another during a difficult time. God is sovereign, and our trust is placed in Him. If I left anyone off the list, please pass this note along.

Todd

Robyn and I left for the hospital a few minutes before seven o'clock in the morning. The boys were still on Christmas break, and Grandma and Grandpa would provide a necessary distraction to Payton's illness with Mom and Dad gone. We arrived at the hospital and immediately proceeded to Payton's room. There was a beehive of activity between seven and seven thirty during shift change as the day team took over. During the days ahead, we would learn the best time to access the medical staff was right after shift change and report outs.

We went directly to Payton's room, somewhat oblivious of the staff around us. I do not know if we had an expectation as to what we were going to see. Was Payton better? Were the doctors able to get him on some drugs that would give him an immediate boost? How was he feeling? We were anxious to talk to him and reassure him regarding his condition and putting his trust in God and the excellent medical care at Riley. We wanted to just hold him and tell him we loved him.

We passed the nursing station, and in just a few more seconds, we could see Payton. We entered the room. I thought, *Oh my gosh!* I am not sure what we expected to see, but I am certain we were not prepared. Payton was lying in his bed, motionless, with a myriad of machines hooked up to him and a panel of indicators and measurements monitoring his every breath and heartbeat. Robyn knew quickly what was going on—she did not need the medical staff to inform her. Payton was on a ventilator. The resident had mentioned that as a possibility the night before, but we were surprised to see him hooked up to the ventilator first thing in the morning. We walked up to his bed and looked at him. Could he hear us? His eyes were closed. He had a rash on his hands and feet; it looked like a bad case of sunburn. We would learn he had toxic shock syndrome, a result of toxins building up in his body, as the kidneys were not excreting his body's waste.

We stood there for a while and softly said, "Payton," to no response. Our hearts sank, and in a moment, we entered a new relationship wherein we could love and support him without any ability for Payton to engage or reciprocate. At least he could not talk back to us, which was something we had to endure with a typical teenage boy.

A short while later, a young lady in her late thirties entered the room. She introduced herself as Angie. She was petite, blonde, and physically fit. She would serve as Payton's lead nurse in the days to follow and be our primary point of contact for most of our time at Riley. Typically, an ICU nurse would care for two patients. Payton was Angie's only patient. In the days that followed, two nurses were assigned to Payton, given the complexity of his situation. We would come to know Angie as a gifted administrator who was intelligent and focused and had an intent to provide excellent care to her patients. She was not overly warm, nor was she cold. She was like Robyn in certain respects as a nurse, particularly one in a pediatric hospital, guarding personal relationships with her patients considering the gravity of the cases she handled. Angie would later share that her goal was for nothing bad to happen on her watch. *This is somebody's child*, she thought. Inexplicably, I would learn Angie was a close friend of

Tim Doyle, my work colleague at Arthur Andersen and one of my early spiritual mentors.

Angie confirmed the basics of what was going on with Payton. She made it easy to understand. She said the doctor would meet with us soon to share the initial diagnosis and plan. We were free to wait in the room with Payton, or the doctor could meet us in the family lounge. We thanked her, and she checked Payton's readings and left us alone for a few minutes to gather our thoughts. Payton was either heavily sedated or in a medically induced coma, so there was nothing we could do, and after a short while, we decided to go to the family lounge to wait for the doctor to arrive. We were anxious to know the official statement of Payton's condition and the game plan to help him get better.

The family lounge was a smallish room at the entry point of the intensive care unit, located about 100 to 150 feet down the hall from the nurses' station, which was centrally located to the hospital rooms. There was room for about eight to twelve people, depending on the level of congestion you could handle in the room. It housed a couple couches, a few chairs, end tables, and some magazines. It was functional—nothing more. It would become our home away from home for the foreseeable future.

I asked Robyn a variety of questions about Payton's condition. She was polite in her responses and engaged, but reflecting after the fact, I realized clearly, she was in shock. My response, consistent with my technical training and consulting background, was to identify the problem, the response, and how to support our family in our new reality.

About fifteen to twenty minutes later, a tall African American doctor entered the lounge, looked at us, and said in her native Nigerian accent, "Todd. Robyn." It was Ndidi, whom we'd met at a friend's wedding just a few months prior. We were stunned. I walked over to her, and we embraced. A few seconds later, she and Robyn embraced. We'd had no inclination she was a doctor or worked at Riley Hospital. In fact, it was her first day back at work after an extended six-week absence to address a personal medical issue.

Now Ndidi was the doctor responsible for Payton's medical care. We felt an immediate comfort, relief, and joy, as we knew the Lord was at work with that providential assignment. It was an unasked-for answer to prayer. The Lord knew what we needed. We were immediately put at ease as Ndidi spoke about Payton and his medical condition in a measured and supportive tone. Her beautiful smile and countenance were muted as she shared with us the gravity of Payton's illness. She said Payton had sepsis, a potentially life-threatening complication of an infection. We would learn sepsis occurs when chemicals released into the bloodstream to fight the infection trigger inflammatory responses throughout the body. This inflammation can trigger a cascade of changes that can damage multiple organ systems, causing them to fail. Simply put, it is a bacterial infection in the blood. Ndidi went on to say multiple organs were not working at normal levels—the kidneys, liver, and lungs—and Payton had a vegetation, or bacterial growth, on his heart valve. Cultures had been taken to identify the bacteria; however, it would take twenty-four to forty-eight hours to learn the results. In the meantime, the staff had put Payton on a broad spectrum of high-powered antibiotics, including vancomycin. She went on to explain the body had a natural response to sepsis and would shut down nonvital organs to preserve the heart, which was what was happening in Payton's body. Payton's heart was working hard to keep him alive, and we needed time to allow the medicine to work; hopefully, no significant emboli from the vegetation would break off and obstruct the lungs or heart. Instead, the doctors hoped for it to dissolve in his bloodstream over time.

If that were not enough, Payton was put in a medically induced coma to help him breathe without exerting as much effort. That would also aid in his recovery. His blood pressure was dangerously low, and he was getting vasopressors or dopamine to increase his blood pressure. They were also planning to put Payton on a continuous venovenous hemodialysis, which would pull the blood out of the body and remove fluids and electrolytes, as the kidneys were unable to relieve the toxins that had accumulated in his body over the preceding days. Ndidi shared a lot of medical information, which I found helpful. Robyn just wanted to know if Payton was going to be all right. Robyn knew the critical nature of Payton's condition. Her medical training had prepared her well for the situation, but it had not prepared her for the reality of facing her son's mortality.

The initial discussion was not a typical doctor's office consult of a few minutes. I suspect we spent fifteen to thirty minutes—a long time, given the demands of her role as Payton's lead intensivist. Ndidi was the doctor responsible for quarterbacking the Riley medical team on Payton's case.

Ultimately, Payton would require nephrology (kidney), gastroenterology (intestine and liver), cardiology (heart), pulmonology (lung), infectious disease, surgery, radiology, laboratory, physical therapy, and other services. He had a big team of specialists who would work on his case. I would take every opportunity in the days ahead to ask questions of each of the doctors in his or her area of specialization to ascertain what was going on, so we knew what the goal was and what to pray for. Payton's lead cardiologist, Dr. Caldwell, said, after I asked her about Payton's condition, "Todd, Payton is the sickest kid at Riley." If a statement like that does not take someone's breath away, I do not know what does. In a nationally recognized acute-care hospital dedicated to serving children throughout Indiana and neighboring states, Payton was the sickest.

Ndidi wrapped up our discussion and asked Robyn and me if she could pray with us. We both said yes. We would come to realize in the days ahead that Ndidi was an outstanding doctor; however, she was an even greater prayer warrior. We have met few people during our lives who have such fervent prayer lives, remarkable knowledge of the Word of God, humility as they approach His throne, and expectancy to see His will come to fruition. Ndidi then posed the most important question ever spoken to us to this day: "You can trust in what man, medicine, and machines can do, or you can trust in what God can do." Without hesitation, we chose God. Intellectually, we knew what that meant; however, we would learn in the days to come what it meant to live that response and see God respond in ways beyond human comprehension and understanding.

Twenty-four hours earlier, we'd been preparing for what we thought was a relatively routine visit to the emergency room, and now we were in for the fight of our lives. But we have a great and powerful God. We put our trust in Him. Payton was in the right place. Given what we know now, if we'd waited another day, there is a good chance Payton would have died at home.

I sent out my next formal update two days later with the following email:

Thursday, January 04, 2001, 8:22 a.m.

From the book of James 4:13–16: "Come now, you who say, 'Today or tomorrow we will go to such and such a city, spend a year there, buy and sell, and make a profit'; whereas you do not know what will happen tomorrow. For what is your life? It is even a vapor that appears for a little time and then vanishes away. Instead you ought to say, 'If the Lord wills, we shall live and do this or that.' But now you boast in your arrogance. All such boasting is evil."

And from the book of Matthew 6:34: "Therefore do not worry about tomorrow, for tomorrow will worry about its own things. Sufficient for the day is its own trouble."

Robyn and I are blessed the Lord willed Payton to live yesterday—what a blessing. With each hour that Payton stays the same or progresses, we consider that a little victory. We are praying for a series of little victories that will enable Payton to live. We realize that God has all the power, and if He wills, Payton will live to do this or that.

Yesterday [January 3] was a series of little victories. He had a difficult night; however, he made some marginal progress. The staph infection in his body is not resistant to medication, and the medication is beginning to work. The cultures are not growing as quickly as before. The vegetation on his heart is smaller, albeit slightly, than the day before.

His heart rate has declined to 130 beats per minute (80–100 is normal). His heart is working very hard to deal with all the problems going on in his body. His blood pressure has stabilized, with medication, at 120/48. His creatinine, which measures kidney functions, has declined to 7.2 from a high of 8.5. Normal levels are 1.0.

Robyn and I are greatly humbled and blessed to have so many friends offering support and prayers. Literally, there are people from many faiths praying for Payton throughout the country. Specifically, we have a very similar prayer request to yesterday.

- God is glorified during Payton's situation.
- Payton's body continues to respond to the treatments provided, and the antibiotics continue to work on the infection. The infectious-disease doctors do not want large chunks of the infection on the heart to break off and potentially create a blockage in his lungs. Pray the medication will dissolve the infection at a rate and in a manner for his body to respond.
- Doctors to discern the necessary treatment to stabilize Payton's vital systems while the antibiotics address the infection. This is quite a challenge, but we have awesome doctors and nurses caring for Payton.
- And for Payton's family and friends to find comfort in this situation.

We are thankful for your prayers. We need them. Payton has a long road ahead of him. He is basically under treatment for forty-eight hours. We just need your prayers for today. If the Lord wills, we will ask again tomorrow.

We love Payton, and Mom and Dad and his brothers are pulling for him.

Another email followed the next day.

Friday, January 05, 2001, 7:13 a.m.

From the book of James 1:2–8: "My brethren, count it all joy when you fall into various trials, knowing that the testing of your faith produces patience. But let patience have its perfect work, that you may be perfect and complete, lacking nothing. If any of you lacks wisdom, let him ask of God, who gives to all liberally and without reproach, and it will be given to him. But let him ask in faith, with no doubting, for he who doubts is like a wave of the sea driven and tossed by the wind. For let not that man suppose that he will receive anything from the Lord; he is a double-minded man, unstable in all his ways."

Robyn and I are praying for Payton to live and for God to be glorified in this process. We are not sure how to handle this and are asking God for wisdom to respond according to His will. This is the greatest trial Robyn and our family have faced, and we will need patience because Payton is very sick and will need time. Time comes in increments of seconds, minutes, hours, days, and weeks. Each day provides a new challenge and new hope.

Yesterday was another blessing. More little victories. Payton was doing better at the end of the day than at the beginning. We are encouraged it appears the antibiotics are working on the infection. During the day, he did not have a fever (without medication). His platelets are up to 87,000 from a low of 32,000. Normal is 150,000 to 450,000. His heart rate has declined to 122–123, down from 130 yesterday, thus putting less strain on his heart. His creatinine, which measures kidney functions, dropped to 6.5 from 7.2 and a high of 8.5.

The outpouring of love and support is greatly appreciated. The meals, emails, phone messages, visits, balloons, and your prayers and encouragement are a blessing to our family and a great glory to God in this time of trial. Thank you so much.

Our prayer request is like yesterday.

- God is glorified during Payton's situation.
- Payton's body continues to respond to the treatments provided, and the antibiotics continue to work on the infection. And dissolve the infection at a rate and manner the body can respond to.

- Doctors properly discern the necessary treatment to keep Payton's vital systems stable while the antibiotics address the infection. For those who have visited Payton, you understand the challenges this presents with the complexity of the drugs and lines going into his body.
- For Payton's family and friends to find comfort during this situation.

We really do need your prayers. We know people are praying for Payton throughout this country and even abroad. Please pray for him today, and if the Lord wills, we will ask for your prayers again tomorrow.

With much appreciation,

Todd and Robyn

Robyn was trying her best to be a mom to all three of our boys and make sure Blake and Chase were healthy and safe. She made sure she was home shortly after the boys arrived home from school. We made it a priority to have dinner together. If needed, one of us could return to the hospital. Robyn's mood was somewhat dictated by how Payton was doing. She was trying to do her best, but it was hard.

We received lots of visitors during our time at Riley; however, one visit caught me off guard during our first week. Becky Kendall, the general counsel at Eli Lilly, the city of Indianapolis's largest employer, stopped by the hospital to see me. We previously had served together on the board of Prevent Child Abuse Indiana for several years in the mid-1990s. She came as a friend to express her support, but more importantly, she came in her role with Eli Lilly, one of the largest pharmaceutical companies in the world. She was aware of Payton's situation and offered us compassionate use for a drug Lilly had in a clinical trial, Xigris, which was under evaluation for use in treating severe sepsis in high-risk patients. Payton met that definition. I was appreciative of her willingness to come visit during her lunch hour. Unfortunately, further discussions with Riley's infectious-disease doctors indicated we were too far down the path to use the drug. Nevertheless, we greatly appreciated the offer. Many others made similar acts of kindness.

I sent the following email after a long first week in the hospital:

Saturday, January 06, 2001, 8:49 a.m.

From the book of Exodus 15:2: "The LORD is my strength and song, And He has become my salvation; He is my God, and I will praise Him; My father's God, and I will exalt Him." Because we know God and know His sovereignty, we can take strength in Him. We praise Him for simply who He is. Without this knowledge, I am crushed and would not know how to respond. But since we know God, we know all things are possible through Him. If it is His will. Payton is alive for another day, and we are blessed.

A brief update. Robyn and I were exhausted last night after the week. We both rested well and are ready to get back at it. Payton had more little victories. He came close to a bigger victory, but his body could not handle being totally off the blood pressure medicine, and so he reverted initially to higher levels. For those of you who have visited, you can understand how truly intricate the human body is, which points to the wonder of God's perfection in the creation of our bodies.

Please pray for the following:

- God would continue to be glorified in this process. Robyn and I have received notes, emails, calls, and visits from people throughout the world, and we know that God can and will use this to illustrate the majesty of His love and sovereignty for the world.
- Doctors would continue to discern the right treatments and adjustments to enable Payton's body to respond and heal itself.

- There are some encouraging discussions about potential adjustments over the next several days that will move him in the direction of recovery.
- Payton's body would respond to the medication. The prayers would lift his spirits and provide the energy he needs to continue the fight. Specifically,
  - The antibiotics would continue to fight the staph infection (a virulent or aggressive bug), the vegetation on his heart would decline in size, and the body would absorb the fragments in a way that will not block other critical functions.
  - His blood pressure would stabilize, and the doctors can take him off the pressors that are supplementing his blood pressure.
  - The oxygen concentration from the ventilator would continue to decline.
  - Payton's family and friends find comfort during this process.

Robyn and I are truly blessed to have so many friends and families pulling for Payton. We are very early in this marathon. Please continue to pray for Payton, and through God's grace alone, Payton can be lifted from this sickness and healed.

Our complete trust is in Him.

Todd and Robyn

Three days later, I provided the following update by email:

Tuesday, January 09, 2001, 8:45 a.m.

Here is today's update. Also, there is one additional prayer request. Payton will have an echocardiogram on his heart to evaluate the antibiotics' progress against the vegetation (staph infection) on his right chamber. Please pray the vegetation is greatly reduced or eliminated in a manner his body can handle.

From the book of Psalms 86:6–13:

> Give ear, O Lord, to my prayer;
> And attend to the voice of my supplications.
> In the day of my trouble I will call upon You,
> For You will answer me.
> Among the gods there is none like You, O Lord;
> Nor are there any works like Your works.
> All nations whom You have made
> Shall come and worship before You, O Lord,
> And shall glorify Your name.
> For You are great, and do wondrous things;
> You alone are God.
> Teach me Your way, O Lord;
> I will walk in Your truth;
> Unite my heart to fear Your name.
> I will praise You, O Lord my God, with all my heart,
> And I will glorify Your name forevermore.
> For great is Your mercy toward me,
> And You have delivered my soul from the depths of Sheol.

There is much to consider in this passage. We are to praise, worship, and glorify God regardless of circumstance and outcome. Robyn and I are so blessed we had Payton this past week. And thankful to spend the past week in the strength and comfort of our heavenly Father and with the prayers, encouragement, and support from so many throughout the world. Yesterday evening marked one week from the time we took Payton to Riley Children's Hospital. God was very good to us this past week. Let me share with you Payton's progress and our prayer requests.

We asked that God is glorified. He is. We have never had the opportunity to share our faith as we have in this situation. We are encouraged by the response of many to

God's sovereignty and recognition that His mercy and grace are enough. Families praying together; churches lifting Payton up in prayer throughout the world; friends, family, and colleagues sharing their faith and responding to our need prayerfully. We asked God the antibiotics would fight the staph infection, and they are.

The cultures taken on Saturday and Sunday did not show bacteria growing. We asked the doctors and nurses would discern the proper treatment so Payton's body could respond and heal itself. The past three to four days were good, and this is being accomplished. It is extremely challenging and complex, given the infection on the heart, kidney dialysis, and ventilator.

There were two goals for the weekend—to get off the norepinephrine (Levophed) infusion for blood pressure maintenance and to get his PEEP (vent setting) down to 12. We prayed, and Payton was able to accomplish the goal. We asked for Payton's family and friends to find comfort, and they are.

PRAISE GOD ALONE, IN HIS GLORY, THAT HE IS ANSWERING OUR PRAYERS. Robyn and I are so thankful we had this past week, and as we shared with so many of you, each day we leave the hospital and Payton is alive, that is a good day. If we don't receive a call in the middle of the night, that is good too. We are truly blessed. Yesterday Dr. Musa attempted to take him off his paralysis medicine. He was out of paralysis for about three hours, although sedate. It didn't work too well for various reasons; however, it was positive, as the doctors could judge how he responded to certain conditions. He was able to respond to the doctors and us.

PLEASE CONTINUE TO PRAY. THERE IS NO DOUBT GOD IS HEARING OUR PRAYERS. SPECIFICALLY, PRAY FOR THE FOLLOWING:

- God would continue to be glorified in this process.
- Doctors and nurses would continue to properly discern the necessary treatments and adjustments for Payton so his body can respond and heal itself. Specifically, managing Payton's sedation is a big challenge. While he is in critical condition, this is a challenging proposition left to man, but God can do anything.
- Payton's blood pressure would stabilize, and his medication would decline (dopamine at three and off the dobutamine). Getting his blood pressure stable and off medications is critical for the doctors to take him off the ventilator and adjust the dialysis.
- Payton's body would start to heal itself and return to normal. He can get some calories and nutrition (IV). His digestive system is not working as it shut down because of the sepsis.
- Payton can continue to reduce his ventilator settings and make progress toward getting off the vent.
- Payton's friends and family find comfort and peace that surpasses all understanding.
Before I close, please let me share a little about Payton, as many have asked.

He is thirteen and will have his fourteenth birthday on May 15. He is 6'1" tall and weighs about 180 pounds (now about 165). He has a strong will. He is a believer—but as a teenager, application of God's truth and commands is not what it needs to be. He has a girlfriend—Meredith Ress. He plays on the eighth-grade basketball team. He is gifted in music and plays the guitar. He is smart and logical. He looks like his mother and her father. He has two brothers, Blake (10) and Chase (7). He is our son, and we love him. Please continue to pray for him. And Lord willing, we will make the same request of you tomorrow.

And we know, as the scriptures tell us in Psalm 139:14, that Payton is fearfully and wonderfully made.

Praise God, and God bless.

Todd and Robyn

Mike and Ann returned home, as they'd left in a hurry on New Year's Day and were now coming up on day ten away from home, with no end in sight. We were thankful for their help. Keith and Becky Ogorek would take care of Chase. Their daughter Emily was a few years older than Chase and served as a mini-mom. They enjoyed living out their fantasy world together. Dave and Sue Parish would take care of Blake. Their son, Chris, was Blake's classmate. The Parishes had lost a child at an early age to leukemia and knew firsthand the challenge of a critically ill child. Later, Sue shared with me in a loving and supportive way, "You know Payton could die." In many respects, I appreciated hearing that, because the prevailing thought from virtually everyone was that Payton would live. We were good people. God was good. Payton was talented. Surely, he would make it, and when he did, his recovery would testify to God's love. I believed that as a possibility too but appreciated Sue's willingness to share a difficult message.

Intellectually, we knew Payton's situation was grave. We were confident the Lord could deliver Payton. We never expected the blessings that would flow out of that trial in spectacular and significant ways.

⇜ Biblical Principle ⇝

Paul said in his letter to the church at Philippi in Philippians 4:6, "Be anxious for nothing, but in everything by prayer and supplication, with thanksgiving, let your requests be made known to God; and the peace of God, which surpasses all understanding, will guard your hearts and minds through Christ Jesus."

God tells us to make our requests known to Him through prayer, and His peace will comfort us as we focus on His truths in Christ Jesus. We need not worry but must commit our problems and circumstances to God. The passage does not say He will fix our problems as we would fix them or help us to figure out how to fix the problem, but He will provide us a peace that surpasses our human understanding.

Upon reflection, I see that He provided that peace during the days in the hospital and our life to follow. It was by no means easy. It hurt a lot, but He cared for us in ways we could not understand.

CHAPTER 12

BLESSED

I sent the following email to share the battles at hand and the Lord's response:

Thursday, January 11, 2001, 7:19 a.m.

We will claim big victory #1 ... but battle #2 is a BIG ONE. Victory #1 is the blood cultures show no positive readings for the staph infection since last Saturday, which means the antibiotics are doing the job. We praise God alone for that victory. Battle #2 is HUGE. Payton's body must now heal itself.

He is on dialysis, as his kidneys do not function. He is on a ventilator for breathing and on blood pressure medicines, as his heart is weakened. Imagine running a marathon. You are tired, exhausted, and the body is depleted. Now you must gradually build the strength back up. Payton has a similar challenge. The initial goal was to stabilize the body functions while the antibiotics did their job. We praise God Payton has lived the past ten days and now can fight battle #2. Payton is a big, strong kid, and undoubtedly that will help him in his fight. He also has a very strong will.

The past two days were stable. Some encouraging signs and some that make one anxious. The vegetation on his heart appears stable to smaller. Certain ventilator settings went up slightly, while his PEEP stayed the same. One blood pressure medicine stayed the same, and one went up slightly. We know we must put our entire trust in God and the team of doctors and nurse He has provided. Otherwise, one tends to micromanage every situation and blood pressure and medication adjustment. We simply need time and for the body to respond and heal itself.

PLEASE CONTINUE TO PRAY FOR PAYTON. WE KNOW GOD IS HEARING OUR PRAYERS. THE OUTPOURING OF LOVE AND SUPPORT IS A GREAT BLESSING, AND WE ARE HUMBLED THAT GOD LOVES US SO MUCH. SPECIFICALLY, PRAY FOR THE FOLLOWING:

- God would continue to be glorified in this process.
- Doctors and nurses would continue to discern the necessary treatments and adjustments for Payton so his body can respond and heal itself. The doctors are taking very small steps and do not want to put Payton at more risk than he can handle at this time.
- Payton's body would begin to heal itself.
- Payton's blood pressure would stabilize, and the doctors can wean him off the medications.
- Payton can get some nourishment from a feeding tube inserted into his intestines.
- Payton would not retain fluids. Last night, he started to retain unnecessary fluids.
- Payton can reduce his ventilator settings and make progress toward getting off the ventilator.
- Payton's friends and family find comfort and peace that surpasses all understanding.

Payton's eighth-grade basketball team, New Augusta North, dedicated their game to him on Tuesday night. The coach had a feeling they would score 55 points (Payton's jersey number) and hold the opposition under 30. The final score was 56–21. Undoubtedly one of the best games of the year.

Let me close with the following scripture, which provides us with some comfort during this time of suffering. From the book of Romans 8:18–21: "For I consider that the sufferings of this present time are not worthy to be compared with the glory which shall be revealed in us. For the earnest expectation of the creation eagerly waits for the revealing of the sons of God. For the creation was subjected to futility, not willingly, but because of Him who subjected it in hope; because the creation itself also will be delivered from the bondage of corruption into the glorious liberty of the children of God."

We believe in life eternal and understand this suffering is very slight compared to the glory which comes later through our salvation in Christ Jesus. This provides us with some measure of comfort during a time which is testing us like none other.

Thank you for your prayers and outpouring of love for our son and family.

Love,
Todd and Robyn

We were overwhelmed with love and support from so many during that time, including meals, cards, and messages. Every personal need was taken care of. Our children were cared for. Everyone wanted to do something to help. Pike Township School District, where the boys attended (Payton: New Augusta, Blake: Guion Creek Middle School, and Chase: Fishback Creek Public Academy), was incredibly supportive. Chase was thrilled to receive some new uniforms from Fishback. My employer, Arthur Andersen, told me not to worry about work at all. The office managing partner and friend Derrick Burks visited us almost every day. Our church, Zionsville Fellowship, and many other churches and families were covering us in prayer, and it was evident.

During that time, there was one visitor who was on the "A" list, the person we hoped would come to the hospital: Joey Stein, Payton's Sunday school teacher for the junior high. Robyn, her mom and sister, and others loved when Joey came for a visit. The time usually ended up being an hour or more of funny stories and laughter, which was a great thing for those gathered and allowed us to take our minds off the crisis at hand, albeit momentarily. We had other memorable visits as well. Our neighbor Becky Ogorek, during one of her visits, teared up as she looked at Payton in his bed and noticed his cracked and chafed lips, and she said, "He needs some lip balm." I thought I was going to die laughing. I thought, *Seriously? He is the sickest kid at Riley, barely staying alive, and you are concerned about chapped lips?* But that is Becky, who has a nickname for the reality she lives in: Becky's World. But more importantly, the comment reflected her love and care for another human being, which is awesome. Another neighbor, Ana Carlsgaard, made her first visit to see Payton and burst in to tears, sobbing. I am not sure she expected to see Payton in that condition. We gracefully told Ana we were not sure what Payton could hear and did not want him to have any unnecessary stress.

It was clear we were loved by many, and they were grieving alongside us and groaning to the Lord in prayer to save Payton. We were receiving a deluge of support, prayers, and Bible passages to encourage us in our journey.

There was one other significant marker or blessing for me each day as I headed out of the house to go to the hospital: I would grab the same hat to wear. It was from the PGA golf championship held the prior August at Valhalla Country Club in Louisville, Kentucky. It was a visible reminder to me of my dependency on the Lord for Payton. The letters represented Payton Alexander and God, with God at the center.

We were blessed!

My friend Jeff Terp, who served as our crisis communications point person, shared the following email update with our ever-increasing email list and website:

Monday, January 15, 2001, 5:05 a.m.

Todd just called from the hospital and asked we pray for Payton. His blood pressure is doing better. In fact, it is in the general area of 120/54. Both numbers are consistent and the highest, which is a great improvement, since he entered Riley. Heart rate is doing well also.

However, and this is where we need your prayers, Payton is having some challenges with his liver. Todd said the liver is inflamed, and the doctors do not know why. If the liver does not function properly, it could be counterproductive to the medications and allow toxins to enter the bloodstream. As you know, these toxins could be very harmful.

Please pray for Payton to have the strength to overcome this liver issue and grant the wisdom and knowledge to his doctors so they know the proper treatment and how to address the latest challenge. Please also pray for Todd and Robyn to give them peace and understanding through this process.

Thank you for your prayers.

Jeffrey A. Terp

Later that morning, I provided a more thorough update on Payton's situation via the following email:

Monday, January 15, 2001, 8:17 a.m.

From the book of Hebrews 4:12–16: "For the word of God is living and powerful, and sharper than any two-edged sword, piercing even to the division of soul and spirit, and of joints and marrow, and is a discerner of the thoughts and intents of the heart. And there is no creature hidden from His sight, but all things are naked and open to the eyes of Him to whom we must give account. Seeing then that we have a great High Priest who has passed through the heavens, Jesus the Son of God, let us hold fast our confession. For we do not have a High Priest who cannot sympathize with our weaknesses, but was in all points tempted as we are, yet without sin. Let us therefore come boldly to the throne of grace, that we may obtain mercy and find grace to help in time of need."

We have a God who knows us. Everything about us. His Word can strengthen us—whether we face trials like this or in living our lives according to His plan for us. In this time, we are strengthened and assured, not in knowing what tomorrow brings but rather through the knowledge that His mercy and grace are all that we need. In that, Robyn and I and our family find peace that surpasses all understanding.

I want to share with you the many blessings we have had in the past two weeks. Payton was admitted on January 1.

1. God prodded my wife to take Payton into the emergency room on January 1, when he did not appear to be in an emergency, rather than wait until the doctor's office was open on January 2. Thankfully, we did, as Payton crashed quickly after getting into the hospital.
2. God provided us with excellent care. St. Vincent's transferred Payton to Riley not fully knowing his condition. Both are excellent hospitals; however, Riley is one of the top children's hospitals anywhere, and given the nature of Payton's situation, this is exactly where he needed to be. The medical team is outstanding.
3. God provided us comfort through Dr. Ndidi Musa, a member of our church, as his primary physician. Great comfort comes in

knowing God directed Payton to her. This was her first full week back on the job after a six-week leave of absence due to a surgery.

4. God provided an infection which was easily identified and treatable. However, it is awful bacteria, perhaps one of the worst, *Staphylococcus aureus*. But it could have been a virus (not treatable) or resistant to medications. His bacteria were growing rapidly, so the doctors knew the enemy and could begin treatments.
5. God poured out His awesome love on our family. Hundreds of emails, cards, gifts, and calls. Wonderful meals brought to us. Help with our other two boys. It is difficult, if not impossible, to describe the prayer support Payton and our family are receiving from this community and beyond.
6. God kept us away from the hospital during two or three nerve-racking situations. Payton's second night was very challenging—touch and go. Even this past Saturday night required significant changes to his blood pressure medicine; however, by the end of last night, his medication levels were basically at the same level as Saturday afternoon.
7. God has provided us with two weeks. With each day, there is hope. Payton's body now can heal itself. As I shared with you last week, the first battle was won. The doctors kept Payton alive, so the antibiotics could get the infection under control, and the vegetation on his heart is smaller.

God's grace and mercy are sufficient. As Dr. Musa told us early in this process, there are two ways you can look at this situation: everything man, medicine, and machines can do or what God can do. We chose God and know He can do anything.

Lastly, God knows what we need and provides us comfort. From the book of Matthew 11:28: "Come to Me, all you who labor and are heavy laden, and I will give you rest." And from the book of James 1:2–3: "My brethren, count it all joy when you fall into various trials, knowing that the testing of your faith produces patience."

Overall, Payton is much better than he was two weeks ago; however, he still has a long way to go. His heart is requiring help (blood pressure medicine), as are his kidneys (dialysis) and lungs (oxygen), and he is not getting the nourishment he needs. But he is moving in the right direction. His blood chemistries are improving, and this weekend, the doctors took him out of a medically induced state of paralysis and now have him in a heavy state of sedation. This means he can technically move but not very much. He can hear and does respond to us through his eyes. Sometimes we get distracted at a certain medication level or how Payton is responding moment to moment. We are reminded our trust must remain fully in God, and He alone can provide.

We humbly ask you to pray for the following:

- God would continue to be glorified in this situation. We know this is happening and give thanks.
- Doctors and nurses would continue to discern the necessary treatments and adjustments for Payton to enable his body to respond and heal itself (a few of Payton's doctors will rotate to different assignments this week).

Payton is now on his third week, and the doctors also spend time in research, administration, and other matters. God continues to provide the caregivers we need. As Dr. Macke explained this weekend, Payton's body has a significant amount of inflammation from fighting the infection and must heal, and it can, for his body to respond. We pray the blood pressure medication levels will decline; the vegetation on his heart will decline and be absorbed in a manner Payton's body can handle; and he can tolerate his feedings (his digestive system is not currently working—he has a feeding tube, which needs to eventually anchor in his stomach). And Payton's family and friends would find comfort and peace that surpasses all understanding.

A friend developed a website for Payton, which will provide daily updates and information about Payton and provide an opportunity for Payton's friends to keep in touch. As Payton is in intensive care, his friends are not able to visit. You can visit the website at www.getwellpayton.com. The site should be complete with information by the end of the day.

For the next couple of days, we are limiting visitors to family and close friends, as Payton is getting adjusted to this state of heavy sedation. His sedation level is one of the bigger challenges for the doctors, and we are hopeful he can adjust.

Our family thanks you for your love and support of our son Payton and each of us during this time of need.

Love,
Todd and Robyn

We were certainly blessed with so many who loved us and cared for us during our greatest time of need, not to mention the expert care of Riley Children's Hospital. However, we were about to embark on the most difficult day of our lives, one that would rattle us to the core.

Biblical Principle

In Matthew 5:1–12, Matthew records one of Jesus's most famous sermons on the Mount:

> And seeing the multitudes, He went up on a mountain, and when He was seated His disciples came to Him. Then He opened His mouth and taught them, saying:
> "Blessed are the poor in spirit,

For theirs is the kingdom of heaven.
Blessed are those who mourn,
For they shall be comforted.
Blessed are the meek,
For they shall inherit the earth.
Blessed are those who hunger and thirst for righteousness,
For they shall be filled.
Blessed are the merciful,
For they shall obtain mercy.
Blessed are the pure in heart,
For they shall see God.
Blessed are the peacemakers,
For they shall be called sons of God.
Blessed are those who are persecuted for righteousness' sake,
For theirs is the kingdom of heaven.

Blessed are you when they revile and persecute you, and say all kinds of evil against you falsely for My sake. Rejoice and be exceedingly glad, for great is your reward in heaven, for so they persecuted the prophets who were before you."

It is illogical, apart from God, to consider yourself blessed when your child is in critical condition and fighting for his or her life. However, we were overwhelmed with the love and support of so many who were praying for Payton and our family. The medical team was working hard to keep Payton alive. My employer fully supported my time away. Friends and colleagues came to minister and support us, and we attempted to do the same. Every physical need was covered.

Upon reflection, God provided through His people an overwhelming love we never had experienced before and likely never will again. We are richly blessed.

CHAPTER 13

FISH OR CUT BAIT

The next day, I sent the following email with a deeply personal message and plea:

> Tuesday, January 16, 2001, 9:03 a.m.
>
> I have shared much with you about Payton's medical condition and God's Holy Word, which provides us comfort and understanding in this time of suffering. Allow me to share a personal message which was on my heart last evening:
>
>> Father, my heart aches to see my son suffer so,
>> yet your grace and mercy are all we need.
>> It is our honor and privilege to raise Payton to be a man,
>> one that will reflect the glory of your light to this world.
>> We know not why this time and place is before us;
>> Our soul rests in your loving arms.
>> To see the prayers and adoration to you, Father,
>> illuminates your love that flows out to this world.
>> Some may question the need to honor and obey our Creator God,

but for you, we owe our earthly and eternal life.
You gave your Son to take away the sins of the world,
I can now feel the anguish of the preciousness of life.
O Lord, I ask that Payton live another day,
to heal and recover through your glory and power.
We do not know the path of our earthly life
but to accept, serve, and bow down before your heavenly throne.
Take my concerns and questions, and bring peace to my heart,
for you alone are sufficient for my every need.

Yesterday was a roller coaster with great excitement and Payton's blood pressure improvement. Yet by midafternoon, we had another big battle on our hands. Payton has not had any digestive capabilities since he was admitted. His liver and spleen are enlarged. The doctors began giving him one-ounce fluid every four hours through his NG tube, in addition to IV feedings, to stimulate his digestive system. The liver and gall bladder are accumulating bile, which needs discharged. Today the doctors are going to take Payton off the ventilator and dialysis temporarily to have a CT scan of his abdomen. Please pray the doctors can identify the source of Payton's problem and determine the necessary treatment. Payton is very weak, and I do not know how much strength he has for the fight. Please pray God provides Payton with the strength to continue this fight while his body recovers. Above all, pray for God's healing touch on Payton. Surgery is very risky for Payton, given his blood pressure and low platelet count. God has answered our every need, and we ask for your prayers for Payton's total healing. Please continue to pray God is glorified in this situation, Payton's doctors and nurses can discern the proper treatments, and for Payton's family and friends to find comfort during this situation.

We will never be able to fully thank each of you who is praying and supporting Payton and our family.

Love,
Todd and Robyn

Given the gravity of Payton's situation, Jeff Terp sent two additional updates later that afternoon.

Tuesday, January 16, 2001, 4:10 p.m.

Payton had a CT exam today and did very well during this process. The doctors determined a portion of his large intestine is swollen and inflamed. There are many possible reasons for this, but the most likely is a portion of the bowel is decaying. This decaying process causes toxins to release into the body and can affect other bodily functions. If the bowel is decaying, it will explain the toxic liver and Payton's most recent setback. At 5:00 p.m. today, Payton will have surgery. The doctors plan on exploring the bowel to determine if in fact it is decaying, and they will remove it. If it is only a portion of the bowel which needs removed, this will not limit future activities or result in a restricted diet. Please pray for Payton to remain strong during the surgery and grant the doctors the skill and wisdom to help Payton and determine the proper diagnosis. Also, please thank God that Payton did well during the CT scan, and the doctors may now have the answer for Payton's recovery. Please understand this is a major surgery for anyone, especially Payton. But there are blessings in he is stronger today than fourteen days ago.

We will keep you posted.

Jeffrey A. Terp

Tuesday, January 16, 2001, 8:17 p.m.

Payton went into surgery at 5:30 p.m. The doctors expect the surgery to last for five hours. We may not send an update until morning.

Thanks for your prayers.

> Jeffrey A. Terp

The next morning, I sent the following email, the fourth update in a twenty-four-hour period:

Wednesday, January 17, 2001, 8:08 a.m.

From the book of Philippians 4:13: "I can do all things through God who gives me strength."

One of our prayers each day is that God give us another day with Payton to heal and get stronger. And that each night we don't get a call from the hospital in the middle of the night. For seventeen days, God has answered that prayer. Praise God and Him alone.

Yesterday Payton had CT scans of his abdomen and brain. The brain scan came back clear. Praise God. The abdomen showed a potential issue with the colon. After much consultation among the medical team and surgeons, Payton went into surgery at 5:30 p.m. Surgery is always risky; however, this is something the doctors wanted to avoid, given Payton's very weak and unstable state. We praise God the team's diagnosis was correct. The ileum, a section of the colon, had a section which was decaying: a virtual roadblock with blood clots and waste products. The surgeons removed this section and put in an ileostomy. The surgery went well by all accounts. Praise God. Payton returned to ICU around 9:00 p.m.

For those of you who have seen Payton and his condition, you can truly understand what a blessing this is to have God's hand over Payton today. He has a dialysis machine, a ventilator, blood pressures, medications, feedings, and morphine to control the pain. The staff had to move him twice attached to these machines with assisted breathing from a manual device—this was no small feat. As Payton and I prayed yesterday, I asked Payton to find comfort, as God can provide him with whatever strength he needed to go through this process. Keep in mind, Payton has been ill since December 21 and fought a long battle with a virulent staph infection.

The next twenty-four to forty-eight hours are critical. Recovery is as difficult as surgery. Payton is very likely to get worse before getting better. Payton's body must respond to the surgery. Stabilization is critical. Once he's stabilized, we pray the combination of three weeks of antibiotics and removing the obstructed bowel will enable Payton to recover. It is likely Payton's colon lost blood during his battle with the staph infection and began to atrophy. The inability of the colon to work backed up the liver, and he accumulated toxic levels of bile in the liver. Once the colon is stable in two to three days, the doctors can start feedings which hopefully will enable the liver to resume its function.

If I may, I would request the following:

- Please thank God for all He has done. He has and continues to show His love for Payton and his family and friends.
- Pray God continues to be glorified in this process.
- Pray Payton can stabilize over the next twenty-four to forty-eight hours. The doctors and nurses can make the right decisions regarding blood pressure and fluids (blood products, saline, etc.), and Payton's body can respond properly.

- Pray Payton finds strength from God to win this next battle.
- Pray the doctors have found everything which is preventing Payton from full recovery.
- Pray the vegetation on his heart continues to decline in a manner which the body can absorb.
- Pray for Payton's family and friends to find peace which surpasses all understanding.

Yesterday the medical team was awesome. The nursing team was focused like a laser. They are working so hard to keep Payton alive.

We appreciate all the love, prayers, and support we are receiving in this process. Your prayers mean so much to us and to our Father in heaven, who tells us to pray without ceasing.

Payton is not able to have visitors for the next couple of days. We will spend substantial time with Payton, as he is in a lot of pain. The pain medication tends to drop blood pressure, and thus, they can't give him everything he needs.

I would encourage each of you to visit the website created for Payton: www.getwellpayton.com. You can leave messages for Payton. Please read the glory section, which speaks to God's role in this situation.

We are thankful for yesterday and the blessings of the day and hopeful for a good day today.

Love,
Todd and Robyn

Throughout Payton's hospitalization, I wanted to share the reality of Payton's medical situation, let people know what to pray for, and share our hope in the Lord and His promises in His Word. Emails were sent and posted on www.getwellpayton.com for all to see. However, I did not fully disclose in the message above the full picture from Payton's surgery, as it was too difficult for even me to handle. The rest of the story follows.

Dr. Jeff Macke, the second of Payton's lead intensivists, had posed a high-stakes choice to Robyn and me during our normal consult early the previous morning, January 16: he said we needed to "fish or cut bait." In layman's terms, Payton was not getting better, and the longer one is in a medically induced coma, the more difficult it is to come off the ventilator. We already faced the likelihood of Payton missing the remainder of his eighth-grade school year. Dr. Macke recommended we take Payton down for a CT scan to try to figure out why he was not making progress. After all, the infection was now under control due to a high-powered cocktail of strong antibiotics. He explained there was significant risk just in getting him down to the CT scan, given his medical condition, let alone in a potential surgery if they found a problem they needed to address. Doctors walk a delicate tight rope with critically ill patients, not taking unnecessary risks, for fear of losing their patients. However, Dr. Macke explained this was a risk he recommended we take.

The first order of business was to disconnect the various tubes and lines attached to the machines, which were vital to keeping him alive. A team of four or five specialists gathered around Payton. One was manually bagging Payton, providing him the life-giving oxygen needed to keep him alive. It was a difficult task for a human to replicate the precise pressure and inhalation and exhalation rhythms of the ventilator.

Angie was at the helm, at the base of the bed, forcefully directing the team as they headed down the hallway to hopefully find out what was wrong with Payton, making sure his vital signs did not fluctuate to any significant degree. I walked behind and marveled at the precision and intensity of the operation. They had to navigate a myriad of doors and entryways as they carefully moved him to the ICU 4 South, where there was an elevator large enough to fit Payton's bed and the team. Angie made sure Payton was not jostled or agitated, as any significant disruption could have caused his already challenging condition to crash. It was a well-orchestrated process, one they were prepared to do; however, I knew it was anything but routine. Angie later shared the simple task of transporting

Payton was one of the most stressful situations she would encounter as they tried to keep him alive without the machines so vital for his every breath.

The results of the CT scan revealed a dying and decaying colon, which was causing waste and blood to accumulate in Payton's stomach. Dr. Macke told us surgery was necessary, and he would arrange it for that afternoon. Later that day, they would redo the drill to take him off the myriad of machines and life support to transport him for surgery. Surgery was risky, but the risk was off the charts for someone in Payton's condition. Keeping him alive was challenging, but now the stakes were significantly raised. Payton had struggled with his blood pressure from the time of arrival. The doctors warned me Payton would have some level of consciousness for the next twenty-four hours, as they could not sedate him to the level necessary in light of the recent surgery, which meant they could not give him the amount of pain medicine needed, for fear it would significantly depress his blood pressure.

The afternoon following Payton's surgery, we were at his bedside. It was his seventeenth day in the hospital. He'd just survived a difficult surgery less than twenty-four hours ago. He was now slightly alert for the first time since we'd left him the evening of New Year's Day. The best analogy for his condition would be the state of a person who wakes from a deep sleep in the middle of the night: barely alert, groggy, and wondering if he is awake. That described Payton for a few hours that afternoon.

We knew Payton was hurting. He was trying to mouth something to us but could not speak due to the tube down his throat. We tried to comfort him. We told him we loved him and said he'd done a great job with the surgery. I told him the doctors would try to increase his pain medicine soon. Robyn said, "The doctors found the problem. You are going to be okay." Payton softly, with the limited strength he had, shook his head. Was he telling Robyn something he already knew—the outcome that would play out in the days ahead? Our hearts sank as we realized he was hurting, and there was nothing we could do. I had never felt so helpless in my entire life. Yet we were thankful he made it through another day, and that was our prayer.

We sent out a brief communication the following day, given Jeff's deadline.

Eyes of the Father

Thursday, January 18, 2001, 6:32 a.m.

From the book of 2 Chronicles 16:9: "For the eyes of the LORD run to and from throughout the whole earth, to show Himself strong on behalf of those whose heart is loyal to Him." I received this message of inspiration from a member of Payton's medical team. I am thankful for all the inspiration and scripture shared by so many of you.

A quick update, as my friend Jeff has a deadline. Payton is still alive almost thirty-six hours after surgery—praise God. The prayer requests are the same. The medical team is devoting substantial focus to balancing various elements of Payton's medical support in the postoperative process, including blood pressure. So far so good. The postoperative process causes certain stresses, fluid buildups, and inflammation, which create challenges for anyone, let alone Payton. Payton is a fighter. It was sad to see him in pain yesterday. Particularly as he tried to talk to us but was unable due to his breathing tube. He did have a small complication yesterday with a collapsed lung. The doctors did a quick surgery and were able to stabilize him. Pray Payton will stabilize over the next twenty-four to forty-eight hours so he can start to move forward. Pray God's plan is fulfilled, and God is glorified throughout this process. Thank you for your prayers. Also, you may check out www.getwellpayton.com for more information and to leave Payton a message.

Love,
Todd and Robyn

Finally, we sent an upbeat communication to share joy in Payton's progress.

Friday, January 19, 2001, 12:18 p.m.

From the book of Psalms 33:1–11:

> Rejoice in the LORD, O you righteous!
> For praise from the upright is beautiful.
> Praise the LORD with the harp;
> Make melody to Him with an instrument of ten strings.
> Sing to Him a new song;
> Play skillfully with a shout of joy.
> For the word of the LORD is right,
> And all His work is done in truth.
> He loves righteousness and justice;
> The earth is full of the goodness of the LORD.
> By the word of the LORD the heavens were made,
> And all the host of them by the breath of His mouth.
> He gathers the waters of the sea together as a heap;
> He lays up the deep in storehouses.
> Let all the earth fear the LORD;
> Let all the inhabitants of the world stand in awe of Him.
> For He spoke, and it was done;
> He commanded, and it stood fast.
> The LORD brings the counsel of the nations to nothing;
> He makes the plans of the peoples of no effect.
> The counsel of the LORD stands forever,
> The plans of His heart to all generations.

We are to praise God. Yet we are to notice the plans of the Lord stand firm forever. God has plans for us. We are strengthened in times of trial and suffering as we seek to serve Him. God loves us even in our sinful nature and disobedience to Him.

Eyes of the Father

We praise God for each day Payton is alive. And each day, we ask for another day. PRAISE GOD! THE DOCTOR SAID THE PAST TWENTY-FOUR HOURS WERE PAYTON'S BEST YET! WE PRAISE GOD AND HIM ALONE. God provided Payton with strength. Payton does not have much strength after fighting to stay alive for twenty-seven days, the last seventeen at Riley. He had a horrible infection, *Staph aureus*, and sepsis, which means his whole body was infected and most (it seems like all) of his organs were not functioning or were at severely distressed levels. For those who like numbers, his blood pressure is now 145 over 50 with a fair amount of blood pressure support (dopamine—15, dobutamine—15). The doctors will try to reduce those levels today. They are trying to get the right level of sedation and blood pressure support. His bilirubin is down 2.5 points to 9.5. The elevated bilirubin indicated the liver is not functioning at full capacity and not getting rid of the waste in Payton's body. The level is much higher than it should be; however, it is moving in the right direction considering the significant amount of blood Payton received. Payton's chemistries and blood gases (measures of oxygenation) are improving. Payton's heart rate is around 110. His positive end-expiratory pressure, or PEEP, is 10. The PEEP measures the amount of pressure in Payton's lungs after his exhalation or end of breath. Payton's lungs are very sick, and the air sacs can become stiff and not open. The pressure is intended to keep his air sacs open to ensure they do not collapse. His PEEP was 14–16, and we need it down to 4–5 before he can get off the ventilator. Payton's vegetation on his heart is smaller, and thus, the antibiotics are working. Payton is making progress. He is still very sick; however, he is moving in the right direction and with measurable progress.

Please thank God for His love and guiding hand on Payton. Please pray for the following:

- God continues to be glorified in this situation.
- Doctors and nurses continue to discern the necessary adjustments to help support Payton's body as he recovers. Payton's body, for the first time, appears to be turning the corner.
- Pray Payton's vegetation continues to decline in a manner the body can absorb.
- Pray his lungs, which are fragile from the ventilator and infection (the infection on his heart gets sent directly to his lungs), can repair themselves. He has two chest tubes related to his collapsed lung from Wednesday.
- Pray Payton can start feedings through his NG tube and get his digestive system going again and help the liver recover.
- Pray Payton can eliminate excess fluids over time as his blood pressure stabilizes.
- Pray Payton's family and friends find comfort in this situation.

Robyn and I can't begin to thank all the people who helped over the past nineteen days with meals, our kids, gifts and cards, and support. Keith Ogorek is coordinating our kids' schedule. Mary Wertz is coordinating meals. Most importantly, we ask for your prayers not only for Payton but for the needs of your family. God wants to be a part of our lives, but first we must recognize He is in charge. Our plans are not His.

Even though Payton is in a paralytic state, we read several cards and emails to him. Lord willing, we will read him the many messages from the website. You can send him a message at www.getwellpayton.com. I would like to thank Ron Brumbarger and Bitwise Solutions for developing this website and for their support.

We still have a long way to go. We will not claim victory based on a day. We will continue to ask God for another day. And we are thankful for the past day. We are thankful for Payton's medical team, who have worked very, very hard. I suspect there are well over one hundred Riley and Clarian Health employees who have worked with Payton over the past nineteen days. I hope to provide you with more encouraging news on Monday. If something comes up in the meantime, I will keep you informed. No matter what happens, whether Payton leaves Riley or not or has full use of his vital organs as he did before coming to Riley, we know one thing: God loves us and cares for us. And in that, we take great comfort.

Love,
Todd and Robyn

We had quite a team of friends, family, and even individuals we had never met providing support for us during that time. As I said, Jeff Terp became our crisis communications coordinator, and he made sure email messages got out and posted on the website. Jeff's business career had prepared him well for the seemingly insignificant role that God used to communicate Payton's condition and prayer needs to so many. Barb Grahn, Jeff's sister-in-law, had stopped by our house the prior weekend to pick up baskets of laundry that needed attention. What a gracious act to do someone else's laundry. Loved ones did countless other things that brought us joy as we struggled to live this new life, one in which our attention was directed on Payton's health, the Lord, and trying to maintain some sense of normalcy for Blake and Chase.

Four days elapsed before our next communication, which was quite remarkable; however, the tide would soon turn.

Tuesday, January 23, 2001, 9:09 a.m.

From the book of 1 John 5:14–15: "Now this is the confidence that we have in Him, that if we ask anything according to His will, He hears us. And if we know that He hears us, whatever we ask, we know that we have the petitions that we have asked of Him." To some, this may seem like a great paradox, but it is God's plan we want to fulfill. Our desire is to serve Him and understand His plans and desires, and then we will achieve the fullness of life which is ours for the asking.

Praise God. Payton is making progress. Each day, I realize how thankful we are and comforted in our faith in Jesus Christ. And thankful for the support and prayers of many. And for the dedication and excellence of Payton's medical team. Payton "observed" his three-week anniversary at Riley last night. Today marks one week since his life-saving surgery. Payton has made very good and solid progress since his surgery. The doctors noticed measurable improvement this past Friday. And he is progressing nicely each day. There are still concerns no doubt; however, we must give thanks for the progress made. He is on two medications for blood pressure support. He is almost off one (dobutamine at 2) and stable on the other (dopamine at 6). This is counterbalanced against his sedation drugs, which depress blood pressure, and the doctors are taking 50cc of fluid an hour through his dialysis (roughly two pounds per day). He has approximately twenty pounds of excess fluids which need to come off. His lungs have received a fair amount of damage due to the infection. The vegetation on his heart releases the emboli to his lungs. His ventilator settings are stable, with a PEEP of 10 and an oxygen level around 60 percent (normal is 21). Reducing the fluids will potentially help his lungs. His chemistries are getting better. His platelets are hovering around 50,000. He is receiving platelets every day or two. His body is making them and using them. Normal platelet levels are 150,000 to 350,000. The vegetation on his heart is smaller in dimension, and we know the antibiotics are doing their job. The original estimate was for six to eight weeks of antibiotics. Probably more numbers than you want to know, and there are many more I could share with you.

Please pray for the following:

- God is glorified in this situation. It is nice to see and hear the number of messages from individuals who are sharing how this is impacting them or their family or friends. God wants us to know He is with us in good and bad times. We must seek a relationship with Him.
- Pray the doctors and nurses are strengthened through Him and make the necessary decisions for Payton to achieve a full recovery, if that is God's will. We are now in week four and on our third lead doctor. All are excellent. Very caring and competent. Having spent a significant amount of time with each, and the nurses and specialists, I understand the intricacies and challenges of adjusting and modifying multiple bodily systems. It is extremely challenging at best.
- Pray for Payton's body to continue to heal itself. Pray he can fully come off the blood pressure support while still taking off fluids. Pray the vegetation on his heart continues to decline in a manner the body can absorb.
- Pray Payton's platelets will go up without the need for transfusions and his wounds heal properly without excess blood loss.
- Pray Payton's spirit and strength remain strong. The doctors will consider taking him out of his medically induced state of paralysis as his ventilator settings decline.
- Pray this transition works smoothly and Payton can adjust to this situation without extreme agitation. Pray for the continued support for his family and friends and all those praying for Payton.

Let me close with a personal note. As I thought the other day about this situation and our response, I wanted to give thanks to five individuals in my life who made a major impact in my faith in Jesus Christ. Without these five individuals playing such a role, all in different ways, I can't imagine how I could handle this situation. I know each would not desire credit or recognition; however, there is a reason I choose to do so. Tom Blossom, Laura Byers [now

Mayhall], Tim Doyle, Keith Ogorek, and Robin Gore. I praise God for each of them as they have truly given themselves to God and His plans. They are an inspiration to me and others. I would like to share with you a brief message about one of them, Robin, and her son, Brandon Gore. Perhaps I can share about the others at a future time.

Robin Gore provided the scripture referenced above. Jim and Robin's son, Brandon, was diagnosed with leukemia five years ago. I ran in the Leukemia Society marathon in the summer of 1999 in honor of Brandon. Immediately upon returning from the marathon, our team learned Brandon had relapsed after three years and his last treatment. This past summer [2000], he acquired aspergillus, an infection in his lungs that someone in his condition can't fight and had a new tumor in his stomach. The doctors gave him days or perhaps a week or two to live. He lives today! His family desires he lives a long life. I do too. Yet they put their entire trust and faith in God that His plans surpass ours. I am thankful the Gores came into my life. Their strength, commitment, and conviction in Jesus Christ is truly remarkable. I have dealt with this situation for twenty-one days. They have for five years. Please pray for Brandon and the other children who battle cancer. If you would like more information on Brandon or his specific prayer needs, please send an email to care2crop@fieldsfam.com.

Love,
Todd and Robyn

Every day the Lord delivered. Payton was alive against improbable odds. But we were told the longer one was on a ventilator, the harder it was to get off. For twenty-three days, a machine had been doing the work for his distressed lungs. God breathed life into Adam in the Garden of Eden, and we desperately needed that life-giving breath now.

⁃ Biblical Principle ⁃

The apostle Paul wrote in Romans 15:13, "Now may the God of hope fill you with all joy and peace in believing, that you may abound in hope by the power of the Holy Spirit."

The Greek word for *hope* is *elpis*, which means "confident expectation or anticipation," not "wishful thinking," which is the common understanding today. God alone will provide us with joy and peace through His Holy Spirit.

Payton's health crisis was His battle, and we needed to seek Him and His will during that most difficult time. Upon reflection, I realize we had an unsurpassable peace in knowing God was in control. Otherwise, our lives and family would have struggled mightily in the years to follow.

CHAPTER 14

THE BREATH OF LIFE

Wednesday, January 24, 2001, 11:45 p.m.

From the book of Isaiah 50:7: "For the Lord God will help Me; Therefore I will not be disgraced; Therefore I have set My face like a flint, And I know that I will not be ashamed."

Let me paraphrase the above. The Lord is our only source of help. We must focus on Him like a laser. In Him, we are honored. We must stay determined in the face of opposition.

WE HAVE A HUGE BATTLE IN FRONT OF US. BATTLE #3. Through God's grace and mercy, we won the first two battles. Victory #1 was staying alive long enough for the doctors to fight the staph infection while Payton's body was in a distressed state. Victory #2 was going to surgery and surviving the recovery process at a time when Payton's blood pressure was low, and he was on a high level of blood pressure support.

Battle #3: Payton's lungs must get better. Lungs heal slowly. Payton's ability to generate sufficiently oxygenated blood declined over the past two or three days to a level which is borderline acceptable. A bronchoscopy was done this afternoon. Some "junk" was taken, which will show if there is infection other than staph in his lungs. A potential infection might be *Pseudomonas aeruginosa*. This is an infection typically picked up in the hospital when your immune system is low. Payton's white cells are high, which could indicate he is battling an infection. As a precautionary measure, the doctors have started Payton on ceftazidime, an antibiotic, to treat the potential infection. We will likely know within twenty-four hours. In the meantime, the doctors have added nitric oxide to Payton's ventilator, which is typically used for pulmonary hypertension. The blood vessels in the lungs are constricted, so the heart must work harder. The doctors are hoping the nitric oxide will dilate the pulmonary artery and blood vessels in the lungs to provide better blood profusion to the lungs. The blood going to his lungs does not have enough oxygen. Payton's ventilator support prior to nitric oxide was near the maximum level of support. Hopefully, the doctors can reduce oxygen support to 35–60% and maintain oxygen saturation levels (SATS) of 90 or more and PO2s in the 50s. Currently, he has a PO2 of 64, with 95% oxygen support. I am sharing these details as there are several medical professionals receiving this email.

Payton's lungs are very sick or, in the words of his primary physician, diseased. Lungs heal slowly. The doctors need to determine the cause of his continued decline in lung capacity. It could be continued dissolution of the vegetation on his heart, with emboli going to his lungs. Or another infection. Or perhaps something else.

God has provided many blessings in the past twenty-three days. I have shared many of these with you. Candidly, Payton could not have dealt with this blow a week ago after the surgery. Praise God we can fight the battle now. We are about to embark on another day. After the bronchoscopy, the doctor who performed the surgery said, "What a stud." Payton responded to yet another situation with potential complications without blinking. Payton has fought for over a month and keeps winning. Satan keeps bringing more battles for him to fight. This leads me to the primary prayer request for tonight. Refer to the opening scripture. We know not where this battle ends for Payton. Nor do we know future battles each of us will face. We do know this: we cannot turn away from God. When we do, Satan wins. We will all leave our earthly bodies at some time. While we are here, we must stay faithful, focused, and dedicated to God. Every situation we encounter in life, from an unkind remark to Payton's fight for his life, provides an opportunity for us to turn our back on God and allow Satan to have his way with us. Therefore, I would ask you to pray for the following:

- God receive all the glory and praise for supporting Payton's fight the past twenty-three days. For the strength He has provided to Payton and the guidance provided to Payton's medical team and the peace, comfort, and hope provided to so many.
- The medical team determine the source of Payton's lung deterioration and identify the proper course of treatment to stabilize his lungs while they gradually heal themselves. And for God's hand to direct the team to make the right decisions at the right time.
- Payton's lungs heal and get better. And Payton's other bodily functions continue to improve: blood pressure, digestive functions, kidney, and liver.
- Payton's family and friends continue to find peace and comfort in God alone.

This is a big battle. We are prepared. We ask for God's grace and mercy. And for God's will to be done. His plans are bigger than ours. He understands the total puzzle—we don't. We are so thankful for the prayers and support of so many. Hopefully, someday I can share with you how God has ordered so many events in our life over the last several years and is providing exactly what we need right now to deal with this situation. And the many things ordered during his hospitalization, commonly thought of as coincidences, but I know better. And thank you to Ndidi Musa, who shared the scripture with me tonight. Thank you for your prayers. We are so richly blessed.

Love,

Todd and Robyn

PS Robyn is asleep; we discussed the contents of this email prior to her going to bed.

I was reminded of the Lord's timing and my need to remain focused on Payton, the Lord, and my family. Everything else was taken care of. Unlike the rest of my professional life to date, I had no work or appointments. My employer had told me my attention needed complete focus on Payton. During Payton's time in the hospital, I scheduled only two meetings: one with Paul Willis Dunker, our marketing head, on January 16 at 11:30 a.m. and another with Bryon Parnell, my future business partner, on January 24 at 4:00 p.m. On January 16, at the time of the meeting scheduled with Paul, Payton was taken for a CT scan, and he would ultimately have a four-hour surgery later that day. On January 24, during the time of the meeting scheduled with Bryon, Payton had an emergency bronchoscopy. Both meetings were canceled. God's message was clear: *There is no work during this time.* I needed to maintain a singular focus on the situation at hand. Ultimately, the reason I was able to see God's hand and hear His voice was clear: there were no distractions.

Jeff Terp provided a brief update on Payton's lungs in the following message:

Friday, January 26, 2001, 5:43 p.m.

Todd called me from the hospital, and Payton's last two days were relatively stable. Payton has a new infection in his lungs, *Enterobacter cloacae*. It is unknown whether the bacteria are causing the problems with Payton's lungs.

Please pray Payton's lungs get better. His oxygenation levels are acceptable, but the lungs are badly diseased. This is a big battle, and we need time and continued stability or improvement.

Payton's original problem, *Staph aureus*, is the subject of a front-page story in today's *Indianapolis Star*, except Payton's staph infection is not resistant to antibiotics.

Todd will provide a more detailed update tomorrow, January 27.

God bless.

Jeffrey A. Terp

We continued to ask for prayer in the following email update and were thankful for the prayers and scriptures offered up from many on our behalf.

Saturday, January 27, 2001, 10:19 a.m.

From the book of Romans 8:28: "And we know that all things work together for good to those who love God, to those who are the called according to His purpose." To paraphrase, despite the sufferings of this present time, for those who love God, we are assured His overarching plans are accomplished through us. We do not fully understand His plans or perhaps seek the situations we encounter; however, we are called to respond considering His glory.

Payton's last two days were relatively stable. His lungs are diseased and functioning at less than optimal capacity or barely above minimum needs. He is currently receiving a significant amount of support for oxygenating his blood through the ventilator. Nitric oxide is providing support to dilate his blood vessels and particularly the pulmonary artery. Normal air oxygen is 21%. With 70% oxygen support, Payton's lungs are oxygenating his blood at acceptable levels. He has an oxygen saturation rate of 91 and PO2s of 51. Payton's blood pressure is relatively stable, and other bodily functions are in acceptable ranges.

The cultures taken from the bronchoscopy on Wednesday identified new bacteria in his lungs: *Enterobacter cloacae*. The doctors do not know if this is contributing to his lung distress. This is a form of pneumonia. His lungs have remnants from the staph infection, emboli from the vegetation on his heart, and anticipated distress from prolonged ventilator use. The doctors are treating this pneumonia with piperacillin. He now has almost three days of antibiotics in his system. Lungs heal slowly, and it will take time to recover from pneumonia.

Please pray for the following:

- God continues to be glorified in this situation. And we respond according to His plans and His love for us.
- The doctors and nurses continue to discern the proper decisions to keep Payton stable or improving. For those who have visited, you know this is no small task.
- Payton's body would heal—specifically his lungs.
- The piperacillin will effectively treat the *Enterobacter* pneumonia.
- No significant emboli from the vegetation on his heart go to his lungs during this time of great distress.

- His other bodily functions continue to improve in a manner which will allow the body to recover fully.
- Payton's family and friends continue to find comfort during this time of trial.

Recently, I shared five individuals who have greatly impacted my walk with God and acceptance of Christ as Lord and Savior. I would like to share with you the story of Tim Doyle. Today's verse is from Tim. Tim has worked with me at Arthur Andersen for sixteen years. He was a great athlete in high school, in baseball and wrestling. But he did not know God. Tim was diagnosed with muscular dystrophy when he was a sophomore in high school. Tim fought hard and was wheelchair bound at thirty. Tim has six siblings; all but two have MD as well. Tim realized he had MD on his sixteenth birthday, hearing God's voice to go to the hospital. Tim accepted Christ since the time of his diagnosis. He is one of those individuals everyone gravitates toward. He is friendly and personable and has a warm spirit. It takes a lot of effort for Tim to do simple things most of us take for granted. Tim created a website: www.suffering.net. It is an excellent source of strength and hope for those who suffer. I encourage you to visit his website and pray for Tim and his family. Tim has "suffered" for almost twenty-four years. We have suffered for twenty-six days. I draw great strength from men like Tim.

We thank God again this trial is presented now and not on the heels of surgery last week.

God bless.

Todd and Robyn

Tomorrow would mark four weeks in intensive care for Payton, presumably as the sickest patient, living with massive amounts of machines, drugs, and seasoned health-care providers doing the jobs naturally done by his body. We were thankful for each day with Payton. In the coming days, Payton would approach to the precipice of a fatal fall only to be yanked back in miraculous fashion time and time again.

Biblical Principle

The apostle Peter wrote in 1 Peter 4:11, "If anyone speaks, let him speak as to the oracles of God. If anyone ministers, let him do it as with the ability which God supplies, that in all things God may be glorified through Jesus Christ, to whom belong the glory and the dominion forever and ever. Amen."

Throughout Payton's hospitalization, our first prayer request was for God to be glorified. It was not our choice to enter that crucible, but once we entered, our only hope and source of strength was God.

We harken back to Ndidi's question: Do we trust in man, medicine, and machines or God? Upon reflection, we know God is faithful to His promises. It was ultimately not the answer we wanted, but we wanted to share with others the reason for the hope we had during an exceedingly difficult chapter in our lives.

CHAPTER 15

THREE CRASHES AND THREE REBOUNDS

I shared the following email update, not knowing the close call that would occur two hours later:

Monday, January 29, 2001, 4:22 p.m.

The apostle Mark, writing primarily to the gentile Christians, especially Romans, wrote in Mark 11:22–24, "So Jesus answered and said to them, 'Have faith in God. For assuredly, I say to you, whoever says to this mountain, "Be removed and be cast into the sea," and does not doubt in his heart, but believes that those things he says will be done, he will have whatever he says. Therefore I say to you, whatever things you ask when you pray, believe that you receive them, and you will have them.'"

I believe, and I am asking you to pray. Man, and statistical probability might not agree. One of Payton's primary doctors said today, "Our backs are against the wall. I don't fault him for that assessment. It is a medical assessment." Two weeks ago, Dr. Macke said, "It is time to fish or cut bait."

His lungs are badly damaged. The doctors are giving him almost maximum respiratory support, and his oxygen saturation levels are borderline acceptable. The doctors began an experimental therapy to provide steroids that could potentially reduce the inflammation in the lungs. The lungs are battered. The impact of prolonged ventilator use at high settings, staph infection, recent bacteria that likely came from the colon surgery, and emboli from his heart vegetation has impeded his ability to breathe. Before we get mad or cry, we could not have won this battle at the time of the surgery. If the heart vegetation was on the left side of his heart (his vegetation is on the right side), then the vegetation could shower the brain with emboli and result in mini-strokes. This is a blessing. It is clear Satan is at work. I ask your prayers for the following:

- God is continued to be glorified in this situation. There was an unbelievable situation today I may share at an appropriate time.
- Payton's doctors and nurses discern the exact treatments needed and execute in an excellent manner until Payton is more stable.
- Payton's lungs would stabilize and ultimately heal. God would provide the necessary healing and oxygen sufficient for his body to live.
- Payton's family and friends to find comfort, peace, and hope in this battle. It will not be a short one.

I will leave you with a closing thought as a small dose of comfort God provides in this tremendous struggle. Yesterday Payton's girlfriend, Meredith, and her mother came to visit. Meredith is a very nice young lady. She indicated every time she saw the number 55, she began to cry—55 is Payton's basketball jersey number. Then she decided each time she saw the number 55 (speed limit sign, clock, etc.), she would pray. She said you will be surprised how often you will see the number 55. I was drinking a can of Dr. Pepper and turned the can and noticed the amount of sodium was 55 milligrams. When I left the nurses last night, I shared this story and said we wanted to get the oxygen support down to 55 from 84 and for PO2s to get to 55. The doctor's goal was a minimum of 50; they have run in the 40s. Payton's primary nurse said it was highly unlikely we could drop the oxygen from 84 to 55 (I agree) but would work on the PO2s. When I arrived today, Payton's other nurse read the PO2s, and it was 55. Praise God for providing some comfort and indicating He is in charge, and we thank Him again for each day He provides us with Payton.

We thank all of you for your prayers and support. We are humbled and blessed.

Love,
Todd and Robyn

It was clear God was testing our faith in Him to deliver a miracle as Payton's life was at risk. Prayer is always important, but it was increasingly apparent there was nothing more anyone could do but plead before the throne for Payton's life to be spared. The doctors seemingly had done everything they could.

Tuesday, January 30, 2001, 9:19 a.m.

From the book of Psalms 23:

> The LORD is my shepherd;
> I shall not want.
> He makes me to lie down in green pastures;
> He leads me beside the still waters.
> He restores my soul;
> He leads me in the paths of righteousness
> For His name's sake.

Yea, though I walk through the valley of the shadow of death,
I will fear no evil;
For You are with me;
Your rod and Your staff, they comfort me.
You prepare a table before me in the presence of my enemies;
You anoint my head with oil;
My cup runs over.
Surely goodness and mercy shall follow me
All the days of my life;
And I will dwell in the house of the LORD
Forever.

Yesterday, around 6:30 p.m., I was driving to the hospital (Robyn had called me in a panic: "Payton is crashing; you need to get here right away"). I was praying and pleading to God for Payton's life. For yet one more day. I knew the hour was upon us. The doctors began the steroid treatments in the morning, but it would take several days to see the impact on his lungs. There was nothing more the doctors could do. Payton's ventilator support was very high, and around four or five o'clock, Payton had another pneumothorax (collapsed lung). The doctors said it is hour to hour. When you are in a clinical state of acute respiratory distress (ARDS) and high ventilator settings, there is no room for error. I began pleading to God for Payton's life with a passion and fervor which is not my normal prayer request to God. I pulled up to the stoplight, the last one prior to getting on the interstate, and was anxious to get to the hospital. The car in front of me stopped at the yellow light. I was upset, as I needed to get to the hospital. I looked at the license plate on the car. It said, "PSLAM 23," for the twenty-third psalm. My heart wept for joy, and I started to cry. I reached into the backseat to grab my Bible and read the above passage as I drove to the hospital: "Yea, though I walk through the valley of the shadow of death I will fear no evil; for You are with me; Your rod and Your staff comfort me." Our God is good. And no, this was not another random chance event, but another God-ordained event to provide me assurance and comfort in our darkest hour. For you see, I knew, and the doctors knew, Payton's life hung in the balance. He was either going to be delivered from that hour, or he was going to join the Lord in heaven.

We left the hospital last night at midnight. And for the twenty-eighth day and now for the twenty-eighth night, God has delivered. And Payton was sick for ten days prior to entering the hospital. God alone has provided Payton with the strength and resources necessary for Payton to win each of these battles. Yesterday I was angry. Angry at Satan for trying to destroy my son. But I know it says in the book of John 10:10, "The thief does not come except to steal, and to kill, and to destroy. I have come that they may have it more abundantly." Satan came to destroy, and Jesus came to give us abundant life. The choice for me is clear. I have observed too much over the past twenty-eight days and before as I have seen God order our lives to prepare us for this time of greatest need. And I praise God for everything He is doing to help Payton live.

Please pray for the following:

- God continues to be glorified in this situation.
- The doctors and nurses continue to make the right decisions, and God's hand would direct them during these critical next days. Not only do we have great doctors and nurses, but we have very caring doctors and nurses (and staff). Payton's two primary doctors were at the hospital well past ten o'clock last night. Payton's primary nurse (Angie), who is very talented, was tearful as she came to get

Eyes of the Father

Robyn yesterday when Payton had another pneumothorax. We are blessed to see the entire team working so hard.

- Pray for Payton. Ask God's comfort and peace for him. I cry as I write this, thinking how much he has endured. Outside of his brain, almost every other part of his body was attacked and under some form of distress. Kidneys—dialysis. Lungs—ARDS. Colon—surgery. Liver and spleen—enlarged and not yet working, as feedings are not underway. Left and right chest—chest tubes. Body—excess fluids, although down 15 pounds with another 5 to 10 to go. Pressure sores on his feet and hands. Blood—sepsis and more. Throughout all this, God is providing.
- Pray Payton's lungs deteriorate no further, and they begin to heal.
- Pray the steroids help the inflammation and fibrosis on his lungs.
- Pray he does not acquire a new infection while his immune system is depressed from the steroids.
- Pray for one more day of healing. Because each of us only gets today.
- Pray for comfort and the peace which surpasses all understanding for Payton's family and friends.

And most importantly, give thanks to God. Whether it is for Payton or for your or your family or anything God is doing in your lives. If you desire, please share with us your thanksgiving on the website www.getwellpayton.com. If you would like to support Payton through an around-the-clock prayer chain, please check the website or contact Leisa Ress.

As we left the hospital, I gave a high five to my good friend Nick and told him and Robyn today was the best day of my life. I saw God's power, majesty, and love in a way never revealed to me before. I do not know what tomorrow brings. I can just thank God for each day He provides for the needs we have at that time.

God bless.

Todd and Robyn

We sent the following critical update to hundreds, if not thousands, who were praying on our behalf:

Thursday, February 1, 2001, 1:44 a.m.

From the book of Psalms 118 (with some personalized wording):

> Give thanks to the Lord, for He is good;
> His love endures forever.
> Let his doctors and nurses say:
> His love endures forever.
> Let those who fear the Lord say:
> His love endures forever.
> In our anguish I cried to the Lord,
> And He answered by setting us free.
> The Lord is with us;
> We will not be afraid.
> What can man do to us?
> The Lord is with Payton; He is his helper;
> He will look in triumph on His enemies.
> It is better to trust in the Lord,
> Than to put your confidence in man.
> It is better to trust in the Lord,
> Than to trust in princes.
> Diseases surrounded him,
> But the Lord cut them off.
> He was pushed back and about to fall,
> But the Lord helped him.
> The Lord is Payton's strength and his song;
> He has become his salvation.
> Shouts of joy and victory resound in the schools,
> churches and homes of the righteous;
> The Lord's right hand has done mighty things!
> Payton will not die but live,
> And will proclaim what the Lord has done.

> The Lord has permitted him this suffering,
> But He has not given him over to death.
> O Lord, save Payton;
> O Lord, grant us success.
> Blessed is he who comes in the name of the Lord.
> From the house of the Lord we bless you.
> The Lord is God,
> And He has made His light shine upon us.

I received the above from Psalm 118 from Leisa Ress, Meredith's mother. It substantially follows Psalm 118, personalized for Payton. I encourage each of you to read Psalm 118 from your Bible. I received this email tonight when I got home from the hospital. Leisa mailed it yesterday morning at 10:00 a.m. I was with Leisa most yesterday, and we discussed many scriptures but not this one. Yesterday (Wednesday) we received a call from the hospital at 8:40 a.m. Payton was crashing. He had bleeding in his lungs. His oxygen levels with full support went down to 72 with full ventilator support (100% oxygen). Normal oxygen levels without support are 98 or 99. Upon my arriving at the hospital, Payton's initial primary doctor shared with me a scripture which was on her heart regarding Payton. It was Psalm 118. My plan tonight (early this morning) was to use Psalm 118. I will tell you why in a minute. Then I got home and saw Leisa's email. I suppose this is another of those strange coincidences. For those not familiar with the Bible, there are 66 books, and in the book of Psalms, there are 150 psalms. No, this is not another coincidence but another example of God visibly demonstrating His control in this situation.

Let me explain why I want to share Psalm 118. "It is better to trust in the Lord than to put your confidence in man." On January 3, Ndidi said there were two ways to look at this situation: everything man, medicine, and machines can do or what God can do. We chose God at that time. Since then, we have asked for a day. Each day and God have faithfully delivered. There have been many ups and downs. Yesterday Payton's doctors gave us the following medical assessment (paraphrased): there is nothing more we can do, and the odds of Payton surviving this situation are not good at all. Now, should we start to question God? No! Should we put our faith in man over God? No! Does this mean we believe Payton will live? Yes! Could Payton die? Yes, and unfortunately, so did 160 healthy people in the Oklahoma City bombing, people killed by drunk drivers, and so on. Life is precious. Our God loves us. But there is suffering and death in life. For all of us. We PRAISE GOD He alone delivered Payton this morning when there was bleeding in his lung and he was crashing. Yet sometimes we want to know everything is going to work out in the end. But do any of us really know what our future holds during this life? Of course not.

We now set our sights on February 1 and winning February one day at a time. Do we need a miracle by medical standards? Yes. Has a miracle ever happened? Yes. Miracles are those unexplained events which medicine can't explain. My friend Brandon Gore had a couple miracles. Can God provide miracles? Yes! If He can create the universe, He can heal Payton's lungs. Is that part of the plan? We will find out. I continue to believe Payton will live. Payton is a fighter, and God went 31 and 0 in January.

Please pray for the following:

- God continues to be glorified.
- Doctors and nurses to continue the excellent care and support for Payton. And for comfort for them. It is not easy for them to go through the emotional roller coaster with critically ill patients. To

see so many of them praying for Payton and checking on his status is a great blessing.
- Payton's lungs to heal completely.
- For God to provide a miracle and God alone to receive the glory and praise. For man has now said, "I can do no more."
- The rest of Payton's body to heal and Payton to walk out of Riley Hospital of his own strength.
- Payton's friends and family to find comfort in this situation.

To the many friends and family that are praying and supporting our family in this time of need, thank you. We are humbled and blessed.

God bless.

Todd and Robyn

~§ Biblical Principle §~

From Psalm 118:8: "It is better to trust in the LORD, than to put confidence in man."

Within an hour of the above email posting on the website, I received an email from our neighbor and friend Ana Carlsgaard. The email was entitled "The Center of the Bible." She'd received the following summary of Psalm 118 earlier in the week. Again, was that another coincidence? No, I don't think so. And let me be a little dogmatic. When God continually tries to reach us and we ignore the perfectness of His creation and plan for us—in this life and eternal life—my heart aches.

The Center of the Bible
What is the shortest chapter in the Bible?
Psalm 117
What is the longest chapter in the Bible?
Psalm 119
Which chapter is in the center of the Bible?
Psalm 118

> There are 594 chapters before Psalm 118
> There are 594 chapters after Psalm 118
> For a total of 1,188 chapters
> What is the center verse in the Bible?
> Psalm 118:8
>
> Does this verse say something significant about God's perfect will for our lives? The next time someone says they would like to find God's perfect will for their lives, and they want to be in the center of His will, just send them to the center of His Word! "It is better to trust in the Lord than to put confidence in man."
>
> God blesses.
>
> Ana

The New King James commentary says the following regarding Psalm 118: it is "a psalm of declarative praise, the climax of the group of psalms called the Passover psalms or Hallel psalms. Hallelujah comes from this word. These Psalms were probably sung by the Savior (Jesus) on the night before His death." Verse 22 captures the essence of the passage as follows: "the stone which the builders rejected has become the chief cornerstone."

New York Times best-selling author Jonathan Cahn elaborated on this passage as follows:

> So the despised and rejected man on the cross would end up becoming the cornerstone of faith … of civilization … of history … and of the world. Think about it … kings and queens, generals and emperors, bow down to a man nailed to a cross. The most pivotal, world-changing life on this planet is that of a crucified Jewish Rabbi … the stone of rejection. And that crucified Rabbi becomes the cornerstone of history. In God, the object of man's hatred becomes the center of His love, and the object of man's despising becomes the vessel of His glory. How amazing is that?[4]

Just as it was foreordained before the foundation of the world that Jesus was to die for our sins, so too was the number of Payton's days determined. Twenty-four hours later, we would receive the dreaded phone call in the middle of the night that Payton was crashing, and once more, we would head to the hospital needing a miracle, or God had another plan in store for us and Payton.

Upon reflection, no man can see God's plan and purposes through the eyes of the Father. In the days, weeks, months, and years to follow, we would begin to see through His eyes the plans He had for us—or, as Keith would say, "the glorious unfolding"—and give thanks to the Lord for making it so clear through Psalm 118 that we, like Jesus, can sing songs of praise even when we face the most difficult circumstances imaginable.

PART 5

THE GLORIOUS UNFOLDING

CHAPTER 16

THE LORD SPEAKS, AND HIS PLAN UNFOLDS

A moment frozen in time. Payton was gone.

Only a few minutes after Blake, Chase, and Meredith left Payton's bedside, Dr. Seferian said we needed to make a decision—one no man or father should ever have to make. God answered immediately and in dramatic fashion. Thirty-three days of trips to the hospital to watch our oldest son fight for his life were over. Hundreds of friends, coworkers, and family no longer would come to visit and console us. Thousands of prayers for healing had been lifted up to the Lord throughout Indianapolis, Indiana; the United States; and even around the world, apparently to no avail. But were those petitions not heard? Did God not respond to or ignore the prayers of so many? Our daily prayer and hope always started with the desire for God to be glorified through Payton's situation. His plans and purposes are often impossible for us to comprehend, certainly different than what we hoped for. How could a healthy teenager have contracted a bacterial infection that would somehow make its way to a small hole in his heart and cause his vital organs to shut down with sepsis? Would the Lord answer Robyn's prayer from the early hours of the morning that Payton's life would have meaning?

After saying goodbye to our neighbor Cindy and her friend Diane, we began the process of leaving the hospital. We gave many thank-yous, hugs, and goodbyes to the wonderful staff. Payton's lead nurse, Angie

Schroeder, was providentially scheduled off the day of Payton's passing. We were thankful she was not there to see him, a patient she had fought so hard for, pass. Angie's daughter Lindsay had a swim meet that afternoon at the IU Natatorium on the IUPUI campus about a half mile from the hospital. Angie arrived unexpectedly at the hospital minutes after Payton passed. She wanted to see us and check on Payton. We were blessed to see her and thank her, and by God's grace, she'd avoided Payton's final hour.

Before we left, I told Robyn I needed to go to the other ICU unit at Riley, 2 South, to visit my dear friend Robin Gore. Her son, Brandon, had been admitted on January 29, just a few days prior, with a problem with his lungs, and he was on a ventilator, fighting for his life. A sixteen-year-old boy whose body had been ravaged by almost five years of cancer treatments for acute lymphoblastic leukemia was now struggling to breathe.

It was an odd feeling to walk down the cold, sterile hallway to go see another patient, but it was something I knew I needed to do. I was eerily at peace as I navigated the corridors between the two units. I arrived at ICU 2 South and went to the nurses' station to find Brandon's room. It was about 6:20 p.m. It was strange. Everything was the same, but everything was different. The wing housed critically ill patients, and the rooms and machines were similar, but the staff didn't know me, and I didn't know them. I did not know what to expect, but it struck me as odd, the juxtaposition of leaving the ICU at 4 North as a father whose son had lost his battle for his life and then going to the other ICU unit as a friend to visit a young man a few years older fighting for his own.

I walked from the nurses' station down to the end of the hall to Brandon's room. My body was full of raw emotion. I was thankful the Lord had put the Gores in our lives. Robin's son had defied the odds and overcome aspergillus on his lungs and a tumor in his abdomen to survive when the doctors had given him a week or so to live.

As I approached Brandon's room, I saw Robin with the same joyful countenance she always had. Robin and the Gore family had many bad days by man's standards, yet her joy in the Lord was remarkable. Her unfailing trust in Jesus was unwavering despite five difficult years. I looked at her and realized I was experiencing something for the first time in my life: the unspeakable hurt of losing my firstborn son and the peace that transcends this world and our human experience in knowing he was no longer suffering and was in the presence of the creator of the Universe, Almighty God. Without so much as a hi or hello, I said, "Payton is with the Lord." We embraced, and tears streamed down our faces. We knew Payton was with Jesus. Not only had the Lord introduced me to a woman and family who'd taught me what it meant to go through suffering with an absolute trust in Christ, but God also had Robin and Brandon in the hospital the week of Payton's passing to provide comfort and support during my time of greatest need.

I asked Robin, "Who won, and who lost?" as heaven is where we desire to be. Robin and I agreed neither Payton nor Brandon won or lost if we were secure in our faith in Jesus as our Lord and Savior. We were thankful that Payton was with the Lord and that Brandon remained with us. The Lord used both of our situations at Riley to share the good news of His gospel and our faith in Him, regardless of circumstance or outcome. We'd both had remarkable opportunities to share our faith in Christ to many who desperately needed to hear the good news of salvation in Jesus Christ and Him alone. The doctor gave Brandon a 1 percent chance to live, but two months later, Brandon left Riley Hospital on April 9, my birthday. At the time, his doctors said they were not aware of any other bone marrow transplant patient who'd been intubated and able to come off the ventilator. Today Brandon has a good job; a wife, Erica; and a young family. He will have lifelong challenges with his hips and his lungs as a result of years of cancer, chemotherapy, and their ravaging effects, but he lives as a true testament to the power of God. We did not get the same answer to prayer that Jim, Robin, and the Gore family received, as our son did not live. We did get a powerful witness through the Gores to show us how to put our trust in Jesus during an incomprehensible trial. In life and in death, Brandon and Payton both served as a testament to God's love for us and impacted many lives for Him.

Almost two years prior, the Lord had placed the Gore family in my life. I'd thought I was doing something for them—running a marathon to raise money for cancer survivors—but the Lord was doing something for me: showing me a family and a mother with a 100 percent commitment to Christ during a significant trial that almost cost their son his life. Their example was a huge blessing to me; it prepared me for the difficult road ahead and showed me how to put my full trust in the Lord.

After saying goodbye to Robin, I returned to find my Robyn in the hallway outside the waiting room. Inexplicably, she was by herself. We gathered our things, including the bag of Payton's belongings, to make the trip home. As we made our way toward the nurses' station, Robyn saw Dr. Seferian, who, two hours earlier, had been at the center of the life-or-death decision. Robyn, an unemotional woman not prone to hugs, reached out to hug Ed. The embrace contained a mixture of bewilderment, disappointment, sympathy, and friendship all rolled up into one. Ed was caught off guard, as he was part of a team who'd worked hard to keep Payton alive for weeks. By that standard, he and his colleagues had failed. They'd been unable to keep the patient, our son, alive. I suspect Ed, who was quiet and introspective, did not have deep friendships with his patients and their families, but I know he deeply cared for us and Payton, which made the embrace even more important and difficult. We expressed our thankfulness, said our goodbyes, and committed to staying in touch. We did, including seeing him years later when he was on the medical staff at Mayo Clinic in Rochester, Minnesota.

It was a few minutes before seven as we headed to the parking garage. Twelve hours earlier, we'd been pleading with the Lord for Payton in the chapel. Now we were heading home to begin life as a family of four. I pulled out of the parking garage and gave the attendant, a young man in his late teens or early twenties, my ticket to pay the daily charge. I said, "Do you need to pay if your son passed away today?" I suspect humor was a mechanism for me to handle my grief. He looked at me and then appeared to glance at some papers in his hut. Perhaps he was trying to figure out if there was a policy addressing that situation or whom to call. I doubt anyone had asked him that question before. I interrupted his search and said, "That's all right. We are fine to pay. Don't worry about it." I told Robyn I had not been trying to create a problem.

We made the familiar trip home and pulled into our driveway, not knowing what to expect or thinking much about what was next. We would learn in the coming hours that planning a funeral, particularly given the extraordinary circumstances surrounding Payton's illness and our large community of friends and relationships, was like planning a wedding but with little time to do so.

We gathered our things from the car, opened the door, and headed into our house. We knew the boys were at the school carnival. Robyn's mom and dad, Mike and Ann Scott, were sitting in our family room. There were more hugs and tears, followed by quiet. Of our three boys, Payton had been most like Robyn's family, the Scotts. He'd looked like Grandpa Mike. He'd been big like Mike, and he'd had an ornery streak like his as well. Mike was the ultimate tough guy, but he was not prepared for that situation. Grandma Ann was special. She'd been there when Payton was born and supported Robyn and me as first-time parents, and she'd been with us often as the boys were growing up. They were hurting. They were people of faith; however, their life experience and knowledge had not prepared them for a time like that.

It was quiet as we waited for the boys to come home. Our time was interrupted by a call to my friend Keith to arrange a time to meet the following morning to discuss funeral preparations. Keith mentioned the idea of a memorial for Payton. It was surreal that Payton had been alive only a few hours earlier, and now we were talking about a memorial. He mentioned something having to do with Fort Wilderness and a medical facility in Payton's honor. I mentioned an initiative led by David Musa, Ndidi's husband, called Sierra Leone Agape Voluntary Effort, or SAVE. SAVE had been established a few years prior to provide support to the people of that poor African nation, where the average life span was around fifty years old. Sierra Leone was a country replete with civil war and brutal crimes committed against its citizenry. For several reasons, we decided on Fort Wilderness. After all, that was the place where the trajectory of our lives had changed dramatically just four years ago. It was a place with a mission to impact lives for eternity through God's Word, creation, adventure programming, and warm Christian fellowship. Certainly, it had impacted us, and sadly for us, Payton was now part of eternity, separated from us for a time.

A little before nine o'clock that night, we saw a car pull into the driveway. We suspected it was Uncle Scott—my younger brother by eleven months—with Blake and Chase. If there was one person in the entire world I would have wanted with my boys during that time, it was Scott. He was a man who loved unconditionally. Scott could also keep things light and fun. I am certain the boys had fun at the carnival, even with the specter of their brother's health situation hanging over their heads.

It was like a surprise birthday party, when a group of family and friends anxiously waited for the unsuspecting guests to arrive home. Our family room was shaped like a long rectangle, with views of both the front yard and backyard. A fireplace adjacent to the garage and dark cedar panels lined the walls, with three large casement windows overlooking the wooded front yard. It was a comfortable room, with a couch in front of the window and another across from the fireplace. I sat on the couch across from the fireplace with Robyn. Ann and Mike were in chairs directly across from us, with Ann closest to the front window.

The walkway to our front door was a slightly rounded *S* that meandered in front of an apple blossom tree. The tree would spring forth to life in the following month, but that day, it was dark and cold, and the unthinkable had happened. What could one say to his ten- and seven-year-old sons in a situation like that? As they passed in front of the apple blossom tree, Scott glanced into the front family room, and Ann shook her head to imply the situation was not good. Scott then had a few seconds to grasp the enormity of what he'd just seen as he brought the boys into the house.

The boys walked through the front door, oblivious to what had happened. It was apparent they'd had a good time at the carnival, which had been a much-needed antidote to the circumstances at the hospital. Blake, the born competitor, had won a few stuffed animals and other prizes. Chase, on the other hand, with no competitive desires or instincts, was pleased to reap the bounty of Blake's winnings.

We gathered their coats and asked them to sit down on the couch. Scott was on the far left side, with Blake in the middle and Chase on the right. I told them Payton was now in heaven. He was no longer suffering. God had taken him home. I shared briefly, and would explain in greater detail in the days and months to come, the story of how the Lord had made the decision to take him at the exact moment we'd asked Him to declare Himself. Scott started to bawl. Blake was in shock. Chase did not know what to do. He stared blankly and tried to process what he'd just heard. Blake, with his deeply analytical mind, had posed questions and ideas for the past several weeks about how to help Payton get better. "What if they put something into his heart to suck the infection out?" he'd asked, along with other similar thoughts. Blake was an optimist and never had seen that day coming. Perhaps it was a triggering event for Chase that led to his adolescent and teenage pessimism and contrary view on most matters. All we knew right then was that the situation was not fair. It was one thing for a parent, an adult, to lose a son, but what was it like for a ten- and seven-year-old to lose their brother and now face their own mortality?

Robyn and I went over to the couch to embrace our boys. Scott hugged Mike and Ann. Tears flowed from what seemed like an endless well. Robyn sat on the couch with both boys draped over her, engulfed by her two living sons, whose weight did not even equal Payton's. After a few minutes, Blake, a young man with a keen interest and a talent in sports, asked Uncle Scott if they could go up to Payton's room. Payton had received a lot of great swag and memorabilia with get-well wishes in the preceding weeks: a signed Peyton Manning Indianapolis Colts jersey; an autographed Purdue men's basketball; an autographed Indiana University soccer ball; an Indiana Pacers basketball jersey signed by Austin Croshere, his favorite player; and much more.

They walked up the stairs, and it seemed they were gone only a minute or two before we heard them coming back down the stairs. There was no way they could have gone through all of Payton's stuff that quickly. His room was full of gifts, memorabilia, and well-wishes. Scott came around the corner; Blake was next. Scott had a look like the puzzled "What just happened?" expression we had seen on Ed Seferian's face just a few hours ago. Scott spoke, his voice quivering with emotion. We listened intently. He said, "I opened Payton's door. I heard the perfect strum of a guitar. I wondered, *Did I just hear what I think I heard?* I looked at Blake and asked if he'd heard anything. He said yes. The strum of a guitar."

Was that God's way, perhaps through the angelic heavenly hosts, of providing comfort to Scott and Blake to let them—and us—know Payton was okay? I wept with joy upon hearing of the Lord's love for us; He was clearly speaking to us and telling us He loved us. Growing up, I'd had a very analytical mind, trying to live with congruence to my beliefs, which for many years were self-taught and did not include the Lord. Now the Lord was clearly showing me His plans and purposes. I was in awe.

Over the past thirty-three days, a team had mobilized to address many needs: caregivers for Blake and Chase, meals for our family, a website for friends and family to receive updates and offer their prayers and support, communication channels to share urgent messages and prayer requests, and even help with our laundry. I needed to post a message letting everyone know what had happened. I relied heavily on my friend Jeff Terp, a communications expert who'd spent years in the political process, to spearhead a lot of our crisis communication. That evening, I asked Jeff to coordinate certain key telephone calls to family and close friends. When you go through a process like that, you find you cannot possibly spend thirty minutes or more with everyone you know—it is simply exhausting. I was thankful for Jeff's support in helping us get the word out. Knowing that, I could go to bed and send out a message first thing in the morning to let the world know of Payton's passing.

For thirty-three days, the Lord had supernaturally provided additional strength—mentally and physically—to keep me going. The days often had been long, but I never had been sick, and Robyn and I had been remarkably in sync throughout Payton's hospitalization. As I got ready for bed that evening, I was tired. We had been up since three thirty in the morning, and it was now going on eleven o'clock at night. Who knew what the next several days would bring, with a calling and funeral service and friends and family traveling in from around the country to offer their condolences and support? As my head hit the pillow, my mind was spinning with many things to think about. I was hopeful for a good night's sleep, yet one thing kept coming to my mind throughout the night—one of the last things I would ever have expected.

Eyes of the Father

◆ Biblical Principle ◆

The apostle John wrote in the last chapter of the Bible, in Revelation 21:1–5,

> Now I saw a new heaven and a new earth, for the first heaven and the first earth had passed away. Also, there was no more sea. Then I, John, saw the holy city, New Jerusalem, coming down out of heaven from God, prepared as a bride adorned for her husband. And I heard a loud voice from heaven saying, "Behold, the tabernacle of God is with men, and He will dwell with them, and they shall be His people. God Himself will be with them and be their God. And God will wipe away every tear from their eyes; there shall be no more death, nor sorrow, nor crying. There shall be no more pain, for the former things have passed away." Then He who sat on the throne said, "Behold, I make all things new." And He said to me, "Write, for these words are true and faithful."

All creation groans, as this is not how it was supposed to be. Mankind paid a huge price for Adam's original sin against God in the Garden of Eden. There is a day coming when everything will be made new, and the pain and suffering of today will be no more.

Upon reflection, although Payton's life was not spared and we grieve our loss greatly, we know the Lord has a plan for us, and we look forward with great anticipation to the day when we are reunited with Payton.

CHAPTER 17

A RESTLESS NIGHT AND A SURREAL PHONE CALL

It was one of those restless evenings when it seemed I got little sleep—and certainly not any deep, comforting sleep. My mind could not turn off. One reflection, moment, and thought kept coming to me. It related to our former church, Garfield Park, the church we'd left five months prior when it was clear the Lord was calling us to Zionsville Fellowship and the church where Payton had been confirmed the prior year—a sort of Christian catechism. Pastor Tom Blossom had become a good friend during the past ten years, and that was where I'd come to know Jesus Christ as my Lord and Savior. It was where I'd spent significant time in church leadership roles, including church renewal efforts. It was also a church where we had established some friendships—perhaps not deep ones but important ones, nonetheless. As I lay in my bed, drifting in and out of sleep, I thought about our friends back at Garfield Park. How would they respond to the news? I was concerned it would hit them hard, as some did not have the biblical knowledge or equipping to understand the Lord's plans for Payton.

During 1999 and 2000, I'd led many of the teaching and praise-and-worship sessions at Garfield Park, the same ones started by Keith and Becky after our initial trips to Fort. In December 1999, I'd been convicted to teach on salvation, a topic that, to my recollection, had not been explored in any depth during my ten years at the church. In advance of my leading the sessions, Pastor Blossom offered me simple and sage advice:

- What do you want them to know?
- What do you want them to do?

My teaching centered on the following two central tenets drawn from scripture:

- Jesus Christ was sent to earth to take the sins of the world through His death on the cross.
- Will you accept Jesus Christ as your Savior and Lord of your life?

It was a conversation I'd had with Jim Granneman, an elderly man in our church choir, after one of the teaching sessions that was drawing my attention most and causing me not to sleep. Jim was a quiet man who was faithful in his attendance and participation in the church choir and a man I knew little. Including the above conversation, he and I probably had had one or two other conversations during our ten years at the church. Jim once had asked me, "How do we know the Lord's will?" A deep and profound question. He'd chosen a simple question to raise his point. He said, "Todd, there are lots of worthwhile charitable causes who request support. How do you know which ones to give to?"

Why were Garfield Park, our relationship with the church, the question of the Lord's will, and my conversation with Jim Granneman coming to mind over and over throughout the night? I woke up around seven o'clock the next morning, Saturday, and knew I needed to work on the message regarding Payton's passing prior to working on funeral arrangements. I continued to reflect on my restless night and Jim's question. I knew we needed to return the next day to attend the Sunday morning service at Garfield Park. I suspected many were hurting over Payton's illness and passing, and I wanted to share the news directly with them and let them know we were okay.

Over the years, Robyn and I had grown in our marriage, relationship, and communication. We now speak candidly with one another. That was one conversation I did not want to have with her. I dreaded sharing my thoughts about going back to Garfield Park. I had a much deeper relationship with many of the people there than she did, but our son had just passed away. I knew she would think I was half-cocked for wanting to return to the place we'd just left. But I knew—no, the Lord was making it clear—we needed to return.

But first, how could we share news with hundreds, if not thousands, that a young man had lost his life? It was hard. I posted a message at 8:11 a.m. on February 3, 2001. I had to relive the story of the phone call in the middle of the night, Chase coming to visit Payton for the first time, God's response to my demand that He declare Himself, and the scripture we'd shared as he drew his final breaths and somehow provide hope to many who did not know the truth of Christ and how He used suffering to bring glory to Himself. I closed with the following:

> Payton fought the good fight. He battled for 33 days, until he knew his work was done. I know this situation and Payton have touched many hearts for Christ. To some, God's love and our salvation through Jesus Christ has been strengthened, and to some, it has been exposed. God's sovereignty (control) was seen. The plan for Payton was for 13 years. Thirteen wonderful years. We will miss him. Our heart aches with sorrow, yet we are so comforted at how God has poured out His love on us in a way that we could never imagine. It is our prayer that many of you will examine this situation considering God's truth. God has so much for us. If we thought this life was all there is, we would be very sad and emotionally devastated. Romans 6:23: "For the wages of sin is death, but the gift of God is eternal life in Christ Jesus our Lord." This is a sinful world—our hope and salvation are in Christ Jesus and eternal life. We know that Payton is in heaven right now, playing his guitar. Goodbye for now. We love you, Payton.
>
> Todd, Robyn, Blake, and Chase

About nine o'clock, I called Keith on my cell phone to arrange a time to meet to discuss the funeral. He and Tom Streeter, the senior pastor at Zionsville Fellowship, would come to the house at ten o'clock. When I first had met Keith, he'd been in advertising for a good-sized firm and had a good grasp of scripture and matters of faith, and he'd shared them with me as we watched my son Blake and his daughter Emily on the soccer field. Now, five years later, he was a member of Zionsville Fellowship's pastoral staff and would officiate our son's funeral. Keith had shared a brief conversation he'd had with Fort Wilderness about a memorial, and he would share more once they arrived. While talking with Keith on my cell, I heard our home phone ring—it was the first call of the morning. A few moments later, Robyn yelled up the stairs to tell me there was someone on the phone for me. I told her I was on my cell phone and asked her to take a message.

After wrapping up my conversation, I went downstairs and asked Robyn who'd called. She said, "Jim Granneman called to ask how Payton was doing and when we would be back at Garfield Park." I was stunned. If I'd made a list of a thousand people who would have called me or our family, Jim Granneman would not have been on the list. That was the only time Jim ever called us. The Lord was making it clear to us through Jim that Garfield Park was hurting, and we needed to return to see them the next day, which made the dreaded conversation with Robyn a whole lot easier. I shared with her my restless night and the thoughts running through my mind about Jim and the conversation we'd had the year prior. God is so good! It was certainly a confirmation that we can, in fact, know God's will.

Our pastor, Tom Streeter, and Keith arrived around ten o'clock. It just kept getting harder. It was bad enough to lose our son, and now we had to make plans to bury him—and make lots of decisions that did not seem very important. Death certainly changes your perspective on a whole lot of things. We quickly decided the service would be a celebration of Payton's life, not a funeral. We were not in denial but wanted to focus on the life Payton had lived and bring glory to the Lord and hopefully to a grieving community of family and friends. Payton had been gifted with music, often playing his guitar, so we identified eight individuals representing our current and former churches, his school, and musicians he'd played with during the praise worship service at Fort Wilderness the prior summer to lead the worship at his service. We picked the songs for the band to play. Payton was a big fan of Creed, and we selected the song "Arms Wide Open" as the music to play when guests arrived for the service. One significant challenge remained: where to hold the service. Our church, Zionsville Fellowship, did not have the physical space to accommodate a large crowd. We had no idea how many people would attend, but we expected a lot of people to show up. Traders Point Christian Church was pleased to offer their facilities. Payton had attended school there from third through fifth grade. They had a large facility on the northwest side of Indianapolis, not far from our home.

Keith would officiate the service. He was honored and pleased to do so. I know it was one of the most difficult things he has ever done. We were early in our now twenty-five-year friendship. The Ogorek family is part of our family. I suspect we could write a book simply about our lives lived together and, as Keith would say, "creating family memories."

We would have two other speakers at the funeral: Ndidi Musa and LaMarr Davis. Ndidi had been a source of great strength during our time at Riley. She was a strong woman of prayer, or, more succinctly, a prayer warrior. I have met few, if any, women or men who exemplify lives of humble submission through intimate prayer relationships with the Lord. It is something difficult to describe, but once you see and experience it, you can understand. Ndidi was a great doctor, but she was an even stronger woman of prayer. LaMarr was a good friend who'd lived two blocks away in our old neighborhood. Years later, Chase would refer to LaMarr as the most selfless man he'd ever met. LaMarr, like Keith, had become a pastor in the mid to late '90s. I remember vividly the conversation we had in our cul-de-sac as he shared with me the Lord's stirrings on his heart. Robyn and I were blessed to have those three individuals as representatives of the body of Christ during the service. I would share reflections on behalf of the family. I did not know what I was going to say or how I was going to say it, but I did know I had to share the crushing sorrow of the loss of Payton and the hope we had in Christ.

One more thing remained before Keith and I would head to the funeral home to meet the funeral director and deal with the dreaded details regarding the service: Keith needed to share a discussion he'd had with Fort Wilderness the prior evening. Fort was a special place for us, one where the trajectory of our family had changed dramatically as we were introduced to camping, the Northwoods of Wisconsin, warm Christian fellowship, and the Zionsville Fellowship church community. Keith had spoken with Jean Robertson, wife of the camp director, Tom, and Jean had suggested building a medical facility in Payton's honor. The camp founder, Truman Robertson, always had wanted a medical facility but did not have the funds to build it. Fort had never named a building after anyone in their forty-five-year history. We thought it was a great idea. A goal of $75,000 was quickly established. Providentially, the Fort board had their regularly scheduled quarterly board meeting that morning, February 3, and approved the plan for Payton's Place. Camp had a capital campaign underway, and renderings of Payton's Place were available a few days later at the calling and funeral service.

It was another cold winter morning as I headed out to the garage to get in the car to travel to Crown Hill Funeral Home. Crown Hill is where some of Indiana's most famous or infamous citizens are laid to rest, ranging from former President Benjamin Harrison to John Dillinger. I was going to meet the people and the funeral director who would care for us with the final arrangements. I was thirty-seven years old and had no practical experience with funerals. I had gone to a couple funerals when I was in my teens, but the reality was, no one close to me had died. As I drove up to the funeral home on West Thirty-Eighth Street, a busy corridor running across the near north side of Indianapolis, I was struck by the size of the burial grounds: 555 acres spread out on both sides of the road, with a roadway running underneath Thirty-Eighth Street connecting the north and south sections. About two hundred thousand people had been buried there since they opened for business in 1864. Now I was arriving to add one more. It was awful.

I pulled into the parking lot and noticed the mausoleum off in the distance. I walked under the canopy, entered the doors, and was immediately greeted upon my arrival. "Uh, I am here to see James Dixon," I murmured. Keith had a connection with James. Keith would arrive a few moments later. The staff offered me some water and shared their condolences; they were clearly well trained and experienced at putting one at ease.

As I sat in the lobby, my mind wandered to a lot of things: my family, my friends, God, work, and on and on. It was the first time in weeks I'd been alone and not part of the daily hospital ritual. My days of directing my energy toward keeping Payton alive were over. A new chapter was beginning: life on earth with Payton was over. Now the unthinkable was upon us: burying our son. Dr. Macke would later share with us in a poignant and heartfelt moment, "It is not natural for a parent to bury his or her child." Truer words were never spoken. Robyn did not go with me to the funeral home. Going there without her was one of many things I did to protect her and allow her to come to grips with our new reality. Since Payton's passing, she has returned to his grave site only twice—when we buried my grandmother and my father in plots adjacent to Payton's—and in the first year or two following his passing, I handled most, if not all, of the difficult stuff. I was fine with that. It is who God made me to be.

The funeral business is interesting. Everything is done to create a sense of calm, peace, reassurance, and respect and for the comfort of the grieving family. However, the reality is the staff and their actions toward the bereaved are masking the chaos—not literal chaos but the type of chaos described in the book of Genesis, in the first chapter's first two verses: "In the beginning God created the heavens and the earth. The earth was without form, and void; and darkness was on the face of the deep." Theologians and Bible commentators describe "without form, and void" as chaos. Out of disorder, God brought order. That sums up how I felt: we had gone from order to disorder. As much as I could see the Lord's hand in everything leading up to the time of Payton's passing, I was now entering a time of disorder and would need Him more than ever before. During Payton's illness there always had been hope he would recover. Now our hope was to see Payton one day in eternity.

Keith arrived a few minutes after one o'clock. It was nice to have a close friend by my side. Keith and I waited in the lobby for a few minutes, and around 1:20, James Dixon greeted us with a warm smile. We would soon learn James not only had a warm smile but also clearly had been called to his role. He led us downstairs to his office, where we gathered at a small conference table to wade into a myriad of details: an open or closed casket (we chose closed); clothes for Payton to wear (I guess it is not appropriate to bury one naked, although Payton would have found it funny and apropos); the obituary; the order of the service; the program; a photograph of Payton; remembrance items; the casket design, headstone, and inscription; memorial gift instructions; a photo montage and video tributes; plots for additional family members (since Payton had been the first to pass); the funeral service time and calling(s); the grave-site committal service and a meal to follow; and funeral procession logistics. It was simply numbing to handle those details, but James was a pro and made everything easy, and he was a Christian, so he could relate to our perspective on Payton's passing. We anticipated a large crowd of mourners and those paying their respects to Payton and our family. We set the date of the funeral for Wednesday at 10:00 a.m., with a calling the day before from 4:00 p.m. to 8:00 p.m.

Payton's favorite color was orange, which influenced our decision with respect to flowers and the casket and headstone. I cannot think of a more dreadful experience than buying a casket while knowing your loved one will soon be in it. Yet the casket is what everyone will see at the funeral, and you want to show appropriate dignity and respect.

James was in and out of the room as he scurried to get the arrangements made and address a couple necessary interruptions. I guess we were not the only family who needed his expertise and support. His periodic absences did allow Keith and me to have some time together man to man and friend to friend. We'd lived a lot of life together over the past five years, and our families were increasingly close. I looked at Keith and said, "I now have something you do not have." I paused and then choked out the following words with a raw, conflicted emotion: "A desire for eternity and to one day be in heaven." Prior to that day, for me, heaven had been largely an intellectual understanding based on the historical and resurrected Jesus, to believe in Him and accept the free gift offered us through His death on the cross, but now it was real. My intellect now matched my heart for the first time in my life. Ten years before, I had accepted the gospel of Jesus Christ as true. Now I knew it was true and had a burning desire to join Payton one day with Jesus.

Since the funeral would take place within the coming week, there was no need to embalm Payton's body. Even though we'd requested a closed casket, James still had to prepare the body for burial, including his attire. I told James I would return on Monday with Payton's clothes. As much as I appreciated James and his wonderful support, those two hours were some of the most undesirable of my life.

It was about four o'clock, and I was feeling a little hungry. Eating and many other routine activities take a backseat during times like that. We were thankful so many people had provided meals for us during the past month. Food had been one less thing for us to address.

I arrived home and gave Robyn and the boys hugs. It already had been a long day after my restless night spent thinking about Garfield Park and after the emotional finality of posting Payton's passing on the website, the call from Jim Granneman, the meeting with Keith and Tom to plan the funeral, and the dreaded two-hour visit to the funeral home. I wanted to veg out or rest and watch some sporting event or mindless television program, but there was too much to do: making phone calls to family and friends, writing a father's reflection for the funeral, responding to numerous emails, and more.

I shared with Robyn details regarding the funeral and service. She was polite but offered little input or concern. She trusted me to do what was right. She had already shifted gears and was focused on providing comfort to our boys. We each had a job to do. That evening, we enjoyed another of many meals prepared for us. We were thankful for the outpouring of love and support from so many people. If you ever have friends or loved ones who are hurting, just do something: make a meal, give a gift card, cut their lawn, or offer to do their laundry. The little acts of kindness are appreciated. I am certain there were far more of those acts and prayers offered up on our behalf than we will ever know this side of eternity.

After dinner, I went upstairs to my office to work on the funeral service and organize my thoughts on the tribute for Payton's service, but first, I went to the website to see some of the posts. I was overwhelmed by the multitude of heartfelt, aching messages for us, and I'm equally overwhelmed now. This was long before Twitter and use of the phrase "Twitter is blowing up" to describe the reaction to some outrageous comment or event. My best friend growing up summed it up well: "Payton, this guestbook is a tremendous testimony to how much everyone loves you and your family. It also shows how strong God's love is. I will miss you more than I can say. I will continue to pray for you and your family. All my love, Dave Brown." That was what he and many others said: "You are loved by many. God's love is even greater. We will miss you. We will continue to pray." But another message, an email from a work colleague, caught me off guard on the day following my son's passing and provided a bizarre reality twist.

⇛ Biblical Principle ⇚

Luke wrote the following in Acts 9:10–12:

> Now there was a certain disciple at Damascus named Ananias; and to him the Lord said in a vision, "Ananias."
>
> And he said, "Here I am, Lord."
>
> So the Lord said to him, "Arise and go to the street called Straight, and inquire at the house of Judas for one called Saul of Tarsus, for behold, he is praying. And in a vision, he has seen a man named Ananias coming in and putting his hand on him, so that he might receive his sight."

In one of the most famous biblical stories (check it out), God calls Ananias to find Saul, a persecutor of Christians, to heal Saul from his physical and spiritual blindness. Saul subsequently changes his name to Paul and goes on to write most of the New Testament books, minister throughout the kingdom, and ultimately die as a martyr for his newfound faith.

God had given Jim Granneman a message to call us the morning following Payton's passing and tell us to return to our former church. Upon reflection, I do not fully understand the kingdom implications of the call or our return. However, I know the Lord works in mysterious ways, and Jim's question of the Lord's will and returning to Garfield Park had been the things on my mind as I lay restless the night before.

CHAPTER 18

A BITTERSWEET AWARD AND A COMMUNITY IMPACTED

Work takes a backseat during times of personal crisis or, in my case, no seat. I was blessed to have an employer, Arthur Andersen, who cared for its people. In many workplaces, employees develop strong friendships and relationships that make it easy to support one another during a crisis. That was the case at Arthur Andersen. During my previous sixteen years, I'd worked hard and been deemed a high performer, as evidenced by both job assignments and tenure with the firm. As I said before, Andersen was generally an up-or-out firm. Either you were promoted, or you left for another job, typically in corporate America. A professional service firm is driven by billable hours, and I'd generated more than adequate billings, or client revenue, during my career. I enjoyed the opportunity to develop and equip talented young staff. Andersen was often rated as the number-one professional service firm to work for.

But now it was different. I needed to rely on my team to address the necessary work and client commitments.

The incredible nature of providential and God-ordered circumstances continued when I opened an email from Paul Willis Dunker, our marketing head, to find a bizarre reality twist. He said the *Indianapolis Business Journal* had honored me as one of the Indianapolis community's Forty Under 40 award winners, which recognizes individuals who have achieved noteworthy success or recognition in the community. Given Payton's passing, the award meant nothing to me. My thoughts and actions were 100 percent focused on Payton, my family, and everything surrounding Payton's life and impending funeral. The publication profiled each of the recipients, telling his or her story. The stories were nicely done, befitting the honor; however, my story was different from the others, as you will see below.

> People complain that much of technology, including the internet, is impersonal and prevents communities from coming together. But Todd Leyden knows better, personally and professionally.
>
> On January 1, Payton, Leyden's oldest son was admitted to Riley Hospital with a life-threatening staph infection, which had reached his heart and spread throughout his body. As of this writing, the 13-year-old continued to struggle.
>
> Meanwhile, family and friends were at the Leydens' side. Some were at the hospital; others communicated through a Web site established for Payton—www.getwellpayton.com. Hundreds of people visited the site, and they left prayers and messages of encouragement. Payton's name was added to prayer circles stretching from Hawaii to New Hampshire.
>
> "I've been humbled by all of this," said Leyden, who is a principal with the Arthur Andersen accounting firm and a member of Zionsville Fellowship Church. "I never would have chosen this situation to demonstrate our faith. But it's been clear in this situation, if we didn't have our faith, we would be a wreck, and we wouldn't know what to do."
>
> Before the Web site offered so much support to his family, Leyden was already a strong believer in technology's ability to help people.

He served as lead consultant to the Mayor's High Technology Task Force in 1997, helping develop a strategic plan for building a technology-based economy for Central Indiana. Leyden's leadership led to more than $200 million of venture capital becoming available to support new technology, as well as a state government fund, the 21st Century Research and Technology Fund, to help Indiana support technological innovation.

Another highlight of Leyden's career was being the project manager for the privatization of the Naval Air Warfare Center in 1996. The nationally acclaimed effort resulted in saving more than 2,000 jobs for Indianapolis and a one-time savings for the Navy of $180 million.

Caring for youth is not something that Leyden has limited to his own family and church. He's served on the board of Prevent Child Abuse Indiana and the Children's Museum of Indianapolis, for example.

With God's help, Leyden said he would soon be able to return to those professional and personal pursuits. Yet even his family's suffering has helped others.

As one family wrote in the getwellpayton.com. guest book: "Our thoughts and prayers are with your entire family as your battle reminds us all how precious our children are and how blessed we are to have them in our lives."

Leyden Brief Case

Best advice: "Don't be a professional golfer; you and your family will starve to death" (from his grandfather)

Favorite book: "The Winner Within: A Life Plan for Team Players" by Pat Riley

Hobbies: golf, running, study of church world history

Proudest accomplishment: "My family (wife Robyn and three sons) and faith"

The timing of the recognition was not lost on me. Many friends and colleagues would have loved to have had the opportunities the Lord had brought my way. However, such an honor never had felt more unimportant in my life. The day I was planning my son's funeral, I received that significant community recognition. I would have given all of that away in a second in exchange for Payton.

More tears flowed as I returned to reading the posts on Payton's guest book from many family and friends:

> "Although I never knew him, this website inspired me."

> "His zest for life made him a child one could never forget."

> "Through you, I've learned not to take life for granted and to cherish each moment that I get to live, laugh, and cry."

> "God works in mysterious ways, in which many times we cannot understand."

> "I hope you know how much I cared for u, and I'm sorry for what I've done and what I haven't done. I'm going to miss you every day that u aren't with us, and I know we'll be together one sweet day."

> "The spiritual impact your son has had on this community is miraculous."

> "I read the Bible to know God. Your letters have been a way for me to know God more. I've shared your witness of God's unbelievable strength and peace that He gives in times of great trial."

"Though the death of a child would have us look to the skies and scream, 'WHY?' we who know Christ are called to maintain an eternal perspective. Each time I have read the daily update in the past week, my heart has been incredibly humbled by the ministry your family has provided to others in doing just that."

These are but a few of the entries on the day following Payton's passing. The guest book is full of hundreds of posts. Seeing God's love and support for us through so many family and friends was humbling, as was seeing the impact made in others' lives by simply trying to put Christ first. The primary reason I resisted writing this story for so long is the undue attention it brings to us. We would never have chosen this situation, nor would we ever say we could have responded to this unspeakable loss without Christ. We simply tried to live a life congruent with our faith, recognizing that God's plans and desires are far greater than ours.

I turned off the computer for the evening and started to get ready for bed. Tomorrow was day two—more of the same but totally different without Payton. It was getting late. I made some progress on gathering my thoughts for the funeral service. I knew I had a couple days until everyone started to arrive. I could not let my mind wander to consider what our return to Garfield Park was going to be like.

⇜ Biblical Principle ⇝

The apostle James wrote in James 4:13–16,

> Come now, you who say, "Today or tomorrow we will go to such and such a city, spend a year there, buy and sell, and make a profit"; whereas you do not know what will happen tomorrow. For what is your life? It is even a vapor that appears for a little time and then vanishes away. Instead you ought to say, "If the Lord wills, we shall live and do this or that." But now you boast in your arrogance. All such boasting is evil.

Upon reflection, we are thankful for the life we had and the opportunity to impact the community we loved, Indianapolis. However, we rejoice in the Lord's glorious unfolding, knowing that His plans are exceedingly greater than anything we can imagine. Our time on earth short, but the implications of what we do or do not do last forever.

CHAPTER 19

FAMILY OF FOUR: WE NEVER HAVE TO WORRY WHERE HE IS

The next morning, Robyn and I gathered the boys to head to church. For the first time in five weeks, Robyn and I could spend some significant time with Blake and Chase. How were they doing? What was going through their minds? How would they adjust to life without their brother? Or could they? Those were questions we might not have answers to for years, if ever.

We owned two vehicles: a Ford Windstar minivan used for the many weekend activities, including soccer games, and a Toyota Camry sedan. On that morning, we took the Camry. It was my work car, which I occasionally used to take out clients and my staff, and was cleaner. As I backed out of the driveway, I paused as I passed the walkway heading to our front door. An overwhelming feeling came over me: our family never used the Camry to go anywhere. Our three boys had been far too big to cram into the backseat. But now we were a family of four. The realization hit me like a load of bricks. Two years prior, the local Fox News television affiliate had done a special on birth order and middle children and used our family as the centerpiece of their story. Cheryl Adams (Parker), a fellow board member on Prevent Child Abuse Indiana, realizing we had three boys, had asked if we would participate. "Sure," I'd said. The story had shown our three boys playing on the trampoline in the backyard and Payton and Blake taking each other on in soccer. More importantly, the piece had shared typical character traits for the middle child: competitive, generous, diplomatic, social, and flexible. They were peacemakers. As the years passed, we would come to realize that was an accurate description of Blake. As I pulled out of the driveway, I realized Blake was our oldest living child, but he was a middle child. I knew that should never change. I was a little mad, as God had made Blake a middle child, and now he'd been thrust into the role of the oldest living Leyden son. The seemingly simple act of getting in the car had created a flood of emotions.

We made the twenty-minute trip to Garfield Park to see our former church family and worship our Lord and Savior. They were not expecting to see us less than forty-eight hours after Payton's passing. Truth be told, we were in a fog. Garfield Park was the first of many communities we would grieve with in the coming days: Pike Youth Soccer Club; my employer, Arthur Andersen, and my clients; our church, Zionsville Fellowship; boards, including Indianapolis and Central Indiana Technology Partnership and the Children's Museum of Indianapolis; neighbors; friends; and the broader community, not to mention the boys' schools.

It was a blessing to share our sorrow with our friends at Garfield Park. They were surprised and pleased to see us. It was important for us to return. That was where Blake and Chase had been baptized as infants and where Payton had been confirmed. Garfield Park was where Robyn's and my faith had started to grow and where we needed to share in the grieving process with friends. More importantly, our return was also an act of obedience. The Lord had made it clear we needed to return. Often, we do not know the reason or purpose for God's promptings in our lives, but we come to find out as we follow His lead and join Him in His work.

After attending church, we headed home for lunch. We needed to spend time together as a family by ourselves and set aside all the other stuff for a while. We had plenty of food available, as our church, Zionsville Fellowship, had organized meal support at the beginning of Payton's hospitalization. We had a dining room off the kitchen but rarely ate there. Most often, we ate in the breakfast nook on a drop-leaf rosewood table given to Robyn by her dad. We sat down with a view of our smallish wooded backyard area. There was a little bit of snow on the ground surrounding the deck. The drop-leaf table was a little bruised—the result of a project gone awry as Chase, the ever-creative one, drilled a series of small indentations. Now we were a family of four. Both leaves were down—yet another reminder.

There was no hurry at lunch. We were cherishing time together. What to say? What to do? A typical blessing for the meal seemed inadequate. I knew we were all hurting, including me. Earlier that day, Ray Grahn, an elderly member of Garfield Park, had pulled me aside, grabbed me by the shoulders, looked me squarely in the eyes with his steely but soft brown eyes, and said, "Todd, love your wife, and take care of your family." It was wonderful advice, along with counsel I received in the following weeks from Margo Eccles, an elderly and prominent community leader, who said, "Men want to do, and women want to be." In other words, I could not fix this problem. Robyn and the boys needed to adjust to the new reality. It would take time. I took seriously my role as we began our new life together.

Over the weeks and months that followed, I had to gauge how much to talk about Payton and the seemingly endless ways the Lord had worked through his situation and made clear the plan for Payton and our lives. There were too many examples and situations that defied human understanding. At lunch, I shared an analogy with Robyn and the boys. I turned to the kitchen, where Robyn had a couple serving dishes on the countertop. I described to the boys the legal scales of justice, which were perfectly balanced to represent fairness in the judicial process. I said if we could take every great thing that would happen in our lives in the future—vacations, jobs, accomplishments, and more—and put it on one side of the scale, their total would never equal the loss of Payton on the other side of the scale, but I assured them we would see Payton again one day in eternity. Robyn said, "I will never have to worry again where he is." The teen years are challenging, and Payton certainly had caused us angst from time to time. Robyn was grieving, but she knew Payton was in good hands, and for that, she was thankful.

After spending time with Robyn and the boys that afternoon, I knew it was time to get to work. It was Sunday evening, a scant forty-eight hours since we'd left the hospital and less than forty-eight hours until the calling. Family would start arriving Monday night and Tuesday. Most of the funeral arrangements were covered by Keith, Crown Hill, and others. I needed to start writing a father's reflection, perhaps the most important thing I would ever write. It was an opportunity to pay tribute to Payton, reflect on God's love and comfort for us during the past five weeks, and point others to Christ Jesus as we put our faith and hope in Him. There were many things to share. I started the draft of my remarks with the following: "In the midst of sorrow, we can look at Payton's earthly death one of two ways: it stinks, or it is a great blessing." I continued to write. I am certain the Holy Spirit was not only guiding me with the words to share during my countless website posts but also providing me with extraordinary strength and stamina, as I was rarely tired. Maybe it was a five-week adrenaline rush. I worked well into the evening on my reflection and other things to prepare for the days ahead.

The next morning, Monday, I took Blake to school, and Robyn took Chase. We wanted them to return to a sense of normalcy as soon as practical. Also, we knew they would miss at least two days of school for the calling, the funeral, and time with family. Last Friday afternoon, Blake, Chase, and Meredith had visited Payton, and Blake had shared his class's get-well video; now he needed to let them know his brother had died. Blake shared with me that Payton's passing allowed me to present the gospel of Jesus Christ to family members and others who otherwise might not have heard or understood the gospel. In that respect, as Robyn had pleaded before the throne, Payton's life had had meaning.

Blake and I arrived at Guion Creek Middle School, and I put my arm around him as we entered the school. Blake's and Chase's schools were supportive during Payton's crisis. Chase's school had provided him with extra uniforms, concerned with our ability to keep up with the laundry. Blake's teacher, Mrs. Wielenski, was extraordinarily supportive. Teachers are a true treasure to our children. I walked Blake to his classroom and asked his teacher if Blake could share news about Payton with his class. Blake was a loud, happy, and engaging child. On that day, he was quiet, soft-spoken, and reserved. Blake said a few simple words as he shared the news of Payton's passing: "We are happy for Payton and sad for us."

Crown Hill Cemetery was about ten minutes from Blake's middle school, and that was the next stop on my agenda, as I needed to get a lot done prior to the arrival of friends and family. A few minutes later, I was traveling on West Thirty-Eighth Street, and off to my left were thousands of dead people, which gave me pause, as I knew my son would soon be there. I pulled into the parking lot and entered the building, a little more comfortable than I'd been during my visit two days prior. The front office staff took me downstairs to James's office. Robyn had picked out the clothes for Payton's burial. Robyn is fond of clothes; however, that was not an assignment she relished. James greeted me and asked how I was doing. It was a question I would answer often. I always wanted to give an honest and complete answer. Typically, I avoided one- or two-word answers. I wanted to be real and share what was going on and, at the same time, acknowledge our faith, trust, and comfort in the Lord, even though I knew some might have difficulty understanding.

James proceeded to go over a few details related to the calling and service, including our pickup at the house the day of the service. We would take a limousine the nearly five miles to Traders Point Church. James then broached a difficult subject. A funeral director takes great pride in caring for the body, even though the person is no longer there. His or her spirit and soul are in heaven. In that case, Payton's casket was closed. We'd made that choice as a sign of respect and a way to demonstrate dignity to the deceased and support and honor to those grieving his passing.

Indiana University had requested, and we'd approved, an autopsy on Payton's body. The IU Medical Center is a teaching hospital, and Payton's had been a complicated case. Perhaps the autopsy would aid their research efforts in such a way as to benefit future patients like Payton.

Based on the two hours I'd spent with James on Saturday, it was evident he was a caring man. He wanted to let me know he'd spent a considerable amount of time preparing Payton's body for burial and done the best he could. The combination of Payton's illness and effects, along with an autopsy that had addressed multiple organ failures and resulted in swelling in the brain, had left Payton not looking good at all. I appreciated James's concern and thanked him for doing everything he did.

I handed James a small bag of clothes: underwear, tan cargo shorts, and an Old Navy crewneck T-shirt—the outfit Payton was wearing in the picture included in the program for his service. Before I left, I gave James one final item: my watch. On Christmas Day, I'd received two gifts from Payton: a CD by Limp Bizkit (Payton had thought it was funny; I had not) and a watch. He and Robyn had gone to a jewelry store at Lafayette Square Mall near our home, and Payton had negotiated the purchase of a beautiful Seiko watch. It had been expensive, but Robyn had assured me

Eyes of the Father

Payton had done a wonderful job of negotiating and knocked at least fifty dollars or more off the price. He'd had a motive: he'd wanted my watch. I took my old watch off my wrist and gave it to James to put on Payton for him to have for eternity. For the past seventeen years, I've worn the watch he gave me that Christmas, only taking it off to sleep at night. It is a constant reminder of both the time and the time we had together, as well as the preciousness of Robyn's and his thoughtful gift and, more importantly, the gift God gave us in Payton.

Robyn was busy as well. She went shopping with her sister, Cari, to buy some special outfits for the funeral. As I said, Payton's favorite color was orange, and Robyn decided we would all wear some element of orange. Robyn, a renowned fashionista, bought some bright orange boots for herself and an orange sweater for me. She bought suits for the boys, with orange in the shirts and ties.

They also ventured to Mass Appeal, a high-end salon, so she could get her hair and nails done. The trip provided much-needed time for Robyn to care for herself, as the past five weeks had provided little, if any, opportunity to do so. That afternoon, she returned home in pretty good spirits. My wife is generally an upbeat, can-do person like her father. She was taught at an early age that you can do anything you put your mind to doing. Often, she follows the admonition "Just suck it up, get it done, and move forward." While that is noble in certain respects, it can and does mask underlying problems.

She'd received a call earlier in the day from a couple friends, Barb Baxter and Mary Midla, who wanted to come over for a visit. Barb is one of the most outspoken advocates for Jesus I have ever met. She is never at a loss to confront a total stranger with the story of Jesus and the gospel. In contrast, Mary is quiet and reserved. Mary had led Robyn's first Bible Study Fellowship (BSF) class six years prior and had a big impact on her.

I am certain we had a thousand or more hugs, cards, or conversations in the time leading up to Payton's passing, his calling and funeral, and the days to follow. However, there were certain relationships and conversations that were clearly God-ordained for that specific time. For Robyn, that was the case with Mary. It was like my relationship with Robin and Brandon Gore.

In 1994, Robyn had left the workplace and, with her faith journey just beginning, heard through her connections at Traders Point Church and preschool about the nationally recognized Bible study program BSF. Robyn's first leader, Mary, was an ideal woman for Robyn to learn under. She was thoughtful, caring, and compassionate. But again, God knew that one day Robyn would need her for another reason. Mary's teenage son had been tragically killed in a boating accident the year prior to Robyn's starting BSF, so when Mary came with Barb to visit that afternoon, they had a common experience, understanding, and grief they could share together and a joy in their relationship and perspective. Undoubtedly, the loss hurt a great deal, but the relationship God had established for that time brought great comfort to Robyn.

That evening, I went upstairs to my office to finalize my reflections for the service on Wednesday and run through it a time or two. Public speaking is something I enjoy, and I'd had some formal training during my professional career; however, this was entirely different. I had to deliver the eulogy for my son. It was one of the most important assignments of my life. I checked the website to view some of the posts. They were accelerating at a rapid pace—well over a hundred since his passing.

> From my childhood friend Todd Kemerly: "Leydens, you're a blessing to us all. God continues to use your family to demonstrate His love, strength, hope, peace, and comfort to all that you've touched through Payton's battle and victory."

> From our neighbors the Steiners: "Your deep faith and trust in our God is marvelous to observe, not in the time of joy but sorrow. From scripture, through your weakness is My (God's) strength made known. We are blessed to have such an absolute testimony and display of His truth so near. We pray Payton's spark will ignite a holy fire across this world and increase the Word of truth infinitely."

> From Nicole Wenger, a classmate of Payton's: "I know this must be a hard time for you. He is in a better place. I'm jealous that I can't be there. It would be much better than

here on earth. God will be with you and see you through this. Hang in there. I will keep you and your family in my prayers."

We are thankful Nicole was keeping us in her prayers, along with hundreds of others. Tomorrow would soon arrive and with it the calling and a time for tears, reflection, sorrow, joy, thanksgiving, comfort, encouragement, and glory to our Father in heaven all rolled into one.

Biblical Principle

The apostle Paul wrote in 2 Corinthians 5:1–8,

> For we know that if our earthly house, this tent, is destroyed, we have a building from God, a house not made with hands, eternal in the heavens. For in this we groan, earnestly desiring to be clothed with our inhabitation which is from heaven, if indeed, having been clothed, we shall not be found naked. For we who are in this tent groan, being burdened, not because we want to be unclothed, but further clothed, that mortality may be swallowed up by life. Now He who has prepared us for this very thing is God, who also has given us the Spirit as a guarantee. So we are always confident, knowing that while we are at home in the body we are absent from the Lord. For we walk by faith, not by sight. We are confident, yes, well pleased rather to be absent from the body and to be present with the Lord.

Payton's body was ravaged as a result of a microscopic infection that had made its way to his heart. Paul uses the analogy of a tent to describe our temporary physical being. A tent deteriorates in the face of changing weather and storms and needs repair. A tent also reminds us we are pilgrims here on earth, on a journey to our final destination and heavenly home.

Upon reflection, we are comforted to know that while he is not with us and is absent from his body, Payton is present with the Lord.

CHAPTER 20

A CELEBRATION OF LIFE: WORSHIP UNLIKE ANYTHING THIS SIDE OF HEAVEN

The day of the calling, February 6, arrived and with it friends and family who were grieving with us. The calling was from 4:00 p.m. to 8:00 p.m. at Traders Point Christian Church. Payton and Blake previously had attended school there, and Chase would the following year. It was a comfortable venue, given our relationship with the church and the many close friends who attended there. Most importantly, the sanctuary was big, able to seat almost one thousand people. We did not know what to expect, but we anticipated a large crowd.

We pulled into the parking lot a little after three o'clock, and there was a beehive of activity, as school was letting out for the day. As I walked through the parking lot, my mind took me to the field day a couple years prior when Payton and his classmates had enjoyed a spring afternoon on the expansive grounds surrounding the church and school.

We opened the doors and entered the lobby. Robyn was startled, as right in front of her was a sign: Payton Leyden Calling. Intellectually, we both knew where we were going and why we were there, but the reality of Payton's funeral, burial and our loss was starting to set in. After pausing for a few seconds, we headed to the administrative offices. Sandy Whybrew, an assistant on the church staff, greeted us and offered her condolences and help with anything we needed. Her daughter Kris had been one of Payton's teachers. She led us to the room where family could gather. There were snacks and drinks in the room, another act of kindness extended to us. We then walked a short distance to the sanctuary and entered the center doors.

We were familiar with the building but less so with the sanctuary, as we'd attended only a couple Sunday services. The audio-visual technician was playing the music loop that would greet our friends and family in an hour, and we heard the familiar sound of Creed, one of Payton's favorite bands. Our eyes then turned and looked to the front of the sanctuary. The casket was in front of the stage, prominent in the center of the massive sanctuary. It was beautifully adorned with about fifty floral arrangements, with many including Payton's favorite color: orange. We walked slowly up to the front of the room. We did not want to focus on the casket or the fact that Payton was inside it, but it was hard not to. We knew Payton was in heaven, though his earthly body was but feet away. We quickly moved over to the side of the casket where two barstool chairs were situated. A flood of emotions raced through our heads: his school years and time spent on the playground outside, friends and family who would gather soon, the events of the past thirty-three days, and so on. The funeral was tomorrow. Unfortunately, there was no turning back.

The next forty-eight hours were a virtual blur: the calling; the funeral; the burial; the meal that followed; and a special dinner hosted by my employer, Arthur Andersen, for family and close friends. By Friday morning—one week after the phone call in the middle of the night and Payton's passing—it was all over.

Upon reflection, I will share four lasting impressions of those forty-eight hours:

Loved

John 3:16, one of the most well-known verses in the Bible, says, "For God so loved the world that He gave His only begotten Son, that whoever believes in Him should not perish but have everlasting life." It is hard to fathom the Author and Creator of the universe and all things in it sending His only Son to die for us. That is how He showed His love for us. If that was an expression of God's love, we received a taste, a beautiful view of His love, during our difficult time. The best analogy I can provide is this: imagine standing under Niagara Falls, with the approximate seven hundred thousand gallons of water cascading down onto your body every second of the day. That is the love we received during the time of Payton's illness and passing, and it reached a crescendo during the calling and funeral service.

Hundreds upon hundreds of people showed up for the calling. Traders Point is a large facility. The line of well-wishers stretched through the sanctuary and out the door into the hallway for four hours. We wanted to spend time with each person to let him or her know we were okay and rekindle a relationship, but time was not our friend. We would learn later many had to leave, given the length of the wait. Around seven thirty in the evening, prompted by the advice of two partners at Arthur Andersen, Derrick Burks and Tom Ertel, the people in remaining in line, one hundred or more, came into the sanctuary, and I spoke from my heart about Payton, our love for them, and our disappointment we could not greet every person individually. The funeral was more of the same.

After the calling, we returned home to an exquisite meal prepared by a local chef for about thirty family and friends. My seven-year-old son asked who'd provided the meal, and I said, "My employer, Arthur Andersen."

Chase responded, "You are fortunate to work for them—they are a good company."

I thought, *Wow. My seven-year-old son gets it!*

Worship

John 4:23–24 says, "But the hour is coming, and now is, when the true worshipers will worship the Father in spirit and truth; for the Father is seeking such to worship Him. God is Spirit, and those who worship Him must worship in spirit and truth." Jesus is telling His disciples how and whom they should worship, and that truth is in harmony with the nature and will of God. Most importantly, Christ is saying worship is a matter of the heart.

I never had experienced worship like Payton's service before, and I haven't since. Quite simply, I was in the presence of the Lord. There was an intimacy with God beyond my human comprehension. My heart was on fire, wrestling between the profound sadness of the loss and the inexplicable joy of God's care for us, which He'd exhibited in many, many ways.

The *Indianapolis Star* covered the story and dedicated most of the front page of the City / State section. They described the service as follows: "It seemed fitting that musicians invited to play in Payton's honor broke into upbeat Christian rock songs at the memorial, which Zionsville Fellowship Church Pastor Keith Ogorek categorized as 'not like any funeral service you've ever been to.' The audience brightened the otherwise somber occasion with rousing applause and danced and tapped their feet to the music. 'This is a celebration of life,' funeral director James Dixon said. 'This is victory over death. So, I am asking you all to applaud for Payton.'"

The article continued with reflections from Payton's classmates at New Augusta Middle School. Megan Iudice said, "He was the kind of person who always wanted to help people. He was very religious, and I think that's what made him special."

Melissa Gammon said Payton's advice to turn to the church had prevented her from committing suicide a year ago. "He saved my life."

Todd Leyden

"I know he's in a better place now. God has a bigger plan for Payton than me."
Todd Leyden

Teen's short yet full life celebrated

■ Payton Leyden died suddenly of staph infection, but he made a lasting impression with his faith.

By Michael J. Rochon
STAFF WRITER

Todd Leyden slowly approached the small podium overlooking his son's casket, then gazed down for what seemed like an eternity.

"I know he's in a better place now," he said with a smile. "God has a bigger plan for Payton than me."

Words of praise, standing ovations and seemingly endless tears marked Wednesday's funeral for Payton Leyden, an outgoing 13-year-old from the Westside who died last week from complications due to a staph infection.

More than 300 people — including dozens of teary-eyed classmates — packed Traders Point Christian Church to celebrate the life of a youth who affected his peers through his strong faith and Christian upbringing.

"He was the kind of person who always wanted to help people," said fellow New Augusta Middle School student Megan Judice, her eyes red and swollen from crying. "He was very religious, and I think that's what made him so special."

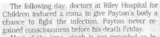
Payton Leyden, 13, died from complications due to a staph infection.

Starnews.com
■ Web link: The online version of this story links to the Web site that friends created for Payton Leyden.

Another classmate, Melissa Gammon, said Payton's advice to turn to the church prevented her from committing suicide a year ago. "He saved my life."

Friends said Payton was a gifted guitarist and hoped to form a band. He talked of becoming a mega rock star one day — just like his idols Jimi Hendrix and Creed.

It seemed fitting that musicians invited to play in Payton's honor broke into upbeat Christian rock songs at the memorial, which Zionsville Fellowship Church Pastor Keith Ogorek categorized as "not like any funeral service you've ever been to."

The audience brightened the otherwise somber occasion with rousing applause and danced and tapped their feet to the music.

"This is a celebration of life," funeral director James Dixon said. "This is a victory over death. So I am asking all of you to applaud for Payton."

Payton was diagnosed with staph on New Year's Day when his family took him to the emergency room with flulike symptoms, said his mother, Robyn Leyden.

The following day, doctors at Riley Hospital for Children induced a coma to give Payton's body a chance to fight the infection. Payton never regained consciousness before his death Friday.

Most of the time, staph is not regarded as lethal. But in Payton's case, the infection coupled with an existing heart condition proved fatal.

During his bout with staph, Payton's family created a Web site so that his classmates could get daily updates on his condition, as well as send him get-well messages via e-mail.

In offering a tribute to his son, Todd Leyden said Payton's friends should view his death as the ultimate reward for all of his good deeds.

"We can look at Payton's death in one of two ways: It stinks, or it's a great blessing," he said. "God's plan for Payton was for 13 years ... and that's OK."

Contact Michael J. Rochon at (317) 444-6083 or via e-mail at michael.rochon@starnews.com

Music had been important to Payton. He'd been gifted. The band assembled for the service comprised eight members, representing our current and former churches and his eighth-grade music teacher. They'd had one opportunity to practice prior to the service. They hit a home run! Their performance was beautiful, and God honoring and will live with me for the rest of my life.

Worship is more than music. We worship God with our tithes and offerings, the way we represent Christ, the lives we live, and the words we share. All we do is an act of worship to our Creator God. Keith officiated the service and did a brilliant job. LaMarr Davis and Ndidi Musa were the other principal contributors offering reflection and prayer. They are two of the most fervent people of prayer I know.

Impact

First Peter 1:6–7 says, "In this you greatly rejoice, though now for a little while, if need be, you have been grieved by various trials, that the genuineness of your faith, being much more precious than gold that perishes, though it is tested by fire, may be found to praise, honor, and glory at the revelation of Jesus Christ." That had been the teaching at family camp at Fort Wilderness six months prior. Now we were seeing it lived out. If we are placed in a situation of trial, how will our faith point people to Jesus? Intellectually, this is challenging scripture. Living this out is seemingly impossible. What if the trial results in your oldest son's death? With a medical condition that typically results in death in a few days to a week but plays itself out in dramatic fashion over the course of thirty-three days? In God's economy, what if this situation only brings one individual to a saving belief in His son, Jesus? How many people would need to come to a saving faith in Jesus for this to be worth the cost? Thankfully, we do not have to answer that question, because we are incapable of doing so. We just need to seek Him with our whole heart, as Moses records in Deuteronomy 6:5: "You shall love the LORD your God with all your heart, with all your soul, and with all your strength. And these words which I command you today shall be in your heart. You shall teach them diligently to your children and shall talk of them when you sit in your house, when you walk by the way, when you lie down, and when you rise."

I shared the following during my time of reflection at the funeral service. A classmate of Payton's shared the following post: "Dear Leydens, right now I have such a deep jealousy of Payton because he was able to escape this sinful world. But we will be there someday too."

Another classmate, Abby Maci, wrote, "Dear Leyden family, I was very sad to hear of Payton's death, but thank God he is in heaven now and feels no more pain. He is in the greatest place imaginable. I know I can't wait to be up there with him. Payton was lucky because for him, he only had to spend a short time on earth before he was able to go to heaven. We will all still miss him but rejoice that he is in heaven. I will continue to pray for you and your family that God will watch over you and comfort you."

Those two young ladies, one fourteen and the other thirteen, both understood the brevity of life here and our eternal home and reward.

There were other notable impacts. James Dixon told me he'd participated in many funerals but could only recall one other service with a longer processional to the grave site, a service for a fallen officer. In addition, there was the possibility of building a medical facility in Payton's honor at Fort Wilderness. Fort was in a capital campaign, and renderings of Payton's Place were available the day of the calling and for the celebration-of-life service.

Dr. Ndidi Musa questioned in the days ahead why Payton had lived so long virtually on the edge of death to ultimately lose his life. As his cardiologist had shared, he'd been the sickest kid in Riley Children's Hospital. Typically, patients in his condition live a few days, perhaps a week. He had overcome huge obstacles during his hospitalization: a staph aureus infection, which had created a vegetation on his heart that had pumped toxins through his bloodstream, ultimately shutting down and damaging many of his vital organs; a five-hour surgery when the staff did not want to transport him for a CT scan; multiple collapsed lungs; and so on. Each day, his life had hung by a thread, yet he'd continued to survive. Ndidi ultimately concluded, "Todd, Payton lived so long to reach so many for Jesus Christ." Amen.

Since Payton's passing, I have had a personal mission statement to further the gospel of Jesus Christ in the community in which I live. The situation with Payton was not my idea of how I would accomplish the

Lord's purpose. To describe the position I was put in, I have shared with many an analogy of a game we played at recess while growing up. The game was called red rover and there were two teams. Each team would form a line with interlocking arms. One team would yell out the name of a team member in the other line, notably someone viewed as a weak link, and shout the following: "Red rover, red rover, send so-and-so right over!" That person would run across and try to break the chain. If successful, he or she returned to his or her side. If unsuccessful, the individual joined the chain he or she had tried to break. In the same way, I never would have considered stepping out in faith with the loss of my son for the advancement of the gospel. But that is exactly what Christ expects of us if we are put in that situation.

The impact continued in the days, weeks, and months to follow. There is a popular adage about things happening in threes. Robyn and I were humbled and brought to tears when we heard from three former classmates seventeen years later, during the time of my writing. Their stories are as follows:

- We received a letter dated February 2, 2018, from Liz Maci. We have known Liz for twenty years. She is the mother of Abby, the young lady referenced above. In her note, she shared the following:

  I was doing some cleaning / purging and came across this treasure. I was reminded of what a beautiful boy Payton was. I was also reminded of the way the two of you led so many young people and their parents through a difficult-to-understand event with such love and grace. If I remember correctly, February 2 is the anniversary. I hope that time has made his passing more bearable for you. With Abby's permission and love, we want you to have this sweet note. We hope that it is a blessing to you.

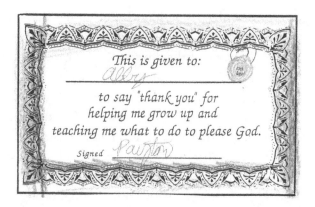

- The same month, Robyn received an instant message from someone asking if her son had played the bass guitar at New Augusta North Academy and worn black-rimmed glasses. Robyn was a little leery and, after talking it over with me, proceeded cautiously with her response. She said, "Yes. Why do you ask?" The person, Stacy Saunders, said, "Payton used to stop by to look at my Van Gogh painting and was so complimentary of my work." She went on to say, "One day he stopped coming by, and I wondered if he did not like me." Robyn was perplexed, as Payton's illness and passing had been widely known to the public, and she thought Stacy surely would have known. Robyn shared with Stacy that Payton had passed away and then told her more of the details of what had happened. Stacy had gone on to high school and always wondered about Payton. Robyn provided her with additional comfort, including sharing about her journey of faith, and said she hoped Stacy had closure. Stacy said she was sorry for our loss. Payton had meant a lot to her.
- On September 14, 2018, I received an email message from Donna Bays. Donna and her children, Jennifer and Steven, were neighbors and lived on the same cul-de-sac where Payton had lived most of his life. Payton and Steven often had conspired to do interesting things together that would cause us to pause at their ingenuity and gumption. Donna shared the following:

Eyes of the Father

On two separate nights recently, I woke up in the middle of the night with a message beaming out, telling me to reach out and share the following with you. It felt a little odd the first time because we haven't spoken in years. But after the second time, I couldn't ignore it and decided that I was supposed to reach out to you. Steven and his wife, Jessica, are expecting their first child. It's a little boy. They plan to name him Payton Alexander, in honor of your son. And the due date is December 25—the day we celebrate Jesus's birth. I get emotional when I think about the fact that little Payton picked Jesus's birthday for his own. That feels so significant, even if the birth ultimately occurs on a different day. I can't convince myself that it's any type of coincidence and just keep getting the message that you would want to know this: that baby Payton and baby Jesus are sharing that special date.

Steven sent a letter to us a few days later and shared the following:

When Payton passed away, I made a promise to him that I would name my firstborn son after him. I never wanted to forget him and all the fun, joy, and occasional mischief I had with him when we were growing up. I can't say how my son will turn out, but I hope that he grows up with the same love and passion for the world I remember your son having.

Words cannot describe our joy upon seeing the impact Payton's life continues to have to this day.

Time: Earth and Heaven
Psalm 39:4–8 says,

Lord, make me to know my end, And what is the measure of my days, That I may know how frail I am. Indeed, You have made my days as handbreadths. And my age is as nothing before You; Certainly every man at his best state is but vapor. Surely every man walks about like a shadow; Surely they busy themselves in vain; He heaps up riches And does not know who will gather them. And now, Lord, what do I wait for? My hope is in You. Deliver me from all my transgressions; Do not make me the reproach of the foolish.

This was the scripture we included in the bulletin for Payton's celebration of life.

Understanding our purpose and our time on earth in the context of the Christian scriptures was what had convicted me for Christ ten years prior, specifically the book of Ecclesiastes. Solomon, the author of the book, was deemed the wisest man in the world. The book addresses questions, such as the meaning of life and our time on earth and declares the futility of an existence apart from God. Once I read Ecclesiastes, I was able to understand and accept the Christian faith and our short time here on earth.

Thousands of books are written analyzing and dissecting the Christian scriptures. Old Testament prophecies proclaiming the coming of Christ were fulfilled exactly as foretold. There is no logical explanation for the creation of the universe and all that is in it except Almighty God. Unfortunately, people of faith, Christians included, are not always good representatives of God and His teachings in the biblical scriptures. We are not God. We do not have the mind of God. We do not have the desires of God. God created us to live under Him and His authority. Outside of eternity, this life is not fair. The Rolling Stones song "You Can't Always Get What You Want" ends with the following: "You just might find you get what you need." In my family's case, God gave us what we needed, even though it was not what we wanted. Robyn, a big fan of the Rolling Stones, shortly after Payton's passing, remarked, "I will never have to worry where he is." Robyn had great comfort in knowing he was in heaven. She missed him desperately but also recognized she would not have to worry about a precocious teenage boy and what he was doing.

I shared the following at Payton's service: "Some might say Payton was too young to die. Yeah, I would agree. But at what age is it okay? Twenty-five, forty, sixty, eighty-two, or ninety-eight? Life is precious each day. Payton is in heaven with the Lord, and we know this, as Payton confessed Jesus Christ as his Lord and Savior." Regarding his earthly days, I remarked, "Typically or hopefully, a father gets eighteen years to live with his children before the child moves out of the house. As Keith shared with me, a father is called to do four things: prepare, protect, direct, and enjoy your children." We were able to prepare, protect, direct, and enjoy Payton for thirteen years. That was God's plan for Payton.

Perhaps the most prescient message I conveyed was God's gift of the time we could spend with Payton during his hospitalization: "We had thirty-three more days with Payton. To love him, support him, and spend time with him. Now, he could not talk to us, and that was sad, but he also could not talk back to us either. And thirteen wonderful years!"

I closed my eulogy with the following tribute on behalf of Robyn, Blake, and Chase:

> It hurts more than you will ever know,
> To see your firstborn son, go.
> But with God, there is a perfect plan
> That man cannot understand.
> We love Payton with all of our heart,
> Yet now it is time to part.
> We are proud of your life here on earth
> And cherished each moment from your birth.
> You will always be a special part of our lives,
> And we look forward to seeing you when we die.
> But through death and Christ's ultimate sacrifice,
> You gain life eternal in paradise.
> So for now, we must say goodbye.
> To say it does not hurt would be to lie.
> We look forward to seeing you again.
> You are our son, brother, and special friend.
> We love you, Payton!
> Dad, Mom, Blake, and Chase

Too often, funerals are the end of the story. But there were amazing things waiting for us after Payton was gone. Yes, the day of the funeral was a horrible day, but God was continuing to work on a bigger plan.

CHAPTER 21

LIFE IS FOR THE LIVING

What now? Thirty-three days in the hospital were over. Planning and preparations for the funeral were done. The calling and service and emotion-filled embraces with hundreds of friends and family now were in the rearview mirror. Payton had been gone but a week. Robyn would remark in the days following Payton's passing, "Life is for the living." There is nothing we can do to change or erase the past. She could only manage the pain. Profound? Yes. Insensitive? No. We needed to move forward while we grieved the loss of our beloved Payton, and equally important, we needed to support our boys, family, and countless friends and community members who were also struggling with Payton's passing. We also needed to adjust to our new reality. It did not seem fair, but no one ever said life was fair, and as I'd learned the prior summer, if suffering brings glory to God through the revelation of Jesus Christ, we are to rejoice. That had been the furthest thing from my mind as I walked the hallway back to meet Robyn and leave Riley Hospital for the last time.

Our family and friends were leaving, but there was one more thing to do. My grandfather Dale was good at calling command meetings. When I was growing up, he'd been a great example for me of a man who worked hard and cared for others. He was German and not prone to a lot of emotion, except for the night I'd called him to tell him Payton had passed away. He'd sobbed like a baby. He wanted to meet me for breakfast before he and his second wife, Verlene, headed home to Michigan. He was intrigued by the memorial for Payton. About seven years prior, he'd finalized a multiyear fund-raising effort to build a new ATO chapter house at his alma mater, Iowa State. He and Verlene had spent countless hours, including sending forty thousand letters to ATO brothers, to raise $1 million. He wanted to share his insight with respect to raising money and offered his and Verlene's personal support. First, he wanted to talk to me about the importance of a lead gift. I had a good amount of experience with serving on the boards of several not-for-profits and was familiar with traditional fund-raising strategies. I was polite as I listened to him and Verlene, but I knew Payton's Place was going to happen. The Lord's hand was evident in everything else. Surely, He would provide the necessary funds. We needed to do our part. Nevertheless, Grandad sent me a letter several weeks later with the following questions.

> Dear Todd and Robyn—re: Payton's Place
>
> We need answers to these questions as a guide to our financial participation. Please be factual.
>
> - Total cost of building?
> - How many square feet?
> - Total money donated through March 31, 2001?
> - Any unpaid pledges?
> - What use will be made of the building?
> - Who will own the building?
> - Who will pay for building maintenance?
> - Who and what is camp wilderness?
>
> Love,
Grandad and Verlene

Some might question Grandad and Verlene's letter (we know it was Grandad's letter), but he wanted to make sure the project was a success and, more importantly, provide a legacy to Payton through a much-needed medical facility at Fort Wilderness. Sure enough, the goal was raised and then some in the following month: $85,000, including a $10,000 gift from Grandad and Verlene. I guess we had been able to satisfactorily answer his questions. We made plans to travel 520 miles to Fort Wilderness on

September 7–9, 2001, with a crew of volunteers, including family, friends, and members of Zionsville Fellowship, to frame the building and roof.

The following weeks and months would result in a gradual reentry to normal life. Robyn needed to take down the Christmas decorations on display—about six weeks later than normal. Various girlfriends offered to take her to lunch. One of the most difficult tasks was to return Payton's Christmas gifts. Peggy Macke, Scott's stepmother, accompanied Robyn to Meridian Music to return a hundred-dollar gift certificate and explain the reason for doing so. She made shopping trips, including buying the boys new comforters for their rooms—anything to keep her mind off the past month. Most everyone was kind and supportive. I did have an odd phone call when I contacted our internet provider and explained my desire to cancel our service. The customer service agent, as was often the norm, kept pressing me, trying to keep me on their plan. Finally, I said, "My son died, and he was the one who used the internet almost exclusively." The representative then said he was sorry for our loss and asked what had happened. I explained, as I always wanted to take an opportunity to share the story and our faith. My explanation did not end the conversation, as the representative asked if we'd considered suing the hospital. That quickly ended the conversation!

My employer was gracious in allowing me whatever time I needed prior to returning to work. Dick Culp, our human resource manager, agreed to my request of a February 26 return date. Andersen was swamped with the year-end audit and tax busy season. That date would allow me ample time to deal with a myriad of details, including filing for death benefits, notifying Social Security, and so forth, let alone returning to the normalcy of life, including caring for our family. My scheduled return date was exactly two months after I last had worked.

The extended time would also allow me to travel to Lansing, Michigan, on February 23 to see my grandmother Violet. I was close to my grandmother, and she had been unable to attend the service, given ninety-three years of life. My grandfather, her ex-husband, had requested my help in negotiating a revision to his alimony agreement that would allow him to liquidate or release assets in exchange for a lump-sum payout to my grandmother. He figured that would benefit both parties. I am certain that addressing a financial transaction between my grandparents, who'd spent thirty-nine years together in marriage, was not on the top of my to-do list, but I agreed to do so.

Grandma Vi became severely ill a couple days before my planned trip. Her bus driver, concerned she was not at the stop as per routine, went to the front door, saw her lying on the floor, and called for emergency help. She was severely dehydrated to the point she was unable to lift herself off the floor. My brothers and I quickly agreed she was in no shape to continue living on her own, so with Robyn's support, I brought Grandma Vi and a few belongings back to Indianapolis to stay with us until we could figure out what to do next. We were less than three weeks removed from burying our son, and now my grandmother was coming to live with us. It was the right thing to do, even if it was the worst time for us to take on the added responsibility. I loved my grandma, and she needed our help. Her situation did cause me to reflect on when the proper time was to check out of this life. Salvation in Jesus Christ and the promise of an eternal home with our Lord is the only answer. Affliction can and does happen at any age.

We met Dr. Seferian a few weeks later to review the autopsy results. Our rationale, in large part, was a desire to continue the relationship with someone who had done so much for our son. We were not particularly interested one way or the other about the cause of death.

On a March morning, Robyn and I headed back to Riley for the first time since Payton's passing. I had an odd feeling devoid of anticipation or a sense of urgency; rather, the meeting was just another thing to check off the list.

We arrived at the hospital, and unlike prior trips, we did not immediately head to ICU 4 North. We met Dr. Seferian in one of the common areas. Before we got to the business at hand, we got caught up on life, as friends do. After all, Ed was now a friend. I think starting our time together that way put him and us at ease.

Dr. Seferian spoke in a measured and scholarly tone as he shared the results of the autopsy and primary cause of death: sepsis, acute respiratory distress syndrome, and bacterial endocarditis. He then said, "It is rare for an airplane to fall from the sky, but it happens. And it is rare, perhaps one in a million, that a staph infection would make its way to the VSD in Payton's heart." His voice trailed off. The vegetation on Payton's heart had showered emboli throughout his body and into his lungs. Essentially, Dr.

Seferian concluded, Payton's death had been inevitable. It had been as if a bomb went off in his body. It was evident Payton had endured significant damage to his body and vital organs. Payton had been a picker, and Robyn and I surmised some scab he'd picked open had allowed the staph infection, which is present on many of our bodies, to enter his bloodstream and make its way to his heart.

The National Institute of Health describes sepsis as "the presence in tissues of harmful bacteria and their toxins, typically through infection of a wound. Severe sepsis strikes more than one million Americans every year and between 15 and 30 percent die. In the worst cases [like Payton's], blood pressure drops, the heart weakens, and the patient spirals toward septic shock, which then can result in multiple organ failure."[5] The Mayo Clinic describes acute respiratory distress syndrome (ARDS) as "a condition in which fluid collects in the lungs' air sacs, depriving organs of oxygen. This is a rare condition occurring in less than 200,000 patients in the US each year."[6] The American Heart Association website describes bacterial endocarditis as "an infection caused by bacteria that enter the bloodstream and settle in the heart lining, a heart valve or a blood vessel. It is uncommon, but people with some heart conditions have a greater risk of developing it."[7]

In retrospect, it was medically surprising he'd lived so long. But as Dr. Musa had concluded shortly after Payton's passing, "Payton lived so long to reach so many," like the countless examples of lives impacted throughout this story. That was the miracle—not the miracle we'd been looking for but perhaps God's miracle to provide those thirty-three days for us to love Payton, care for him, and put our trust in the One who'd created him. For that, we are eternally thankful.

One of the most difficult things to handle was any special day: a birthday, a vacation, Christmas, Thanksgiving, and the date of Payton's death. We decided we were going to use those dates to celebrate, as best as we could, Payton's life.

Payton's birthday was May 15, a little more than three months after his passing. We made big plans that required some help from Robyn's dad. Mike was an excellent cook particularly accomplished in hosting hog roasts to benefit a needy family or organization. We thought a hog roast with all the trimmings was the perfect way to celebrate Payton's birthday with the staff at Riley Children's Hospital and to thank them for their efforts. After all, more than two hundred staff had worked on Payton. It was the least we could do. Riley's administration was appreciative of our offer and graciously did the necessary legwork to obtain the required permits for the event to take place on their campus. It was a great joy for our family to see the staff again and profoundly thank them for the love, care, and excellent support they'd provided to our family and son. In the years to come, I was a frequent speaker at certain events and on various radio programs in support of their annual fund-raising efforts, particularly an annual dance marathon with college students.

That evening, we continued the celebration and headed a couple blocks south to watch our local AAA baseball team play in their beautiful downtown stadium. It was a crystal-clear evening to go to the ballpark with about forty family and friends. I do not remember much about the game except for two things: our ten-year-old son Blake threw out the first pitch, and one of my closest friends and spiritual mentors, Tim Doyle, had his first date with Becky Senter. Nine months later, they would marry, and we found out she was from Bremen, Indiana, the same small town of five thousand people in north central Indiana where my wife grew up. It is a small world.

The biggest hurdle would arrive in July: our annual family vacation to Fort Wilderness. Friday, July 13, our stuff was packed, and we would leave the next morning to journey to Fort Wilderness for our fifth year in a row of family camp—but our first without Payton. Our bags were packed, and we were ready to go. Late that afternoon, Robyn came to me in tears and said, "I cannot go." She had my attention, as she rarely cries and is an advocate for sucking it up and getting over your problem. She said, "I just can't be around all those people. I need to go somewhere where nobody knows us, and we can spend time as a family. It is too soon."

We changed course, literally and figuratively, and started searching the internet for other places to go. We decided to go 780 miles in the other direction to Myrtle Beach, South Carolina. We found an available unit in a high-rise on the beach. We unpacked our suitcases filled with clothes suitable for Northwoods camping and cool nights and repacked with shorts, T-shirts, and swimsuits. We were excited and looking forward to spending a week at the beach.

About an hour before we arrived, I asked Robyn about attending church the next morning. She was not thrilled at the prospect of going to a southern Baptist church in a community she did not know while on vacation. We arrived a little after seven o'clock in the evening and threw our stuff in the room, and the boys and I went down to the Jacuzzi and lazy river. Within a few minutes, we heard an African American man singing: "Lord, I lift your name up high. I love to sing your praises. You came from …" He did not know the words. I am downright awful at knowing the words to any song, but I knew that one, and I helped him, and his family sing the rest of the verses—without the hand motions, as we were in the lazy river! He was part of the Bass and Allen families, who'd gathered for a family reunion. I remembered seeing their names on the outdoor sign when we arrived at the lobby to check in. He invited us to join their family the following morning for a worship service on their patio and deck. I agreed. Later, I told Robyn, "Honey, guess where we are going to church tomorrow morning." We joined about fifty Bass and Allen family members, all a different race than our own, and I shared our testimony and the story of Payton. The man who'd invited us shared from Revelation 2:4: "I have this against you, that you have left your first love." The message was about the need to witness to the world.

We had one final surprise in October. Robyn returned from Walmart with pictures she'd dropped off for development from the fall of 2000, almost a year earlier. We are not always the timeliest people in getting things done, but that year, we had an excuse. There were twenty-four pictures—plenty of Blake and Chase but only one with Payton. It was a picture of the three boys on an ottoman in front of the television, playing a video game, looking at something supernatural on the screen. The photo, taken from behind, was a visible reminder we had three sons; however, we could not see one of them right now. Yet we knew he lived with Christ. God comforted us as He provided that glimpse of Payton but protected us from seeing a direct image of him.

Payton was no longer with us, but his spirit would live on. The coming year would bring a new chapter in my business life after seventeen years at Arthur Andersen and with it a highly improbable opportunity to do something to honor Payton and forge a new path in my career.

Biblical Principle

The apostle Paul wrote in Philippians 1:21–26,

> For to me, to live is Christ, and to die is gain. But if I live on in the flesh, this will mean fruit from my labor; yet what I shall choose I cannot tell. For I am hard-pressed between the two, having a desire to depart and be with Christ, which is far better. Nevertheless to remain in the flesh is more needful for you. And being confident of this, I know that I shall remain and continue with you all for your progress and joy of faith, that your rejoicing for me may be more abundant in Jesus Christ by my coming to you again.

Paul was saying the goal is to be with Christ in heaven. However, while we are alive, we have work to do, particularly sharing life together, as well as the joy and progress in each other's faith journey. Upon reflection, while we look forward to a reunion with Payton and our heavenly Father one day, we are thankful for the opportunity to live our lives for Him and share our story to help others who need encouragement in the face of big or small trials.

CHAPTER 22

PAYTON LLC: A PROVIDENTIAL CONVICTION

In the spring of 2001, a few months after Payton's passing, Bryon Parnell, a coworker at Arthur Andersen and key member of my Business Process Outsourcing (BPO) team, came to me to discuss his concern with the strategic fit of BPO within the Arthur Andersen Business Unit. The reason for Bryon's concern was a relatively innocuous remark made by our firm's CEO, Joe Beradino, who had been quoted in the *London Financial Times* and indicated Business Processing Outsourcing, one of nine strategic service lines, was not a critical part of the firm's future growth plans. Bryon and I had launched that practice area a year prior, in April 2000, with Volatus Technology Advisors as our first client. Starting the BPO practice had been a clear answer to prayer, and we'd landed a significant outsourcing arrangement with Midwest ISO (MISO). This project involved a collaboration with Tom Peterson of the Los Angeles office, who had been my first supervisor when I'd interned seventeen years prior in 1984. Migrating to lead BPO had meant foregoing continued leadership of our high-tech practice, which brought with it a significant amount of community visibility and was the "in" thing, coming on the heels of Mayor Goldsmith's High Technology Task Force effort. BPO, on the other hand, was not particularly glamorous or sexy but appeared to have good opportunities for growth and development.

By the summer of 2001, our BPO practice had two strategic clients:

MISO and Covance Central Laboratories, or Covance, with estimated annual billings for outsourced services of $2.5 million, not to mention the lucrative consulting revenues. We provided strategic solutions for both and eventually had about twenty-five full-time staff. However, that size of client paled in comparison to the larger outsourcing clients served by Andersen Consulting, and the firm concluded it was not in their strategic interest to grow that practice area due to the margins generated in that type of work. However, the firm did not say they were closing or divesting the practice.

Bryon asked me how we were going to grow a practice, recruit clients, and develop our staff's careers if BPO was not a strategic practice within the firm. Given Payton's recent passing, it was not the right time to think about a job change or leaving the only firm I had worked for. Furthermore, the leadership and people at Arthur Andersen had been so supportive of me and my family during Payton's illness and passing. Many were friends. But Bryon had a point. I had to address the concern with our local office leadership.

In November, I shared my concern during my annual review with our assurance (audit) practice division head, Tom Ertel, who consulted with the office managing partner, Derrick Burks. Both men, whom I trusted, assured me MISO and Covance were strategic clients. In fact, they were just the type of clients we wanted from their discussions with the central region managing partner, Jim Kackley, a member of the firm's board. That was good enough for me. But Bryon persisted and could not understand how we could strategically grow a practice if it was not strategic to the firm. We agreed to table the discussion, as Robyn and I were planning an extended vacation during the latter part of January and early February, which was the one-year anniversary of Payton's hospitalization and passing. It was the wrong time to take on the matter. I already had experienced the death of a child, which often could result in marital and family challenges, and I did not need to add a job change to the mix. But the Holy Spirit was convicting me to resolve the issue. I assured Bryon I would continue to pray, and we would meet after my family returned from our trip. Bryon was supportive and did not want to add any undue pressure on our family.

Another complicating factor, global in nature, was with the firm itself. Andersen had established a reputation in its eighty-eight-year history as the preeminent professional services firm. Unlike the other Big Eight firms at the time, it never had merged with a sizable firm, and it had a strong culture centered on client service and the founder's maxim: "Think straight, talk straight." As the years progressed, challenged by Andersen Consulting's success and ultimate independence, the audit and tax partners felt increasing pressure to grow revenues and profitability, which put the firm in the crosshairs of a corporate bully, Enron, who wanted to play fast with the accounting rules. There was rampant speculation in the markets relative to Enron's earnings and how they were attained. In October, two months prior, Enron had had a massive restatement of earnings, which had led to a precipitous fall in their stock price. Weeks later, Enron had filed the then largest bankruptcy in US history.

Three days prior to Christmas, I visited Derrick Burks's home. I needed to review the Covance contract with him, which would expand our outsourcing arrangement and hire seventeen Covance employees to join our team. Covance, a marquee client, was a contract research organization that provided the world's largest central laboratory network. It was a win for both of us. Covance was able to restructure its billing and pricing operations, have a contractual guarantee to manage a critical business operation, and manage their headcount. The proposed arrangement would allow us to hire Covance employees who would fit into our team and structure the right solution.

The primary reason for the visit was to get Derrick's assurance our office remained committed to those types of engagements, as we were now hiring client personnel and impacting their livelihoods. I had known Derrick since I started my career at Andersen. I respected Derrick. His integrity, work ethic and commitment to client service was a powerful example to all who worked for him. He had achieved great success in his career despite an embedded disadvantage because of his race. His athletic sleight build and infectious smile belied his competitive and direct manner. I wanted Derrick's commitment. He gave his enthusiastic support. Derrick was a man I could trust. He was not prone to doublespeak and said what was on his mind. So, we moved forward.

Christmas was a somber occasion for our family. Everyone knew the elephant in the room: Payton was not with us. We tried our best, but it was not the same. We celebrated with my brothers and their families and

Robyn's parents, aunt, and sister and her family. My sister-in-law Peggy worked for Arthur Andersen as well, having joined the firm in March 1996 after my introduction to Business Consulting leadership in Chicago, Pat Dolan and Edgardo Pappacena. During our family get-together at Christmas, I said to Peg, "I have more certainty I will see Payton in heaven than Arthur Andersen will be around in one year." At that time, not many, if any, were predicting that a global $9.3 billion firm with eighty-five thousand employees would cease to exist in the coming year.[8] However, my view of Enron's recent bankruptcy, Andersen's involvement and continued fight with the government, and large corporate clients' desire not to get into the crosshairs of a protracted public fight gave me pause, as the dominoes could fall quickly, like the proverbial run on the banks that had occurred in the early twentieth century—and that had been in a pre–social media world!

January brought mixed emotions, as we were now reliving the time when Payton had been in the hospital, and we were anxiously awaiting our family vacation to Florida and a respite from the dreary winter weather in Central Indiana. Andersen, which had approved Enron's financial reports and continued to resist governmental intervention, saw its reputation smeared alongside Enron's massive problems. Major US and international Fortune 500 companies were starting to pause at having a relationship with an embattled CPA firm, and some long-term clients announced their intention to leave long-term relationships with our firm.

Finally, the last week of January arrived, and I could put aside the problems of Arthur Andersen and the future of the Business Process Outsourcing practice and focus on my family. We were going to make a thousand-mile one-way trip to Orlando, the capital of family fun, and stay at the Hard Rock Hotel on the property of Universal Studios. What better way to honor and remember Payton than to stay in a place that was all about music? After five days in Orlando, we would journey farther south to Naples, Florida, and stay in the condominium of Gil and Joyce Viets, who had been gracious to offer their place for us to stay. Gil had been the managing partner prior to retiring and passing the mantle to Derrick.

The twelve days away were exactly what we needed. Chase always had wanted to go to Disney World, and we accomplished that goal in addition to visiting the parks at Universal Studios. But the most memorable part of the trip was arriving at the Hard Rock Hotel around eleven o'clock in the morning on January 30. Weary after a long car trip, I pulled up to the front door and noticed an eclectic fountain of guitars on the driver's side. I opened the car door and started walking toward the lobby, when I heard the song "Arms Wide Open" by Creed. I started to cry. Immediately, I returned to the car so Robyn and the boys could hear it too. It was the same song we'd played at Payton's service to greet everyone when they entered the church. What an awesome and great God we have! I have no idea how many songs were on the Hard Rock playlist—in the hundreds—and for that song to greet us upon our arrival after a thousand miles was beautiful beyond anything I could have imagined. We were at the right place.

Upon our return to Indianapolis, I owed Bryon and my family a decision regarding our future. I could not let go of the following passage in James 1:8, which kept coming to mind: "He is a double-minded man, unstable in all his ways." The NKJV further explains the passage as follows: *double-minded* is literally "two souls." If one part of a person is set on God and the other is set on this world, there is constant conflict within. That was exactly how I felt. I felt double-minded. Bryon was sensitive to the things we were going through and was not pressing me, but the issue lingered. A decision was needed. The answer was obvious: I needed to leave. I was too conflicted.

First, I had to talk to Robyn. We had talked about the matter a little over the prior six months, but now I had to share my heart and get her support. We always talked about major decisions impacting our family. She trusted me, and she told me I never gave her a reason not to. Typically, I brought a highly logical approach to our discussions, often centered on scripture or where and how I saw the Lord working. Robyn is a smart woman with a good sense of timing and how things will play out. We have different strengths and complement each other well. She knew it was our desire to anchor our decisions in God's truth and not human wisdom. God certainly had made a lot of things clear with respect to Payton's passing, and I was confident He would continue to do so with respect to my employment and our provision, as the Lord's Prayer says in Matthew 6:11: "Give us this day our daily bread." We agreed to move forward, and I would leave Arthur Andersen. The decision was huge. But first, I needed to reach out to a couple other men I trusted for their wisdom and support.

Eyes of the Father

One of the great blessings of my life is having relationships with godly men I can engage for counsel on the most difficult of life's opportunities and challenges. In that circumstance, I reached out to Keith to get his perspective on my leaving Andersen. Keith was familiar with the firm, as his college roommate, Jim Pajakowski, was a partner in our office. Jim's eventual wife, the former Sue Hill, was one of two people who'd taken me on my initial recruitment lunch—again, small world. Keith used the following analogy to describe the situation and my decision: "The house is burning and will ultimately burn to the ground. There are four key stakeholders: you and your family, your clients, your employees, and Arthur Andersen. You cannot satisfy all of them. You need to take the family heirlooms and get out of the house." That was the affirmation I needed.

Although it had been easy for Bryon to address with me the issue of the firm's apparent lack of strategic focus on outsourcing, the decision for Bryon to walk away from employment to unemployment was unsettling. Bryon had had a challenging childhood and hitchhiked across the country in his early teens. He knew what it meant to have nothing and was not anxious to put his family on the bread line. Ironically, MISO and Covance were long-term contracts with up to a five-year revenue stream. The work was protected, and we had a good model to support those clients. Frankly, if we'd wanted to take it easy, we could have. We had good job security. But I do not believe one should do what is practically or politically expedient.

I met with Bryon upon returning to Indianapolis, and in late February, we started to contemplate life outside of Arthur Andersen. Should we start a business on our own? Should we partner with another firm? What was the business model? How were we going to structure the firm? What services would we offer? We had no money to capitalize the start-up. We decided to provide outsourced business process and financial accounting services.

We proceeded with caution and did not want to create unnecessary visibility with respect to our decision to leave. Prior to notifying Andersen of our intent to leave the firm, we chose a code name, the Greek word *poiema* (pronounced poy-ay-mah), to reference our business. Many years later, Jonathan Cahn spoke about poeima, the poem of God:

> It is written in the Scriptures. We are His workmanship ...
> in the original Greek it says we are poiema, which means

that which is made, something fashioned, crafted together, someone's workmanship, as in a masterpiece. From the word *poiema* comes the word *poem*. Then the Poem of God is You. Me? If you become His work. You see, you can either live trying to make your life your own work, or you let your life become His workmanship. A poem can't write itself or lead itself. It must be written and led by its author. It must flow from its author's heart. So, to become the Poem of God, you must let your life emanate from the Author of your life. You must let it flow out of the heart of God. You must follow His will above your own, and plan above your own. You must let His Spirit move you and His love become the impulse of all you do. Then your life will flow as it was meant to flow, with rhyme and beauty, and you'll become His masterwork … the Poem of God.[9]

I did not fully understand the significance of the decision to leave or the choice of that word, but it was clear I was heading down a path to seek the Lord in my professional life. I might be the author of this book, but God is the author of my story. Over time, He revealed the story in a manner to allow me to see His plan for our lives through the eyes of the Father.

Poeima was a reference to both the work we anticipated doing for our future clients and the workmanship we were in Christ, with a set of operating principles and scriptures to guide our business. The following month, we would file articles of incorporation with the Indiana secretary of state and name the company after Payton: Payton LLC (**P**rofessional **A**ccountants **Y**ou **T**rust **O**utsource **N**ow). It might have been a little cheesy, but it provided some comfort.

If January had been a bad month for Arthur Andersen, February was worse, as client defections accelerated, and a significant amount of the firm's attention was spent dealing with the evolving crisis. Three Fortune 500 customers of Covance—Merck, Abbot Laboratories, and Wyeth—fired Andersen as their auditor in February and early March. Meanwhile, we were starting to lay the groundwork for a potential exit from the firm and people I loved—a firm that had supported me through my most difficult hour and developed me into the businessman I am today.

Bryon and I initiated discussions with a local consulting firm to potentially join them. Discussions were well on their way but not finalized. We decided, using Keith's advice, to first let Covance know we were leaving the firm, as Bryon and I both had responsibility for that engagement. Bryon was not involved with the MISO engagement. We scheduled a meeting on March 15 with John Riley at Covance to let him know of our plans. John indicated he was leaving Covance effective April 15. He did not indicate the time frame or whether the company had requested his resignation. I enjoyed working with John, as I did virtually all my clients, and was hopeful his situation would work out. He expressed concern about Andersen's ability to serve Covance, as several prominent clients had severed their relationships with the firm. John was nervous and posed the following rhetorical question: Would Andersen be around to continue to perform the billing and pricing work for Covance's contracts with their clients—the major pharma companies?

I scheduled a meeting with Tom Ertel on March 17 to indicate our intent to leave Andersen and start an outsourcing practice outside of Andersen. Tom had a lot on his mind with a busy year-end audit season and the events taking place within the firm. He did not need one more thing to deal with. Nonetheless, we knew we were doing the right thing, and we were called to walk away from long-term contracts with two prestigious clients to start out on our own.

A few days later, John Riley contacted Tom and inquired about the possibility of a three-way transaction among Andersen, Payton LLC, and Covance wherein Bryon and I would purchase the contract and continue to serve Covance outside the firm. The proposal was not met with lots of enthusiasm from the local office. They viewed it as an unnecessary distraction, given the events taking place across the firm. In many respects, I understood why.

We filed incorporation documents for Payton LLC with the secretary of state of Indiana on March 27, 2002. We identified a business purpose as follows: "The initial members were created by the Lord and brought together by Him; therefore, it is their desire to bring glory and honor to Him through the business affairs of the company. It is our desire to serve our clients well, provide outstanding career opportunities for our employees, and benefit the communities in which we work and live."

Tom and I visited our other significant BPO client, MISO, on March 28 to inform the client of my departure, as I was the lead person responsible for that engagement. Tom started out the discussion by saying we'd had a little hiccup that morning, as our CEO, Joe Beradino, had resigned. The firm was in a battle for its life, one it was prepared to fight for.

The next week, on April 2, Derrick and Tom, after conferring with firm leadership, agreed to Covance's request to sell the outsourcing contract to Payton LLC, and we started negotiations to purchase the contract. The process to purchase the contract from Andersen was not an easy one. Bryan Wiggins served as the lead negotiator for Andersen. I'd hired Bryan six years prior to join the Business Consulting practice I was leading at the time. A family friend and local attorney, Charley Grahn, assisted us with the negotiation. Charley was smart but not a big-time corporate lawyer and spent most of his time on individual matters, including wills and estates. He provided great advice: "This will either work, or Andersen will get its way, and this will fail." His point was validated as Andersen used a big-time legal firm out of New York to structure the agreement. Charley proposed a simple two-page agreement, and we received in return a detailed twenty-five-page agreement with lots of protections for Andersen. We tentatively reached agreement to purchase the contract on April 23, and the closing was set for May 1. The firm held open the US payroll for a day to ensure it received the actual signatures to the contract, so it could release the employees. That spoke to the legal sensitivities of the firm.

By May, Andersen was beginning the negotiation process to sell the entire assets of the $9 billion eighty-five-thousand-employee firm, selling countries, service lines, local offices, and intellectual properties. Bryan would later tell me the contract between Payton LLC and Andersen was the template for every other asset sale in the firm.

The Indianapolis office was sold in June to Ernst & Young (E&Y), which served as Covance's auditing firm. Absent the sale of the contract to Payton, that would have created a conflict of interest. E&Y would have had to decide which service it would provide to Covance: auditing or outsourcing. It could not provide both. My former Andersen colleagues were successful at E&Y. Derrick Burks, the managing partner of the Andersen office, would become the managing partner of the Ernst & Young office two years later. More importantly, Derrick and his wife,

Eyes of the Father

Celeste, were our friends and were next-door neighbors and close friends of the Ress family. The Leyden and Ress families had consulted them when it was apparent Payton and Meredith wanted to start a dating relationship.

The decision to leave based on God's truth and the Holy Spirit's conviction of a double-minded man, who is unstable in all his ways, without any corresponding business ultimately resulted in the purchase of a contract that would provide a great launching pad for our finance and accounting outsource business, Payton. If we had waited to play our cards, we would not have had the opportunity to purchase that contract, as entire countries, national practices, and, at the smallest level, local offices were sold in the month that followed in an unprecedented fire sale never seen before.

On May 7, the *Indianapolis Star* ran a follow-up story on our efforts to build Payton's Place, the medical infirmary at Fort Wilderness. There were several ironies in the timing and nature of the article. First, it ran the week following the start of Payton LLC, the consulting business Bryon Parnell and I had started on May 1. Second, in the picture the *Star* chose to use, only one individual was discernible among the forty persons on the project: Bryon Parnell. Third, the article ran the week prior to Payton's birthday. Finally, the lead headline on the front page was "BUSINESS: Arguments Begin Today in Arthur Andersen Case."

Todd Leyden

Payton's Place
Summer-camp infirmary becomes a living memorial to a much-loved teen

"How God has showered his love on us — I am floored, just floored."
— Todd Leyden

For me, the article and its timing continued a seemingly, by the world's standards, providential set of circumstances that were difficult to explain. The *Indianapolis Star* article's conclusion aptly captured my thoughts as I continued to grasp the magnitude of the Lord's working and ordering of events and circumstances during that time: "How God has showered his love on us—I am floored, just floored."

Two months later, we would face the final chapter in a season of firsts after Payton's passing: a return to Fort Wilderness and family camp with Zionsville Fellowship. It was no ordinary trip to Fort or family vacation. The medical facility named in Payton's honor was complete, and a dedication ceremony was planned for Sunday, July 14, the day after we would arrive.

232

~ Biblical Principle ~

Paul, in his letter to the church at Corinth, wrote in 2 Corinthians 5:7, "For we walk by faith, not by sight."

Upon reflection, I am incredibly comforted by this reality. It is easy to manage or manipulate circumstances toward our objective and miss what the Lord has for us. If I have learned anything in my adult life, I've learned it is much easier to see the Lord at work and join Him than to try to figure out life on my own.

CHAPTER 23

A RETURN TO FORT WILDERNESS: DEDICATION OF PAYTON'S PLACE

As May turned to June, our thoughts turned to our family vacation in July and a return to Fort Wilderness. The trip was filled with mixed emotions. We knew we needed to go. We loved Fort and the staff and enjoyed spending time with the other Zionsville Fellowship families. But Payton was not with us. More importantly a ceremony was scheduled to dedicate the medical facility. A small group of friends and family would join about two hundred Zionsville Fellowship family campers and staff for the important event. It was the final major milestone in our season of firsts after Payton's passing—and it was arguably the biggest one.

The boys were excited to return to Fort. There were always lots of fun things to do and lots of kids to do them with. The nine-hour car trip provided ample time for reflection and anticipation of what the week would bring. Robyn and I were looking forward to spending time with the boys and our friends; however, we knew the dedication was one big final hurdle we needed to clear. We were returning to the place that meant so much to our family, the place where we'd spent the most concentrated amount of time together for the last four years of Payton's life.

As we turned onto Wilderness Trail, Fort was a half mile away. Robyn and I welled up with emotion as we saw the familiar Fort Wilderness sign at the top of the hill, with its familiar trademark: "Stronghold of Christian

Eyes of the Father

Adventure." It was impossible for us to forget family pictures taken sitting on the stone ledge underneath the signpost.

We pulled into the parking lot and faced an onslaught of greetings from the Fort staff, one of the most loving and caring groups of people a person could ever meet. The Fort's founder, Truman Robertson, had instilled that love of others in his family and, notably, his sons, Ron and Tom, who'd served on staff for the past three-plus decades. Both men and their wives and the Fort staff loved the Lord and wanted to share that love with others. It was evident.

Saturday evening was a blur as we enjoyed time with many friends, but we had to take a few minutes to wander by Payton's Place. Fort had existed for forty-six years without a medical facility. For a camp that served almost eight thousand campers a year, that was more than a little problem. Kids with scraped knees, viruses or infections, or occasional sprains or broken bones were the norm at any camp, and Fort was no different, but there never had been a dedicated place where staff could perform treatments or care for the kids while they recovered. On that day, a brand-new facility stood in the heart of camp, with three bedrooms, including one for the nurse, and a central room with medical supplies and equipment necessary for treating patients. The inside of the facility was decorated with personal mementos, including items Payton had received during his time in the hospital, such as an autographed Peyton Manning jersey. There were family pictures of our three boys growing up at camp. There were also a book sharing Payton's story, including the daily website posts; a pair of Payton's size 13 shoes—big feet, particularly for a thirteen-year-old; and a framed copy of the article run by the *Indianapolis Star* detailing our trip the prior fall with family, friends, and Zionsville Fellowship members to build the exterior. It was beautiful and a blessing. But it was hard. The emotions never too far beneath the service returned. Robyn and I stood there and wept.

Sunday morning after breakfast was the first of the worship and teaching sessions. My mind was preoccupied with the dedication later that day. It was a picture-perfect and typical summer day in the Northwoods: seventy-five degrees and sunny, with a soft breeze that whistled through the pine trees. A few wisps of clouds were framed against the backdrop of the clear blue skies. Shortly after lunch, Robyn and I decided to go for a walk. It seemed like a typical afternoon at camp. Kids scurried around the camp or played carpetball. Others were at the beach or stables or enjoying ice cream at the canteen. There were always lots of activities and things to do at Fort. In fact, we'd learned our lesson the hard way during our first year at family camp: don't overschedule. It was best to allow some free time to sit by a fire, chat with a friend, go for a walk, or take a nap.

A walk seemed like a good thing to do. The dedication of Payton's Place was scheduled for 3:30. We were particularly reflective as we took a casual stroll to see what was going on at camp and take everything in. We passed the beachfront and headed toward the dining hall, when we were startled by a loud shriek behind us. We were right in front of Payton's Place. We turned around and saw Mary Wertz come out of her pop-up camper, the only building, RV, or campsite with a direct view of Payton's Place. Mary was screaming for help. Robyn rushed over to see what was going on. It was evident Mary was going into anaphylactic shock. Robyn, a registered nurse, administered Mary's EpiPen, and we quickly sought additional medical attention from Steve Siefert, the head of Fort's emergency response team.

A few minutes later, emergency vehicles raced into camp to respond to the situation. Prior to that time, I had never seen an emergency vehicle at camp. Now there was a medical emergency right before the dedication of Payton's Place. The emergency vehicle came around the perimeter road and made its way past the beach and into the heart of camp. The driver's door swung open, and I was stunned to see Mark Fetzer step out. Mark, a former Fort missionary staff member, was now working for the town of Newbold and their emergency response team. Mark also had been the bus driver on Payton's and my trip to the Grand Canyon in 1998 and one of the two guides who'd led Payton and me on our five-day hike in the canyon. I stood in a virtual daze, as it seemed as if I were watching a movie play out in front of my eyes.

We had come to Fort Wilderness five years prior because of an invitation from our neighbor due to a simple conversation with Payton. We'd kept coming back and had many wonderful family memories along the way. We'd continued to grow in our faith and our new relationship with Zionsville Fellowship. During our last camp with Payton, the message had been about suffering. We are to rejoice if trials bring glory to the Lord. Six months later, Payton had been the sickest kid in Riley Children's Hospital. The night of Payton's passing, Keith had called Fort, and a decision had been made to build a medical facility. The board had approved plans the next morning in a regularly scheduled meeting, and $85,000 had been raised a few weeks later. Forty people had traveled to Wisconsin that fall to frame the building. We were now walking in front of Payton's Place an hour before the dedication, and there was a medical emergency one hundred feet away. Robyn, a nurse, was first on the scene to administer the EpiPen. The emergency responder was the person who'd led Payton and this businessman on a five-day hiking trip to the Grand Canyon. It was like something you could only make up in Hollywood. Clearly, God had some sort of plan in mind for us and Fort Wilderness, but that was bizarre. It was humbling. Words cannot describe the overpowering joy and sadness simultaneously flowing through my veins as I stood transfixed, observing the latest situation unfold.

I've left one important part of the story for last. Mary and her husband, Ron, had been one of the four couples in our *Growing Kids God's Way* class when Payton was hospitalized, the course Robyn and I never had finished due to Payton's illness and passing. Neither the book nor life had provided us with a chapter on how to deal with the loss of child. The situation and our relationship caused me to harken back to a question I'd asked Robyn as funds were streaming in from so many friends and family to build Payton's Place. We received one extravagant gift of $2,800 from Ron and Mary Wertz, significantly larger than any individual gift other than my grandfather's and our personal contribution. Robyn and I asked each other why the Wertz's gave such a sacrificial gift to us as we had only known them for a short time. They never could have imagined the circumstances of that afternoon. Had God known? Absolutely. All I can say is God Almighty surely loves us, and we were humbled to see His plans and purposes unfold, even despite one of life's most difficult circumstances.

The following year, the State of Wisconsin came to inspect the facility and said it was the finest medical facility of its kind in the state—a true blessing to Fort and its campers.

⇥ Biblical Principle ⇤

From Matthew 5:17–18: "Do not think that I came to destroy the Law or the Prophets. I did not come to destroy but to fulfill. For assuredly, I say to you, till heaven and earth pass away, one jot or one tittle will by no means pass from the law till all is fulfilled."

In the above verses, Jesus is addressing the religious rulers of His day and speaks to the purpose of His coming: to perfectly obey the law, fulfill Old Testament prophecies, and provide a means of salvation for sinners. He made clear everything will happen as originally intended prior to the completion of history.

Upon reflection, I know I should not be surprised when I see the Lord's plans work out in an unimaginable way.

CHAPTER 24

DEAR HEAVENLY FATHER

I'd spent the first anniversary of Payton's passing in Florida with Robyn, Blake, and Chase, away from the world and anyone who knew anything of Payton and his passing. The second anniversary would result in a return to normalcy and having to deal with the inevitable turn of the calendar to Groundhog Day, February 2. In our case, we will always see a shadow. On that day, I wrote my first formal letter to Almighty God, the God of Abraham, Isaac, and Jacob and the nation of Israel, the one who sent his only begotten Son that whoever believes in Him would not perish but have everlasting life.

February 3, 2003

Dear Heavenly Father,

Hallowed be thy name. I am at a loss as to what is of relevance to say to you other than thank you. For all things come from you. You know our hearts; you know our days. Not one thing happens without your knowledge. Your plans are perfect. There is joy and suffering. Hope and despair. Yet through your Son, Christ Jesus, we are restored to you. I am eternally thankful.

Yesterday, February 2, 2003, was a bittersweet day for the Leyden family. You knew this long ago. Lord, you saw me weep, perhaps as I have not wept before, as I continue to witness your glory and presence in our midst. I wept as I thought of Payton—as we worshipped you, our Creator and Redeemer.

Lord, about a month ago, I asked my wife what she wanted to do on February 2. Robyn, as you know, is a doer and likes to mix it up. She had no answer and did not seem to want to talk about that day. Yet I knew we could not just sit in the house. Robyn has come to not like January and February due to the cold and season of Payton's illness.

Our pastor, Tom Streeter, spoke yesterday about our faith being teleological. There is a **beginning** and an **end**. There is a plan. I continue to marvel at your plans. Not that I always like your plan. But your plan is perfect, and it fits together, and you are always out in front of us.

Midweek, we had no specific plans for February 2, 2003. The infamous schedule was wide open except for our Sunday morning trip to the church building to join with our local body in worship and teaching. Several weeks ago, Robyn and I decided—okay, I nudged her a little bit—to sign up to relieve the Sunday school teachers for eight weeks. I signed up for the drama team, and Robyn signed up as a tribal leader. Yet you knew that the first week, February 2, was a time when I was called to worship with my family. I mentioned this to Jeff Hines, the drama director, and he graciously said I did not need to participate the first week. I said I would and asked if I could join the drama team after the worship service.

On Wednesday, I noticed in the *Indianapolis Star* a seven-mile run in Carmel after church and asked Robyn if she wanted to participate. She said yes. I had never run in this race before—an annual Groundhog Day run.

On Thursday, our close friend Barb Grahn called Robyn and said her son Matt was attending a retreat called Kairos, or "God's time," in connection with his senior year at Brebeuf and asked Robyn to send him a letter. She also suggested we get together sometime soon. On Saturday, I asked Robyn if she would like to get together with the Grahn family the following night, February 2. Robyn said yes, and I called Barb to arrange.

On Saturday, we attended the Institute of Christian Thought seminar. Brian Hudson asked us to share our aha's. One thought came to mind: Brian's homework assignment to Covenant Christian High School students. He'd asked them to take the first chapter of Genesis and identify twenty-five attributes of God's nature or character. The class groaned. Then, after they successfully completed the exercise, he asked them to do it again in groups and find an additional twenty-five attributes. How you reveal yourself to us.

Late during the session, we received a couple of phone calls. Blake had chipped his tooth and was in pain. Robyn assured Blake it could probably wait until Monday. I told Robyn I would ask Ben Adams, a dentist I'd met that day, for assistance, as he and his wife, Nicole, were in our discussion group. Robyn said, "He can't be a dentist, as he looks like he is ten." Ben was helpful. We called Blake and picked up some over-the-counter dental stuff on our way home.

Robyn's sister, Cari, also called while we were gone. Chase asked Cari if his cousin Eric could sleep over. Cari was originally planning to go to Cincinnati this weekend, but there was an illness in the family, and their trip was postponed. We agreed to the sleepover for Eric and Chase and for Blake and his friend Ben Iliff, even though we have a family rule we do not have sleepovers on Saturday night, as sleep usually does not happen.

Lord, yesterday I wept for joy and sadness. I witnessed your plans, not mine, for February 2, 2003. Lord, I marvel at how you control time and place and purpose. That all things are according to thy plan. We have free will and often stray, yet you are leading us out ahead, longing that we will join you in your work to glorify you.

We arrived at the church building a few minutes early. I dropped the family off at the front entrance and drove to the rear of the building to park. I turned off the car, and right next to me, Jeff Hines pulled in, and we got out of our cars at the same time. I reminded Jeff I would meet up with the drama team after worship and communion, if that was all right. He said it was, and I did not have to participate this week. He then said, "It is a bittersweet day." I said, "It is," and shared with him that I had written Robyn, Blake, and Chase a letter with a couple of small gifts to share with them later that day. In my letter, I mention in closing that it is a bittersweet day. This was the **beginning** to our worship time at the church building.

Lord, the worship service was special, and you know why. It is painful to lose a child. Yet, Lord, I was overcome for other reasons. Worshipping with us were the Robertsons from Fort Wilderness. They had journeyed over five hundred miles to attend the ICT conference originally scheduled for January 18 but rescheduled for February 1. Fort Wilderness was the **beginning** to our relationship with Zionsville Fellowship. We went to the Fort for four years before joining the body of Zionsville Fellowship.

We love the Robertson family and Fort. Last July, during family camp, we dedicated Payton's Place. This was an **end** to almost sixteen months of activities and firsts after Payton's death, including the building of a medical facility in memory of Payton. Yet it was a **beginning** to those at Fort who will use the facility and perhaps learn the story about Payton's life and passing.

Worshipping with us was David Musa. David, I presume, had journeyed several hundred miles from Milwaukee to worship with us on February 2. David's wife, Ndidi, was the initial lead doctor when Payton arrived at Riley Children's Hospital on January 1, 2001. This was the **beginning** of Payton's final thirty-three days, which culminated with his passing on February 2, 2001. Ndidi was the one who said after the second day we could believe in what man, medicine, or machines can do or God. We chose you. Ndidi was there at the **end** and the time of Payton's passing. Payton's doctor (Seferian) asked us to prepare to address life-support decisions. God, I told you that you could decide when Payton's life on earth would end, as it is not right for a father to make that decision. Ndidi said you would declare yourself. And right then, you did. Ndidi and I said, "God is good." Lord, I give you thanks for the excellent medical care through Ndidi and Riley Hospital. More importantly, I am eternally thankful that she is a woman of God who gave us strength through her conviction and faith in you.

Lord, our family was served communion by Keith Ogorek. I do not recall Keith serving communion before. Perhaps someone was missing, and for some reason, he served our section. Keith was the **beginning** to our invitation to Fort Wilderness and the **beginning** to my growth in my faith in Jesus Christ. Keith's daughter Rachel was the beginning to our relationship with the Ogoreks, as she was often a target of Payton's and his friend Paul's practical jokes. Keith also served as the **end** of Payton's life at his bed-site as he drew his final breaths this side of eternity and as he officiated Payton's service.

As we left the church building, Robyn was in great spirits. She loved the drama we did for the kids and how the adults were so into their performance. It was meaningful and funny. She had a great partner in Dave Poindexter, and her experience as a tribal leader was off to a good start.

Robyn's sister, Cari, came over after church. We shared the joy of Eric's participation in Sunday school and the start of the eight-week Exodus drama. Cari, who after Payton's funeral began to engage in church life, has fallen away from the church. Yet after learning this was the first session, or **beginning**, of the Exodus drama, she was very interested in Eric's continued participation. Lord, we know that Cari needs much help, and through you and your church, there is hope. We must pray.

Lord, we completed our race in Carmel. Thank you for such a beautiful early February day. I was able to run in shorts and a long-sleeved T-shirt. It was a blessing to run with Robyn, even though we separated after a couple of miles. On our trip home, we stopped at my office. Neither Robyn nor the boys had visited my new company's office. This was the first time Robyn was even remotely close to the office. Payton LLC is the **beginning** of my second career as I strive to lead a company based on your plans and truth.

Last night, our family shared a meal with the Grahns. We enjoyed our time and fellowship and talked about you and your Word and your plans and life's challenges. The Grahns were our closest family friends at Garfield Park

Eyes of the Father

Church. Garfield Park is where I accepted Jesus Christ as my personal Savior. Garfield Park was the **beginning** point for our family as we learned the majesty and grace of the Christian faith. Garfield Park is where Payton was confirmed just nine months before his passing to join you.

You know every thought, and so you know that I sensed early in the day a lot of these events somehow fit together—well beyond my ability to arrange them and well within your sovereign nature to order them. I thought to myself, *what a day*, and we ended the evening with such a nice time at the Grahns'. Yet you had one more important event which needed to unfold.

We arrived home a little after nine thirty, a little late for a school night. However, this is a special day, and we did not live within the norm of our typical rules. Right after we walked in, the phone rang. I thought it was my mother, as she is usually the only person who calls at that hour. I was wrong. Robyn answered the phone. It was Jeff Hines. He asked that I get on the line as well. Jeff said their family took the opportunity to talk about Payton and his passing over lunch. Later that day, Kim saw their son Elliott kneeling on the kitchen floor in prayer. Kim called Jeff into the kitchen. Elliott was praying to you and asking Jesus Christ to be his personal Savior. It seems the discussion at lunch about Payton and his situation prompted in some fashion this to take place.

Jeff was the first person I saw when I arrived in the parking lot at church in the morning. Jeff said he wanted to call all day and tell us about Elliott. We were only home for a little while during the day. Yet when we arrived home late that night, the phone rang. This was the **ending** to our special day—February 2, 2003. And the **beginning** to

Elliott's personal relationship with your Son, our Savior, Jesus Christ.

Your Word states that you are the Alpha and the Omega—the **beginning** and the **end**, who is and who was and who is to come, the Almighty. Lord, I can only say thank you for your precious gift of your Son, Jesus Christ, to us. Lord, I pray that I am faithful to you to share your good news to a lost world with the redemptive message of Jesus Christ for the restoration of our souls.

All my love,
Todd Leyden

Postscript: Lord, you know why I wrote this letter. Another of your servants, Judy Streeter, wife of the senior pastor, suggested after Payton's passing, I journal my thoughts. Judy was the only person to make this suggestion. I have not faithfully journaled; however, I have recorded and written many acts about you that continue to demonstrate your provision and providence amid life's greatest struggle. The story will continue here on earth for as long as I have breath.

☙ Biblical Principle ❧

John, exiled on the isle of Patmos, wrote the following at the end of his life, in Revelation 1:8: "'I am the Alpha and the Omega, the Beginning and the End,' says the Lord, 'who is and who was and who is to come, the Almighty.'"

Our lives are a series of beginnings and endings. Upon reflection, the Lord has a plan for our lives, and our trajectories, here and in eternity, are forever altered as we seek Him.

PART 6
REST ASSURED

CHAPTER 25

PAYTON'S DREAM

What would Payton think about his passing? Did God provide him with a glimpse of the future prior to his entering the hospital? How would God provide comfort and understanding for his countless friends, including his girlfriend, Meredith? It is easy for me to intellectualize his passing based on my knowledge and understanding of the Christian faith or the countless ordered events that provided assurance to me and our family of God's sovereignty over creation, let alone Payton's life and death.

With permission from Leisa Ress, Meredith's mother, I am including the section below, "Faith Lessons from Payton." I asked her to share the one part of Payton's story that is impossible for me to write. Leisa will take you back to the days before Payton entered the hospital, including the final conversation between Meredith and Payton, which took place the day before he entered the hospital. It brings me to tears every time I share it and perhaps answers the question "What would Payton think?"

Faith Lessons from Payton
Leisa Ress

We have all had times in our lives when, despite much prayer and pleading, God did not answer as we wanted Him to. And we have had to wrestle with the "Why?" question. I want to share with you an experience we went through many years ago, when God gave me a new perspective on the mercy and grace of His sovereignty.

It was the last day of school before Christmas break; my daughter Meredith burst through the door and collapsed against the wall in tears. Her boyfriend, Payton, had been absent from school, and she was disappointed they had been unable to exchange their Christmas gifts.

This first boyfriend was a guarded and innocent relationship, one considered only after Meredith's insistence his parents were "worse than you guys" (meaning even stricter in their parenting) and consented to by both sets of parents only after prayer and a joint family meeting. We agreed there was no unchaperoned time together; their occasional visits with one another would be strictly within the confines of family events and outings.

Upon phoning his home, she learned he had some sort of virus and was too ill to speak to her. Nearly a week passed without a word from him. At last, his mother called and told us he had a severe virus but was showing signs of improvement.

To Meredith's delight, Payton phoned her on New Year's Eve, feeling somewhat better. Near the close of their conversation, he shared something that would later prove quite significant to her. He'd had a strange dream about her. He'd seen her in a field of flowers, wearing a white dress. She was an adult and alone. She looked happy, and he was not in the dream at all. He told her he loved her and said goodbye. Neither of them knew, but those were the final words he would speak to Meredith.

New Year's Day brought a serious turn of events. Late in the evening, a phone call came from Riley's intensive care unit. It was Payton's father, Todd Leyden. Payton was considerably sicker that day. He was in renal failure, on dialysis, and heavily sedated, a very sick young man. I consoled Meredith with reassurances of the renown of Riley Hospital and its highly respected medical staff. We prayed with confidence for Payton's quick recovery.

January 2 brought more ominous news from Todd: further testing had revealed that Payton had contracted a staph infection. Worse yet, it had entered his heart through a tiny, seemingly inconsequential congenital hole.

We prayed much and visited the hospital often. I watched my daughter pray at Payton's bedside, really pray like she never had before. Todd's daily updates came like manna, feeding us scripture and hope and charging us with specific prayer requests. Amid this agonizing trial, Todd's first prayer request each day was that God was glorified in Payton's situation. I marveled at his faith, as all I could muster was a desperate begging before the throne on Payton's behalf.

A website was established for the many concerned friends to follow Payton's daily progress. This became a testimony of his family's faith to believers and nonbelievers alike. It became the vehicle we used to facilitate an emergency twenty-four-hour prayer vigil so that someone would be before the throne each minute of the day.

Meredith devised a special prayer plan: each time a friend saw the number 55 (Payton's basketball jersey number), he or she was to pray for him. Prayers were hurled to heaven from young and old alike as reminders were seen everywhere—55 mile-per-hour speed-limit signs were routinely observed, and 55-milligram sodium levels leaped from soda bottles.

Payton's condition was far graver than we had first understood; each little medical victory was soon outpaced by another defeat. I began to understand what it meant to "pray without ceasing."

As days passed, complications multiplied. There were bowel and colon surgeries, lung collapses, and a myriad of close calls. The threatening possibility of Payton's death became frighteningly real.

Then January 19 brought greatly uplifting news. Payton had experienced his "best twenty-four hours yet." All his numbers were improving, and there was measurable progress.

Immediately upon receiving that phone call from Todd, I rushed to New Augusta Middle School. The hallways were crowded with students returning from lunch. I located Meredith and delivered to her and Payton's friends the inspiring update. There was an explosion of joy; high fives abounded in the corridors of New Augusta.

God was surely about to do miracle healing. And oh, how He would be glorified, as many teens would be drawn to Christ through Payton's ordeal.

On January 24, hope plummeted, as we learned that Payton's lungs were severely diseased and in much distress. And now another different infection had been detected.

By January 29, Payton's condition had deteriorated even further. We groaned in prayer for our great God to speak the word and heal Payton.

All along, I was participating in an in-depth Bible study on the book of Matthew. It was with great anguish that I read daily of how Jesus had gone about "healing every disease and sickness" and how "he had compassion on them and healed their sick." Where was this Jesus now? Why did He seem so lacking in compassion for Todd and Robyn? For Meredith?

It was 3:30 a.m. on February 2 when I was awakened by the alarming ring of the telephone. It was a nearly breathless Todd; his tearful voice chilled me with the news that Payton was crashing. I assured him that Meredith and I would meet him at the hospital within minutes and nauseously proceeded to wake her to the grim reality.

We joined Payton's family at his bedside. Together and individually, each had the opportunity to touch and kiss him and to speak cherished departing words. He lingered at death's door throughout the day.

By late afternoon, Meredith decided to leave the hospital with Payton's uncle and younger brothers. She felt it would be Payton's desire that she be with his brothers.

Within an hour of their leaving, we were called again to Payton's bedside. The end was at hand. As Todd lay his head and open Bible on Payton's chest and caressed his hair, he recited these words: "I have fought the good fight, I have finished the race, I have kept the faith. Finally, there is laid up for me the crown of righteousness, with the Lord, the righteous Judge, will give to me on that Day, and not to me only but also to all who have loved his appearing" (2 Timothy 4:7–8).

I clutched my worn green Bible and continued to fervently beg God to burst forth on this tragic scene to miraculously deliver Payton, with complete faith that His mere speaking of the word would accomplish this miracle.

At 5:30 p.m., Payton died, and along with him, I feared, my faith had died. I drove home numb with disbelief and disappointment. How would I deliver this devastating news to my vulnerable young daughter? How would I satisfy her pleas for those unanswerable questions? Why didn't God save Payton? Why did He seemingly turn a deaf and compassionless ear to our constant, fervent, faith-filled prayers? How could I help her when I too harbored these same doubts?

Payton's parents honored their son and their Lord with a funeral service filled with worship and testimony of God's sovereignty and eternal love.

Afterward, I watched my grieving fourteen-year-old daughter kneel beside Payton's casket at the grave site. I saw a bewildered pain in her eyes no one so young should have to experience. I tried to console myself that God would somehow use even this for her ultimate good, though Romans 8:28 seemed a distant promise.

The next day afforded its first real opportunity for me to spend extended time alone. I searched God's Word for answers or at least for comfort. Those ready grief verses I'd so often dispensed to others felt like ice picks in my heart. I wrestled with the question I knew we should not ask: Why?

So I poured out my soul to God and told Him the truth. I admitted I didn't think I could ever love Him again and that I surely could never trust Him. I said I would have left Him if there had been anywhere else to go, sorry that the truth had been embedded within me that there was no other god. My heart ached so badly I could feel the grief in my stomach as I lay on the floor before a silent God.

And then I had a sort of epiphany. A film reel began to play in my mind's eye, showing those last minutes in Payton's room. Only this time, it was as if God came to me at that moment with these words: "I can take Payton home right now; he will be completely healed and eternally blissful. There will be grief for a time on earth among those who love him, but I will be their comfort and hope. And thousands of souls who do not know my Son will come to me through the testimony of Payton's family and friends."

In that moment, I saw the futility of the insatiable "Why?"

"For my thoughts are not your thoughts, neither are your ways my ways."

It wasn't just a matter of my not being privy to His ways; the harsh truth was that I did not want His ways. At that point in time, had I been given the choice of outcomes, I would have allowed those thousand faceless souls to perish for all eternity in exchange for Payton's life to be returned to his loved ones. My prayers were bound in the temporal; His answers are always for the eternal best in His kingdom.

I went to my knees in praise of this merciful God who would never ask us to make such lofty, holy decisions. I felt awash with His love, grace, and tenderness and so grateful that God alone was wise, loving, and good enough to handle the mantle of sovereignty.

Four years later, as I was looking through Meredith's senior school picture proofs, I came across the following picture [reprinted with permission of JJ Kaplan Color My World Studio]. It is a picture of Meredith, grown up, in a field of flowers, wearing a white dress and all alone—Payton's dream.

It has been seventeen years since our peaceful lives were assaulted with this unthinkable grief. Meredith's journey was difficult and took her down a few corridors of doubt, anger, and outright rebellion. But thankfully, today I can say she is healed, faith-filled, and a more compassionate person for it. Payton's family have gone on to live joyful and fruitful lives and anticipate reuniting with him in the life to come.

Author's Note

Prior to Payton's hospitalization, Robyn and Leisa spent little time together. Today they are best friends and have an accountability relationship. The circumstance that brought them together was awful; however, the Lord used Payton's passing to develop a lifelong relationship. Meredith is married to John Walton and the mother of three children. Robyn was blessed, in her late forties, to serve as a bridesmaid in Meredith and John's wedding. Meredith and Robyn remain close to this day. Meredith has a special place in her heart and past for Payton, but she is guarded, like Blake, about sharing her special memories and reflections about this difficult chapter in her life. As Robyn said shortly after Payton passed away, "Life is for the living."

⊰ Biblical Principle ⊱

Paul said in his letter to the church at Philippi, in Philippians 3:20, "For our citizenship is in heaven, from which we also eagerly wait for the Savior, the Lord Jesus Christ, who will transform our lowly body that it may be conformed to His glorious body, according to the working by which He is able even to subdue all things to Himself."

God gave Payton a vision of a future through a dream he shared with Meredith the last day he was at home prior to entering the hospital. As Leisa shared in her message above, we anxiously look forward to the time when we are reunited with Payton in eternity to come.

EPILOGUE

We are all on journeys in this life on this side of eternity. Robyn's and my journeys were interrupted in the early 1990s by a quintessential question: "Whom and what are we living for? For God or for ourselves?" Once we settled that question and chose God, some significant things happened in our marriage, family, and work. Our decision did not mean life was easy, but it provided us direction and purpose beyond ourselves. However, the most profound impact was the Lord's preparation for our son Payton's illness and passing and the days, months, and eighteen years to follow.

It is difficult to lose a child. As one of Payton's three lead intensivists, Dr. Jeff Macke, said, "It is not natural for a parent to bury his or her child"—especially one who was healthy and succumbed to an infection that inextricably made its way to a small hole in his heart. During the preceding decade, we had grown in our faith, but Payton's loss hurt deeply. However, we knew God was sovereign and loved Payton even more than we did.

In the days, months, and years that followed, I wrestled with one question, running it over and over in my mind hundreds of times: "God, why did you make the circumstances preceding and following Payton's passing so clear?" What do you want me to do? Why had there been so many seemingly providential, ordered circumstances that appeared to fit together like an intricate thousand-piece puzzle? The Lord had provided me with one piece of the puzzle at a time (see the Evidence of God's Plan following this chapter) only when I was prepared to see what He had for me. I certainly did not need all the seemingly ordered events for my assurance and comfort or for my family's. Why had God spent His time showing me all those things? Not that I believe He is confined by time, as we are, and able to see or do only one thing at a time. But God sees and knows all things because He exists outside of time.

The answer to this question is seemingly buried within perhaps one of the most well-known passages of scripture. Most Christian weddings refer to Paul's writing to the church at Corinth and specifically to the thirteenth chapter, which speaks about love as God's greatest gift to us. It speaks about love being kind, not envying or boasting, hearing all things, believing all things, hoping all things, and enduring all things. The chapter ends with a familiar refrain known to Christians and non-Christians alike: "And now abide faith, hope, love, these three; but the greatest of these is love."

The two verses that precede the last unlock the mystery to the question "God, why did you make the circumstances preceding and following Payton's passing so clear?" First Corinthians 13:11–12 says, "When I was a child, I spoke as a child, I understood as a child, I thought as a child; but when I became a man, I put away childish things. For now we see in a mirror, dimly, but then face to face. Now I know in part, but then I shall know just as I also am known."

The New King James commentary says the following regarding verse 12: "The mirror is probably the Word of God (see II Corinthians 3:18; James 1:23–25), which can give us only a partial understanding of God. This will all change when we see Him face to face."

In large part, I started to understand the answer to the question of why God made everything so clear as I put away the things of this world and began to seek Him through His Word, prayer, and a life oriented toward His ways and not my own. While scripture speaks of a mirror as the Word of God, we understand a mirror as something that faithfully reflects or gives a true picture of something else.[10] The true picture of us is how God sees us and His plans for our lives, not how we see ourselves and our plans. Our view and perspective in this life are limited. It is my desire to see how God sees, but this requires me to seek Him and His ways for my life. Only then can I truly see and understand the plans He has for me or how the pieces of the puzzle fit together.

The answer to my gnawing question would come into focus in the spring of 2003, two years after Payton's passing. On April 3–4, I went on my own silence and solitude retreat and traveled ninety minutes to a cabin my father-in-law frequented in a small town in western Indiana,

Lizton. The goal was to get away from everything to pray, reflect, and seek the Lord—a time of spiritual refreshment and renewal. During my retreat, I essentially settled the question as to why the Lord had made so many details clear regarding the situation with Payton, and I came to the following summary conclusions:

1. My thoughts are not God's thoughts; neither are His ways my ways.
2. It is not the number of days; it is how we use those days to glorify God.
3. God is in control of every detail in our lives.
4. God will use sin, infection, and, ultimately, death for His purpose and glory.
5. God will and does reveal Himself to us, but we are often too busy to see His plans for us.
6. Death provides a richness to life and expectation for eternity.
7. God reveals His love for us through suffering and affliction in a way we cannot know otherwise.

These are conclusions I could not have reached ten years prior when I started my journey to understand and live for my newfound faith. It was during my retreat that I first contemplated writing this story and journaled the need to do so. For many years, I'd been uncomfortable with the thought of doing so, given the amount of attention and adulation we'd received due to our perceived response to Payton's illness and passing. I knew I never would have chosen that situation and only could respond in that manner due to the grace of God. I am thankful I waited so many years, as I now have the benefit of continued maturity, additional perspective, and God's continued revelation of the impact of our primary prayer request: that God be glorified. I can now see far more clearly how His fingerprints are interwoven throughout our lives.

By writing this book, I hope to offer encouragement and direction to those who struggle to make sense of life, particularly periods of difficulty and darkness. Most importantly, I write to offer the hope that is ours as we seek the Lord and turn our lives over to Him. As with a diet, through which you do not reach your goal weight overnight, you will not reach spiritual maturity overnight. However, as you study His Word, engage in meaningful relationships with mature brothers and sisters in Christ, and seek His will through prayer, you will see the fruit in your life in the years to come. Robyn's prayer was answered: Payton's life did have meaning, as we have shared parts of this story orally with thousands of people and now through this book, and we've seen many lives impacted and changed for eternity along the way.

Admittedly, there is an ache in our gut when we consider life without Payton. Yet the Lord's plan and glorious unfolding continue, and He has subsequently led us to some remarkable and unplanned opportunities to serve Him through our work, community, and ministry, including the following:

> In 2006, I was recruited to a leadership position with the NCAA to start their eligibility center after leading a study to evaluate their prior clearinghouse model. It was a significant opportunity to impact the lives of a hundred thousand young people per year and build and develop a talented team of employees.
>
> In 2010, Robyn returned to Riley Children's Hospital, where she'd started her career, and where Payton passed away, to take a position as a pediatric oncology nurse in the outpatient clinic.
>
> In 2013, the Lord, in a series of supernatural experiences, introduced Robyn and me to Shannon Falls. We bumped into her three times over the course of four days on a hiking trip in Glacier National Park. The park is one million acres, with 750 miles of trails. I said to Robyn, "I wonder what her story is." Why was a young lady hiking all alone when the bears were waking from hibernation? We somehow found her again the following fall in South Carolina, during a chance business trip, without benefit of her name and location, just a distant memory of a single conversation on the trail eighteen months prior. Shannon shared her story with us, without our asking, during a dinner a few months later. Her story was published in

2017, and we wrote the foreword. We developed a close friendship that continues this day. Our interaction with Shannon and now deep friendship confirmed a yearning Robyn and I had started to sense a few years prior to consider full-time ministry through hiking, creation, and knowing one's story.

In February 2016, I had breakfast with Jeff Terp, who knew of our call to ministry through hiking, creation, and one's own journey and story. As we were getting ready to leave the restaurant, he told me I needed to apply for the executive director position at Fort Wilderness. I returned to my office at the NCAA and met with Gary deCastro, who, without knowing of my breakfast with Jeff, greeted me with the following question: "When are you leaving?" Within the same twenty-four hours, I received a text message from Justin Olson, who ran Fort's college-age program. It included a picture of Robyn and me on the tube float, on a marketing piece for the camp. Justin's text said, "The face of Fort Wilderness promotions." The Lord had my attention with three different messengers all pointing us to Fort Wilderness within a twenty-four-hour time period. So, this businessman with no formal camping experience and his wife applied for the job with the blessing of our elders, and in the fall of 2016, we journeyed to the Northwoods of Wisconsin to see what God had in store for us. The move required us to leave behind thirty-two years of life in Indianapolis; our twenty-two-year-old son Chase; Robyn's sister, Cari; our friends and church; and a well-paying and prominent job to respond to the Lord's call. Robyn, as the trailing spouse, eventually took on the following jobs at camp: accommodations manager and camp nurse, with her office in Payton's Place, the medical infirmary we'd built in Payton's honor fifteen years prior. She works for Paul Ziolkowski (pictured with us below), who was a twenty-one-year-old kid when he led the team who constructed the facility. Ultimately, the Lord made it clear He needed us to use our God-given abilities to impact lives for eternity through God's Word, creation, adventure programming, and warm Christian fellowship at Fort Wilderness.

We were taking to heart the lessons Keith had taught us seventeen years prior when we studied Henry Blackaby's *Experiencing God*:

1. God is always at work around you.
2. God pursues a continuing love relationship with you that is real and personal.
3. God invites you to become involved with Him in His work.
4. God speaks by the Holy Spirit through the Bible, prayer, circumstances, and the church to reveal Himself, His purposes, and His ways.
5. God's invitation for you to work with Him always leads you to a crisis of belief that requires faith and action.
6. You must make major adjustments in your life to join God in what He is doing.

7. You come to know God by experience as you obey Him, and He accomplishes His work through you.[11]

I hope our journey and Payton's life will give you pause to perhaps consider how the Lord is working in your life and what you need to see as you reflect on the following questions:

- Does God have your best interests in mind?
- Can you trust Him and His ways in good times and in bad?
- Is it possible God has a better plan for your life than you do?
- Are you able to see how He is at work in your life? If not, consider the following:
  o Are you too busy?
  o Are you distracted with things of this world?
  o Do you lack knowledge of His Word?
  o Are you not seeking Him through a life of prayer?

If you are not seeing the Lord at work or you are stuck in the valleys of life, you need to act now and earnestly seek Him, lest you miss the life He desires for you.

I will conclude with a simple premise: our God is an awesome God. As difficult as it is to lose a child, He has comforted and provided for us in ways beyond imagination. The intricate tapestry of circumstances and events laid out before the foundation of the world provides convincing proof God is at work and cares for us deeply. Robyn and I continue to miss our son and think of him often but rejoice in knowing a beautiful reunion awaits us once our time on earth is done.

EVIDENCE OF GOD'S PLAN

Through my eyes and others', I witnessed a series of events—listed below—that inexplicably defy human understanding and are the basis for this story. One could look at an individual event and say it was coincidence. I understand and respect that view; however, when viewing the events in the aggregate, I find it impossible to conclude such events are simply a series of random occurrences. The likelihood of one of these events occurring in the manner which they happened is astronomically high. Throughout this book, I have attempted to share our story through both my eyes and the eyes of our heavenly Father. It is presumptuous to believe I see what God sees or can comprehend His mind. However, I do know He will reveal His plans and purposes and gives us the eyes to see as we seek Him. Paul, writing to the church of Ephesus, said the following in Ephesians 2:10: "For we are His workmanship, created in Christ Jesus for good works, which God prepared beforehand that we should walk in them."

1. **Trees or a Fireplace (November 1987).** Our decision between two lots led to the Ogoreks' purchase of the other lot with trees. Eight years later, we established a lifelong relationship that would involve an invitation to camp, a call to ministry for Keith, the start of a praise worship and teaching service at Garfield Park, Keith's officiation of Payton's funeral, and my introduction of Keith to Author Solutions. He is now the president of the Author Learning Center, a sister organization to the publisher of this book.
2. **The Gore Family (June 1999).** I ran a marathon to raise money for the Leukemia Society and honor Brandon Gore. Brandon's mother served as a powerful witness for Jesus during his battle with leukemia. On multiple occasions, the doctors said there was

no hope. During Payton's last week in the hospital, Brandon was in the other ICU with a breathing challenge. Two months after Payton passed, he was released, and he is living proof of a miracle. The Lord used the Gores to serve as a powerful example of Christ to prepare us for our trial.

3. **Fort Wilderness (July 2000).** Eric Bobbitt's message at family camp centered on suffering and, specifically, 1 Peter 1:6–7: "In this you greatly rejoice, though now for a little while, if need be, you have been grieved by various trials, that the genuineness of your faith, being much more precious than gold that perishes, though it is tested by fire, may be found to praise, honor, and glory at the revelation of Jesus Christ." The Lord directed this message to us, as six months later, Payton would fight for his life. Would Payton's trial bring glory to God?

4. **Prayer Partner (October 2000).** Scott Cooper, who'd played with Payton on the worship team at Fort during the prior family camp, was assigned as Payton's prayer partner upon our joining the church. A few months later, his office on the fourth floor of the Indiana University Medical Center was seventy-five feet directly across the courtyard from Payton's fourth-floor room and provided a direct sight line for prayer for thirty-three days.

5. **Last Supper (December 20, 2000).** On Payton's last day at school, and the day of his last basketball game, I had a late-afternoon board meeting. I transported barely touched platters of food to the game, and there was an opportunity for a final meal with his coaches and teammates. Payton was sick the next day and struggled for the next ten prior to his admittance to Riley Children's Hospital.

6. **Sunday School Lesson (December 31, 2000).** December 31 was Payton's last day in our home. He missed the junior high school lesson at church: "No one is invincible." Payton would serve as a powerful example of that lesson for the next thirty-three days and for years to come, as each year, the Zionsville Fellowship high school class brings over two hundred area youth to a winter weekend called the Great White North at Fort Wilderness.

Payton's story is shared, and a group picture is taken in front of the medical facility, Payton's Place, built in his honor.

7. **Lead Doctor (January 2, 2001).** We were reintroduced to Ndidi Musa, a woman from Nigeria we'd met and been seated next to at a wedding reception three months prior. Ndidi, a talented physician and even more impressive prayer warrior, led the medical team on Payton's first full day in the hospital and asked the ultimate question: "Do we trust in what man, medicine, and machines can do or what God can do?"

8. **Payton Crashes (January 29, 2001).** Around six thirty in the evening, I received a frantic call from Robyn: "Payton is crashing; you need to get here quickly." I raced to the hospital, and with the interstate in sight, the car in front of me stopped at a yellow light. I was mad. I glanced at the license plate, and it read, "PSLAM 23," referring to the twenty-third psalm: "Yea, though I walk through the valley of the shadow of death I will fear no evil."

9. **Psalm 118 (January 31, 2001).** Payton crashed a second time. The doctor said Payton's odds of survival were not good. Three friends independently shared the following scripture from Psalm 118:8 - "It is better to trust in the Lord than to put your confidence in man."

10. **The Last Day (February 2, 2001).** We received the dreaded call in the middle of the night: Payton was crashing—for the third time in less than four days. Each time, he'd rebounded. At two thirty in the afternoon, Blake, Chase, and Meredith visited Payton in the hospital. It was Chase's only visiting to see and say goodbye to Payton. A few minutes after their departure, Dr. Seferian summoned us to evaluate life support.

11. **"God, Declare Yourself."** Dr. Seferian was leaving his shift at four o'clock on February 2, 2001, and he said we needed to make a decision regarding Payton's life support in the next day or two, as there was nothing more the medical team could do. I said it was unfair for any man or father to make that decision. Keith said, "The sheep will hear my voice." Ndidi said, "God will declare Himself." I said, "I don't care if it is two days, two months, two hours, two weeks, or two minutes. God can decide when Payton's

life on earth is done." Immediately, we heard a series of three or four rapid and haunting beeps in the next room. Robyn said, "Maybe God is speaking right now." Dr. Seferian glanced to the other room and immediately walked over to the machine that was monitoring Payton's oxygenation levels. Dr. Seferian returned, his face pale, and, looking at us in disbelief, said, "Payton is gone."

12. **The Perfect Strum of a Guitar.** Uncle Scott brought Blake and Chase home after the school carnival to hear the news that Payton died. Blake took Scott to Payton's room to show him all the signed memorabilia Payton had received during his hospitalization. Within a minute, they returned downstairs. Upon opening Payton's door, they'd heard the perfect strum of a guitar. Perhaps the sound had been the angelic forces letting them know Payton was okay and with the Lord.

13. **A Memorial for Payton.** The night of Payton's passing, Keith called Fort Wilderness to let them know about Payton. Jean, the wife of the executive director, said Fort always had wanted a medical facility. The board had a regularly scheduled quarterly meeting the next morning and approved plans. Renderings of the proposed building were available at the calling, and $85,000 was raised the following month.

14. **A Restless Night (February 3, 2001).** The night of Payton's passing, I had difficulty sleeping; my mind raced with thoughts of our former church and, specifically, a question posed the prior year by Jim Granneman: "How do you know the Lord's will?" Concerned about the body's ability to respond to Payton's passing, I knew we needed to return the next day for the Sunday service. That was the last thing I wanted to tell Robyn. A little after nine o'clock in the morning, Robyn received a call from Jim. He asked how Payton was doing and when we would be back at Garfield Park. If I'd made a list of one thousand people I would have expected to call us, Jim would not have been on that list. He was the Lord's messenger indicating we needed to return.

15. **One-Year Anniversary: A Trip to Florida (January 2002).** We traveled a thousand miles to Florida for a family vacation. Upon our arrival at the Hard Rock Hotel adjacent to Universal Studios,

I stepped out of the car and heard the song "Arms Wide Open" by Creed, one of Payton's favorite bands. It was the song played as people arrived for Payton's calling.

16. **Leaving Andersen and Starting Payton LLC (April 2002).** I decided to leave Arthur Andersen a year after Payton's passing, prompted by a scripture in James about being double-minded and concern about our ability to grow a practice area deemed not of strategic importance to the worldwide firm. A client requested we purchase the outsourcing contract from Andersen considering concerns about the firm's viability, given the aftermath associated with the Enron debacle. We purchased the contract on May 1, 2002. The contract was the first asset sold and served as the template for all other asset sales in the subsequent dismantling of the $9 billion firm.

17. *Indianapolis Star* **Article regarding Payton (May 7, 2002).** Fifteen months after Payton's passing, the *Indianapolis Star* ran a follow-up story on our efforts to build Payton's Place, the medical infirmary at Fort Wilderness. The article ran the week following the start of Payton LLC. In the picture the *Star* chose, one individual was discernible among the forty persons on the project: Bryon Parnell, my new business partner with Payton LLC. The lead headline on the front page was "BUSINESS: Arguments Begin Today in Arthur Andersen Case." Payton's picture was off to the side.

18. **Dedicating Payton's Place (July 14, 2002).** An hour or two prior to the dedication, Robyn and I were walking through camp and were in front of Payton's Place, when we heard a loud shriek behind us. Mary Wertz was going into anaphylactic shock. Aside from family donors, she and her husband had donated the largest amount to the project. Robyn administered an EpiPen. An emergency vehicle arrived with Mark Fetzer at the helm. Mark had led Payton and me on the Grand Canyon hike three years prior.

19. **Two-Year Anniversary: A Series of Beginnings and Endings (February 2, 2003).** Zionsville Fellowship's pastor, Tom Streeter, spoke about our faith being teleological. There is a beginning and an end to all things. That weekend, an astounding number

of people with whom we had a long-standing relationship, culminated with an improbable series of events which marked both a beginning and an end in our journey of faith.

20. **Payton's Dream (Fall 2004).** Payton had shared a dream with Meredith the day before he entered the hospital: she was grown up and wearing a white dress in a field of flowers all alone. Four years later, Leisa brought Robyn Meredith's senior picture. She was grown up and wearing a white dress in a field of flowers all alone. Meredith did not realize the significance of the picture at the time, but Leisa did. It was Payton's dream.

21. **Glorious Unfolding.** The story continues …

A FINAL WORD

On January 16, 2019, the day finally arrived, I received the final edited copy of my book. Many individuals contributed to this work. It is now eighteen years to the day that Dr. Jeff Macke, posed the question about taking Payton down for a CT scan and ultimately surgery, saying, "We need to fish or cut bait." The book I had contemplated writing for the past sixteen years and a story that needed to be told. Virtually every week I was reminded each time I took the garbage out to the street that another week went by without me starting this important project. However, God's timing is perfect. The combination of my new role at Fort Wilderness, my closest friend Keith's role as President at Author Learning Center and additional years of wisdom and perspective made this the perfect time to write and share the story.

I was anxious to review the editor's comments and suggestions after investing almost a year reliving the story. As expected, there were plenty of recommendations to improve the quality of the manuscript and questions to address. However, it was a personal reflection on the story and what happened after they wrapped up their work that caught me off guard. The exact moment they finished work on their book, they went outside, out of habit, to check the weather. It was 55 degrees which caused them to think of Payton and smile.

I read the note and for what seemed like the one hundredth time was brought to tears as I sat and peered through moist eyes at the computer. Was this one more providential example from the Lord to give me comfort and joy at His providential care for me and those who love Payton? I was excited to share the above note with Robyn, Meredith and Leisa remembering Meredith's special prayer plan: each time a friend saw the number 55 (Payton's basketball jersey number), he or she was to pray for him. Prayers were hurled to heaven from young and old alike as reminders were seen everywhere.

Upon sending the email I received an almost immediate response from Meredith, "So cool! I'm looking forward to getting the book!" And then I looked upon my computer screen and noticed the improbable had happened once again, Meredith's email was the fifty-fifth email in my inbox. Again, I was overcome with emotion and joy and peace which surpasses human understanding. Our God certainly does love us! To God be the Glory!

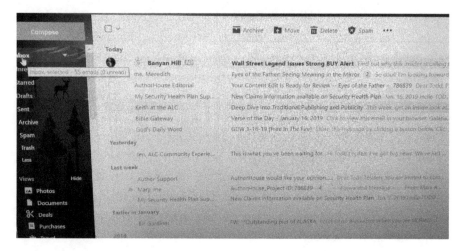

ACKNOWLEDGMENTS

The reality is, the Lord wrote this story. I needed a whole lot of support, commitment, and time to bring this book to life as a source of hope for others. It was difficult to delve into emotional wells largely untouched for many years and to put to bed, in book form, my nagging question since Payton's passing: "Lord, why did you make the circumstances preceding and following Payton's passing so clear?"

I must first thank my wife, Robyn, for her encouragement and support. In recent years, she knew the importance of getting this project done and nudged me along the way. Her willingness to re-visit the period of Payton's illness and passing was a sacrificial gift, as it remains difficult for her to relive certain memories. Our sons Blake and Chase, Payton's brothers, offered support and advice as well. Chase said to be raw and vulnerable. Blake provided critical insight and analysis of my writing with a desire for this work to impact the lives of many.

Following Payton's passing, Robyn's sister, Cari, assembled a comprehensive book of my emails, website postings, newspaper articles, funeral information, messages, and more. This treasure trove of information was invaluable as I revisited documented accounts of the story. Thank you and hot dog, Cari! Also, I am thankful for two awesome brothers, Scott and Tom, who provided invaluable support and care for our family during and following Payton's passing. Your gentle guidance and warm engagement are noticed and appreciated.

I am eternally thankful for the faithful witness of Laura Byers Mayhall, Tim Doyle, Tom Blossom, and Robin Gore. Saint Francis of Assisi reportedly said, "Preach Jesus, and if necessary, use words." Each of these earthly followers of Christ provided me with a desire to seek Him.

Nick Taylor, Leisa Ress, and Jeff Terp are longtime friends and intricately involved in the tapestry of Robyn's and my life. I love Nick and am thankful for our accountability relationship. Leisa is a faithful woman who was drawn into an improbable situation and, ultimately, a deep relationship with Robyn and me. Jeff provided significant support and direction throughout the years. We are blessed by the friendship and care each of you has given us.

Derrick Burks, Kelly Erickson, and Angie Schroeder provided wonderful insight and constructive support with their in-depth review of the manuscript. This book is markedly better because of their willingness to take on this project. A huge thank-you. Please know lives are impacted for the kingdom by the sacrificial gift of your time.

The care and support provided by Riley Children's Hospital were extraordinary. Thank you to Ndidi Musa, Ed Seferian, and Jeff Macke, who led the team of more than two hundred committed health professionals. I'd expected talented medical professionals, but in my wildest dreams, I could not have imagined how much the Riley team truly cared. A special thank-you to Ndidi for your fervent prayers and for demonstrating the truly awesome power that is ours in going before the throne to seek His will.

We are blessed by the body of Zionsville Fellowship. For your love and support for our family throughout the years and your faithful teaching and numerous acts of kindness, thank you.

Robyn and I are thankful for the support of our new family, Fort Wilderness Ministries. To the Robertson family, who created the vision for something special in the Northwoods of Wisconsin; the board; and our fellow co-laborers in the mission to develop relationships for eternal impact, thank you for your support to get this book published.

I was heavily influenced by my former work colleagues at the NCAA, particularly Gary deCastro, Mike Massa, and Bob Fiala, who demonstrated a great love both for Christ and for people. Gary, thank you for your encouragement and support over twenty years at the NCAA and Arthur Andersen and your wisdom to select a word each year for our directed attention. My word in 2016, *ministry*, served as the impetus to respond to the Lord's call for Robyn and me to leave Indianapolis later that year and go to Fort Wilderness.

I owe a huge debt of gratitude to my *pengyou*, or special friend, Keith

Ogorek. The Lord certainly had intricate plans for our families' lives, which emanated from a simple decision: trees or a fireplace. I am eternally thankful for your love, friendship, and counsel for me and my family. We have created tremendous memories over the past twenty-five years. Thank you for the enormous energy you put into this project and for the support of The Author Learning Center and AuthorHouse to get this published. I cannot possibly thank you enough this side of eternity for the gift you have given.

SCRIPTURE INDEX

Old Testament

Genesis 1:1–2
Genesis 1:27
Exodus 15:2
Deuteronomy 6:5
2 Chronicles 16:9
Job 13:15
Psalm 23
Psalm 33:1–11
Psalm 39:4–8
Psalm 86:6–13
Psalm 118:8
Psalm 121
Psalm 139:13–16
Proverbs 18:14
Ecclesiastes 1
Isaiah 40:29–31
Isaiah 50:7
Isaiah 57:1
Ezekiel 36:26–28

New Testament

Matthew 5:1-12
Matthew 5:17-18
Matthew 6:11
Matthew 6:34
Matthew 11:28
Matthew 22:37-39
Mark 11:22-24
Luke 2:8-20
Luke 12:15
John 3:16
John 4:23-24
John 10:10
John 14:1-4
John 17:3
Acts 9:10-12
Romans 6:23
Romans 8:18-21
Romans 8:28
Romans 15:13
1 Corinthians 13:11-12
2 Corinthians 5:1-8
2 Corinthians 5:7
Ephesians 2:10
Philippians 1:21-26
Philippians 3:20
Philippians 4:6
Philippians 4:13
2 Timothy 4:7-8
Hebrews 4:12-16
James 1:2-3
James 1:2-8
James 1:8
James 4:13-16
I Peter 1:6-7
I Peter 4:11
I John 5:14-15
Revelation 1:8
Revelation 2:4
Revelation 21:1-5

NOTES

Every reasonable effort was made to identify copyright holders of excerpted materials. If copyrighted materials were inadvertently used without credit given in one form or another, please notify Todd Leyden at leydentodd@sbcglobal.net so future editions are corrected accordingly.

1. The scripture quotations in this book are from the New King James translation.
2. Henry T. Blackaby and Claude V. King, *Experiencing God: Knowing and Doing the Will of God* (Nashville: Lifeway Press, 1990).
3. Gary and Anne Marie Ezzo, *Growing Kids God's Way* (Simi Valley, CA: Growing Families International, 1993).
4. Jonathan Cahn, *The Book of Mysteries* (Lake Mary, FL: Front Line, 2016).
5. National Institute of Health, National Institute of General Medical Sciences, www.nigms.nih.gov.
6. Mayo Clinic, www.mayoclinic.org.
7. American Heart Association, www.heart.org.
8. *Wikipedia*, s.v. "Arthur Andersen," en.wikipedia.org/wiki/Arthur_Andersen.
9. Jonathan Cahn, *The Book of Mysteries* (Lake Mary, FL: Front Line, 2016).
10. *The Free Dictionary*, www.thefreedictionary.com.
11. Henry T. Blackaby and Claude V. King, *Experiencing God: Knowing and Doing the Will of God* (Nashville: Lifeway Press, 1990).

ABOUT THE AUTHOR

Todd Leyden has spent the past twenty-five years growing in his Christian faith. His innate ability to see how the Lord works through various situations for His glory led him on a providential journey as he responded to the Lord's call to leave Arthur Andersen, a $9 billion global professional services firm, on the eve of the firm's collapse to start his own business. In 2016, another series of God-ordered circumstances led him from his prestigious role with the NCAA and college athletics to a Christian camp in the Northwoods of Wisconsin, where his family had started down a path to forge their identity two decades prior. The move required Todd and his wife Robyn to leave their twenty-two-year-old son Chase; Robyn's sister, Cari; and thirty-two years of life and community impact in the city of Indianapolis to start their next career in Christian ministry.

CPSIA information can be obtained
at www.ICGtesting.com
Printed in the USA
BVHW071920270219
541350BV00001B/3/P